How to Build a Fortune with an IRA

How to Build a Fortune with an IRA

James Michael Ullman
and
Norman Bercoon, C.P.A.

WILDSIDE PRESS

CONTENTS

PART III / Which IRAs Are Best for You?   223

PART I

IRAs: Retirement Fortune-Building Machines

A "fortune" is a relative term. A fortune to one person may not even begin to look like a fortune to another. If you already have piles of money, the sum you can build with contributions to an IRA (Individual Retirement Arrangement) over the years may not seem much to you.

But most people lack piles of money. The amount the average person can build in an IRA or IRAs for retirement truly is a fortune to him or her. If you're starting from scratch, a few hundred thousand dollars or so, added to your Social Security and other pension benefits, would be a respectable retirement fortune—and some people will be able to build seven-figure IRAs.

The main difference between the retirement fortune you can build with an IRA and other fortunes is that you probably will not pass the bulk of it on through generations of your descendants. Sooner or later the money must be withdrawn from your IRA, either by you or by your heirs, must be taxed at ordinary income rates, and, for most people, will be spent on living expenses.

But even if inflation has greatly increased living costs over the years, you probably will have built a larger retirement fortune than you could in any other way. Because you paid no tax on your IRA's earnings while it was growing, if you invested well, its growth should have exceeded the inflation rate. With any after-tax dollars you don't need for yourself after you retire, you can make investments to leave to your heirs. And even if there's nothing left for your heirs, your IRA may have saved them the expense of helping to support you if you hadn't had the IRA.

There has been a lot of confusion about IRAs since they were made "universal," allowing everyone who works to have one. This is due partly to the barrage of IRA promotional materials and partly to the fact that in

2

some respects, IRAs are not quite so simple as some sponsor literature makes them out to be.

This book will tell you how IRAs work and how you can use them to build your retirement fortune—or, if you're starting late, at least how to assure a more worry-free and comfortable retirement. Congress has provided the method. It's up to you to follow through.

1

Now Anyone Who Works Can Have One

The greatest retirement fortune-building mechanism ever devised for Americans who work for a living can now be used by anyone who is paid for services, as opposed to receiving income from investments. That mechanism is the IRA, an Internal Revenue Service abbreviation for Individual Retirement Arrangement.

No matter what kind of work you do or where you stand on the corporate ladder, an IRA allows you to shelter up to $2,000 of earned income from federal taxation each year in your own retirement fund. If you have a non-working spouse, you can elect instead to set up a so-called spousal IRA, which has an annual contribution limit of $2,250. And a working couple can contribute up to $2,000 of earnings each for a maximum of $4,000 a year.

What's much more important, the interest, dividends, or capital gains earned by your IRA will also be sheltered until you're ready to withdraw some or all of the money in it—and then you pay tax only on what you withdraw.

These unprecedented retirement fortune-building opportunities were made possible by the Economic Recovery Tax Act of 1981. Before Congress passed this law,

5

you weren't allowed to open your own IRA if you participated in a pension, retirement, or profit-sharing plan at work. (However, if you received a lump-sum payment from a plan at work, you were allowed to postpone or reduce your tax bill by rolling part or all of the payment over into an IRA.)

The 1981 Act vastly expanded the program by making IRAs universal throughout the American work force. As of 1982, IRAs can be opened by anyone who earns income from services whether covered by a pension plan on the job or not. This includes everyone on the payroll no matter how big or small the company, from people at the lowest pay levels to top management. It also includes people who work for local, state, or federal government bodies and agencies and have government-sponsored pension plans, as well as all members of the armed forces.

No matter how big your income or what your present retirement or profit-sharing arrangements with your employer (or the company you manage, if you're the boss), you can now supplement your other retirement income sources by contributing up to $2,000 or 100 percent of your income each year, whichever is less, into an IRA. And self-employed people with so-called Keogh plans enjoy the best of all possible worlds. In addition to their Keogh plans, they can open IRAs too.

If you are one of the more than 40 million Americans with a qualified retirement or profit-sharing plan at work, you also have the option of making your IRA contribution to your employer's plan if your employer will allow it and then deducting the contribution on your tax return. Many employers, however, won't allow it because it complicates their bookkeeping.

Opening an IRA can be as simple as signing a custodial or trustee agreement with a financial institution, mutual fund, insurance company, or brokerage firm. When you file your tax return, your IRA contribution or contributions may be subtracted from your earnings before income taxes are calculated. There is a special line on the first page of the tax return for listing the amount contributed, and you may use either the short or the long form.

You can invest your IRA contributions in a wide variety of ways—including savings accounts, mutual funds, insurance annuities, and even real estate partnerships—just so long as you invest through a sponsor with a plan that meets IRS requirements. An IRA can also be set up as a self-directed trust held by a custodian, which allows you to make all the investment decisions by buying stocks or bonds.

After Congress expanded the IRA program by making it universal, the public was beseiged by an army of marketers offering a host of IRA investments, some of which may be more appropriate for your temperament and circumstances than others. Under current rules, about the only IRA investments barred by law are life insurance policies, collectibles, and certain instruments that are pledged for indebtedness. The art, coin, and collectible dealers are trying to change the law to make their investments permissible again for IRAs.

When you contribute to an IRA, you have a lot of flexibility in moving the money around if you're dissatisfied (assuming a particular IRA's sponsor doesn't penalize you unduly). As far as the IRS is concerned, you may shift money from one IRA trustee to another as often as you wish so long as you don't handle it yourself. And once a year you can even take money out yourself and move it to another IRA providing the transaction is completed within a 60-day time frame.

Money you invest in your IRA needn't come directly

from your earnings. It can come from savings or any other source. And you can have as many IRAs as you wish, just as long as your total IRA contributions in any year don't exceed the limit.

A word of warning: Money you contribute to your IRA must be money you know you'll be able to get along without for a while. Unless you're disabled, you're not allowed to withdraw money before age 59½ without paying stiff penalties to the IRS. It would not make sense to put money in an IRA if doing so would work a financial hardship on you or your family.

And while Uncle Sam will give you a big tax break with an IRA, he won't pay for your mistakes. If you make a bad investment and suffer a loss, you won't be able to deduct it. Your IRA will simply be worth that much less.

How Big a Retirement Fund Can You Build?

At first glance, being allowed to invest up to $2,000 a year in an IRA might not seem much of an opportunity to build a fortune. But on the contrary, this everyman's (and woman's) tax shelter combines the magic of compound interest with tax-free earnings to expand your capital at a fantastic rate.

Let's assume you're able to invest $2,000 at the start of each year. Here's what an IRA could do for you at various rates of return:

• 8 percent—would grow to $98,884 in 20 years, $244,690 in 30 years, and $559,560 in 40 years.

• 10 percent—would grow to $126,004 in 20 years, $361,886 in 30 years, and $973,702 in 40 years.

• 12 percent—would grow to $161,396 in 20 years, $540,584 in 30 years, and $1,718,284 in 40 years.

• 14 percent—would grow to $207,536 in 20 years, $813,474 in 30 years, and $3,059,816 in 40 years.

• 16 percent—a long-term return indicating either that you're a very shrewd investor or that the future environment will be highly inflationary—would grow to $267,680 in 20 years, $1,230,322 in 30 years, and $5,276,956 in 40 years.

If you're married, have a non-working spouse, and maintain a spousal IRA with a maximum of $2,250 annual contribution, your retirement fund's growth will be that much greater.

In 20 years, you'd have $111,200 if invested at a constant 8 percent, $141,755 at 10 percent, $181,571 at 12 percent, $233,478 at 14 percent, and $301,140 at 16 percent.

In 30 years, your IRA would grow to $275,276 at 8 percent, $407,122 at 10 percent, $608,157 at 12 percent, $915,158 at 14 percent, and $1,384,112 at 16 percent.

After 40 years, you'd have $629,505 at 8 percent, $1,095,415 at 10 percent, $1,933,070 at 12 percent, $3,442,292 at 14 percent, and $6,596,195 at 16 percent.

Working couples able to contribute $2,000 each to an IRA over a period of time stand a good chance of building a retirement fund in the seven-figure neighborhood.

In 20 years, the combined annual $4,000 contribution would grow to $197,688 at a constant 8 percent, $252,008 at 10 percent, $322,792 at 12 percent, $415,072 at 14 percent, and $535,360 at 16 percent.

After 30 years, you'd have $489,380 at 8 percent, $723,772 at 10 percent, $1,081,168 at 12 percent, $1,626,948 at 14 percent, and $2,460,644 at 16 percent.

And after 40 years, $1,119,120 at 8 percent, $1,947,404 at 10 percent, $3,436,568 at 12 percent, $6,119,632 at 14 percent, and $10,553,912 at 16 percent.

However, it's not necessary to invest the maximum

each year in order to build a large retirement fund for yourself with an IRA. Even a modest investment could grow to a surprising size. Investing just $25 a month at a constant 12 percent return would build a fund worth $24,209 in 20 years, $81,107 in 30 years, and $257,242— or more than a quarter-million dollars—in 40 years.

With these numbers, anyone in a position to set up an IRA would be foolish not to do so. Younger and middle-aged workers willing and able to stick to an IRA program can easily build a six-figure—or larger—retirement fund. And older workers can shelter some income during their peak earning years while creating a new retirement income source.

Tables 1, 2, and 3 summarize how $2,000, $2,250, and $4,000 invested at the start of each year would grow at various constant rates of return:

Table 1: How $2,000 Invested at Start of Each Year Would Grow at Various Rates of Return
(Maximum Individual IRA Contribution)

Plan Years Completed	8%	10%	12%	14%	16%
5	$ 12,670	$ 13,430	$ 14,230	$ 15,070	$ 15,954
10	31,290	35,062	39,308	44,088	49,464
15	58,648	69,898	83,506	99,960	119,850
20	98,844	126,004	161,396	207,536	267,680
25	157,908	216,362	298,666	414,664	578,176
30	244,690	361,886	540,584	813,474	1,230,322
35	372,204	596,252	966,926	1,581,344	2,600,054
40	559,560	973,702	1,718,284	3,059,816	5,276,956

Table 2: How $2,250 Invested at Start of Each Year Would
Grow at Various Rates of Return
(Maximum Spousal IRA Contribution)

Plan Years Completed	8%	10%	12%	14%	16%
5	$ 14,254	$ 15,109	$ 16,009	$ 16,954	$ 17,948
10	35,201	39,445	44,221	49,599	55,647
15	65,979	78,635	93,960	112,455	134,831
20	111,200	141,755	181,571	233,478	301,140
25	177,647	243,407	355,999	466,497	650,448
30	275,276	407,122	608,157	915,158	1,384,112
35	418,730	670,784	1,087,792	1,779,012	2,925,061
40	629,505	1,095,415	1,933,070	3,442,293	6,596,195

Table 3: How $4,000 Invested at Start of Each Year Would
Grow at Various Rates of Return
(Maximum Working Couple Contribution)

Plan Years Completed	8%	10%	12%	14%	16%
5	$ 25,340	$ 26,860	$ 28,460	$ 30,140	$ 31,908
10	62,580	70,124	78,616	88,176	98,928
15	117,296	139,796	167,040	199,920	239,700
20	197,688	252,008	322,792	415,072	535,360
25	315,816	432,724	597,332	829,328	1,156,352
30	489,380	723,772	1,081,168	1,626,948	2,460,644
35	744,408	1,192,504	1,933,852	3,162,688	5,200,108
40	1,119,120	1,947,404	3,436,404	6,119,632	10,553,912

These Numbers Don't Tell the Whole Story

These numbers don't even tell the whole story because an IRA is further leveraged by the additional income it can buy after you retire.

At a constant 12 percent return, a 55-year-old worker contributing $2,000 to an IRA at the start of each year for the next 10 years could enjoy an extra annual income for the following 20 years of $5,252—or $438 a month—for a total payout of $105,250. If the 55-year-old's spouse also works and contributes the $2,000 maximum, their $40,000 investment would give them an annual retirement income of $10,504—or $876 a month—for a total $210,500 payout.

A 45-year-old worker could buy a retirement income of $21,606 a year, or $1,700 a month—a total payout of $432,148. A 45-year-old working couple could earn an annual retirement income of $43,212—or $3,600 a month —for a total payout of $864,296.

The earlier you begin, the greater the effect of this leverage. A worker at age 25 investing $2,000 for 40 years would earn a 20-year retirement income of $230,040 annually, or $19,170 a month—a total payout of $4,600,800.

In short, through the mechanism of an IRA, the government is giving most people an opportunity to build a bigger pool of savings than they could on their own— and to use those savings to buy a financially secure retirement.

Let's Put These Numbers in Perspective

Of course, inflation and interest rates could fall sharply in the future, and in light of history, that's a strong possibility. Today's rates are unprecedentedly high. If they fall sharply later in the 1980s, the higher investment returns on the tables in this book may not be available with reasonable safety, or even at all.

But if that happened, it would mean the overall inflation rate would have dropped too, which would be good news all around. A lower and more stable inflation rate would make it much easier to plan for retirement without worrying about inflationary surges eroding your retirement buying power. On the other hand, higher inflation and interest rates in the future could produce even higher returns than shown on the tables. (A more detailed set of tables, showing returns ranging from 6 to 20 percent, is in Chapter 4.)

As far as IRA investments are concerned, the future rate of return doesn't matter nearly as much as earning a tax-sheltered return that at least matches and preferably exceeds the inflation rate, whatever that may be. If you do that, you can still build a fortune with an IRA in terms of real purchasing power.

Why Congress Wanted IRAs for Everyone

One reason Congress made it possible for all workers to have IRAs was to encourage people to save more money. There's great concern over the fact that the U.S. has the lowest personal savings rate among major industrialized nations. More savings are needed to rebuild our aging industrial plants and finance home buyers.

There's also concern over serious inadequacies in the private pension systems. Many people will receive little or no help from private pensions when they retire. In fact, only about one-fifth of all retired persons are paid any income from a private pension.

The President's Commission on Pension Policy, established by the Carter Administration, found that many people now covered by private pensions will never receive benefits, and many who receive benefits will find them inadequate. By 1979, only 45 percent of all private-industry employees were covered by pensions, and only about one-fourth had vested benefits in their current job.

But there's no doubt Congress also viewed IRAs as a way to take some of the pressure off the Social Security system.

The Social Security system isn't likely to go broke, but it has great financial problems. The next few years are sure to bring a reexamination of the whole premise of Social Security and its role. In delivering the annual report of the Social Security Trustees in July 1981, Commissioner John A. Svahn gave a strong indication that changes must be made when he said:

> There is a myth that has grown up in America that Social Security is a program for maintaining everyone at middle-class level in their retirement years.
>
> It has always been a premise of Social Security that it is a base for retirement and a partial replacement for wages lost because of retirement, death, or disability. It was never intended as a full retirement system for Americans.

Social Security's immediate problem is its retirement fund. It may go broke unless Social Security taxes are raised or benefits are slashed, both highly unpopular actions. But somehow Congress and this and succeeding administrations will keep Social Security checks arriving on schedule each month in the foreseeable future.

It's likely, though, that from now on the trend will be toward smaller cost-of-living adjustments and bigger penalties for retiring early. This will increase the need for keeping up with inflation during retirement in some other way, which is the role Congress hopes IRAs will play.

The long-term picture, however—and this is of special importance to today's young workers—is much grimmer. There is what the Wall Street Journal *terms "a time bomb ticking away in the system." It's that the graying of the U.S. population means fewer and fewer workers must support more and more Social Security recipients.*

Without major changes, that time bomb will explode around the year 2030. The bulge of today's young workers—the so-called war babies—will put a tremendous burden on the system as they become retirees. The burden may be so great that their children and grandchildren will find it impossible to pay for their support through Social Security.

Today, every retiree is supported by 3.2 active workers. This could drop to 3.0 by the year 2000, and according to a Social Security Administration forecast, could plunge to just 2.0 by 2055. If that happened without major adjustments in the system, workers and employers combined would have to pay as much as 43 percent of wages subject to Social Security to support retirees— and it's not likely they'd be willing or able to do that.

The message for young workers is clear. No matter how small the amount, start putting money into an IRA if you can. It's money that will multiply many times over the years. You have to assume that when you retire, your Social Security benefits will be relatively less than those enjoyed by your parents and grandparents. Congress is giving you a chance to make up the difference—and then some!

Today's IRA Ceilings Are Just the Beginning

When you start an IRA investment program, here's something else working for you. If history is any guide, there's a good chance your IRA contribution limits will be increased in the future, especially if inflation continues to erode buying power.

Liberalizing rules and expanding benefits over the years has been the history of both the IRA program and the older, do-it-yourself pension plan, the Keogh program for self-employed people (doctors, lawyers, architects, writers, small-business owners, etc.).

In this country, the do-it-yourself pension plan idea began in 1962 when Congress authorized Keogh plans for the self-employed in a law called H.R. 10. The goal was to give self-employed people an opportunity to build tax-sheltered pension plans.

At first there was so much red tape that hardly anyone signed up. And originally, Keogh participants were limited to sheltering $2,500 or 10 percent of their earned income, whichever was smaller. But rules were simplified, and in 1974, Keogh limits were raised to $7,500 or 15 percent of earned income in a monumental law called the Employment Retirement Income Security Act of 1974 (ERISA).

ERISA also authorized the first IRA program. It was aimed at allowing workers without pension plans on the job to build their own retirement funds and have rollover provisions giving them pension portability. In part, IRAs were modeled on the Canadian Registered Retirement Program in effect since 1957.

The original IRA ceilings were $1,500 or 15 percent of income, whichever was less. Later, Congress created the spousal IRA, with a combined $1,750 limit. To qualify, one spouse had to be a worker not participating in a plan on the job and the other had to be unemployed, with no earned income. Congress also simplified IRA rules and allowed employers to set up IRAs for their own employees if they wished.

The 1981 Act established a revolutionary precedent. In addition to raising IRA contribution limits to $2,000 or 100 percent of income, whichever is less, and raising the spousal ceiling to $2,250, for the first time it extended the do-it-yourself retirement plan idea to people who already participated in plans at work. Those rules will probably be simplified as problems arise in trying to follow them. And more inflation might prompt Congress to raise ceilings for all do-it-yourself pension plans.

But the gap between IRA and Keogh ceilings is now so great that pressure for a catch-up move for IRAs could also mount. The 1981 Act also increased annual Keogh contribution limits to $15,000 or 15 percent of income, whichever is less, compared with $2,000 for IRAs—and under present law, people with Keogh plans can have IRAs too.

As IRAs become more widespread, it's likely that IRA sponsors and people with IRAs will try to persuade Congress to narrow that gap. So the more you learn about IRAs now, the better you can take advantage of higher IRA ceilings—and greater fortune-building opportunities—if and when ceilings are raised in the future.

What's in This Book

This book will show you how an IRA can offset the erosion of your retirement dollars through inflation. It spells out some fortune-building rules that will help you maximize the return from your IRA or IRAs. It also has a series of tables you can use to project an IRA's growth for up to 40 years at a wide range of rates of return, either with regular additions or for an IRA to which no further additions are made.

In the beginning, IRAs were a red-tape nightmare.

Rules and procedures have been simplified since IRAs were first authorized in 1974. Nevertheless, in many respects they are still quite complicated. Unfortunately, many people you consult for more information about IRAs don't know nearly as much about how IRAs work as they should. For your own protection, you should become familiar with the basic IRA rules.

This book explains, in simple language, the rules and regulations governing IRAs, and warns of violations and errors in handling or moving IRAs that can result in serious tax penalties and perhaps the disqualification of the entire IRA.

It also explains how the same law that made IRAs universal made it possible for many people to start making voluntary contributions to their employer's pension plan instead of setting up their own IRAs—provided their employers allow them to do so. Under some circumstances, you may also be allowed to move a lump-sum distribution out of an employer plan into an IRA and possibly back to another employer plan later. There are many links and some significant differences between employer retirement plans and IRAs, and if you are covered by an employer plan, you should understand them.

Finally, this book discusses a number of details involved in setting up an IRA, where to get advice on IRAs and IRA investments, and what your IRA investment options are. Those options are far wider than ever because of major changes in how retail investments are marketed, including the creation of investments and savings instruments designed especially for IRAs and other tax-sheltered retirement plans.

2

Why IRAs Are Such Great Investments

An IRA is a great investment because, thanks to the government's help, it allows most people to build a bigger retirement fund than they could in any other way. Some of these advantages are:

• It shelters money from taxation each year.

• It shelters the interest, dividends, and capital gains your IRA earns until you're ready to start withdrawing money—which can be any time after age 59½. The longer tax-sheltered earnings keep piling up, the bigger the retirement fortune you can build.

• It's completely under your control. You decide where to invest your money—and can count on having it when you retire. No matter how often you change jobs, your IRA is always there, making it especially useful for people who change jobs often.

Today the average woman changes jobs every 2.6 years and the average man every 4.5 years. But under federal law, your private pension plan may not be vested until you're on the job for as long as 10 years. You may have earned some deferred pension benefits, but when you leave, you'd have to start from scratch building pension credits with the new company.

• It makes you better prepared for retirement if it's

forced upon you before you're ready. Most people don't retire because they want to, either they must stop working for health reasons or they're put out to pasture before they wish.

• The fund will be inherited by anyone you designate if you die before you retire or before the fund is exhausted.

• You don't have to contribute each year if you can't afford to. As far as the IRS is concerned, you can put as much or as little in your IRA (or IRAs) as you wish so long as you don't exceed the annual contribution limits.

• It gives aggressive investors the same tax advantage held by mutual funds and institutional investors. In making selling decisions, you can concentrate on timing. You needn't worry about whether gains are short or long term because the IRA isn't subject to capital gains taxes.

• You can switch investments from one IRA to another as circumstances change. For instance, you could start by building a cash fund in savings accounts or a money market mutual fund. When the pool of cash is large enough, you could move it into a self-directed IRA and invest in stocks or bonds.

• If you own a business, you can set up an IRA for yourself without having to include your employees, which you must do with a Keogh plan.

• It gives you great flexibility in adapting to changes in your income or financial circumstances during the crucial years between the ages of 59½ and 70½. If you're willing and able, you can continue contributing to your IRA during these years even though you're making withdrawals.

• It can be your basic retirement program if you have no other pension or retirement plan except Social Security.

• It is liquid at all times, and although you may have to pay penalties, it provides easy access to funds in an emergency.

• It gives you the opportunity to further diversify your investments.

• It can be a complement to hard-asset investments that appreciate in value but may not be in an advantageous market cycle when you must liquidate.

How Inflation Erodes Retirement Buying Power

Income from an IRA can help you offset inflation and maintain decent living standards during retirement—and may assure you of them if you start your IRA early enough.

For most people, Social Security and their other pension benefits combined (if you have any other benefits) aren't enough for a comfortable retirement for long, if at all. Many pension plans are of the "defined benefit" type. They spell out the benefits you're to receive. A predetermined formula specifies what your retirement income will be—usually so much per month or year, or a proportion of your past income.

The trouble with this approach is that there's usually no way to adjust for inflation after you retire. Consequently, as inflation continues to erode buying power, living standards for people on fixed retirement incomes fall. Between 1966 and 1977, the average annual per capita pension plan benefits rose from $1,403 to $1,741, a 24 percent increase over the 11-year span. But consumer prices rose 79 percent, a rate more than 3 times as great.

To see how various inflation rates can erode your pension's buying power, see Table 4. Even at a "low" 6 percent inflation rate—the rate many politicians and economists claim would signal a great victory against inflation—the buying power of a $10,000 pension would be reduced to $7,474 in 5 years, $5,583 in 10 years, $4,172 in 15 years, and $3,118—or 31 cents on the dollar—in 20 years.

At an 8 percent inflation rate, a $10,000 pension's buying power would be cut to $6,805 in 5 years, $4,631 in 10 years, and $2,145 in 20 years. At 10 percent, it's cut to $6,209 in 5 years, $3,855 in 10 years, and $1,486 in 20 years. At 12 percent, a $10,000 pension buys just $5,674 in 5 years, $3,219 in 10 years, and $1,036 in 20 years.

As measured by the Consumer Price Index, between 1971 and 1980, the inflation rate averaged 7.9 percent. In the second half of the decade, from 1976 to 1980, it averaged 9.0 percent—and it was 10.4 percent in 1981. If inflation continues at anywhere near those levels, the buying power of pensions based on incomes at the time of retirement will be reduced substantially in just a few years.

Table 4: How Inflation Erodes Retirement Buying Power
Future Buying Power of $10,000 Annual Retirement Income Today at Various Inflation Rates

Years	6%	8%	10%	12%	15%
5	$7,472	$6,805	$6,209	$5,674	$4,971
10	5,583	4,631	3,855	3,219	2,471
15	4,172	3,152	2,393	1,826	1,228
20	3,118	2,145	1,486	1,036	611

Note: Inflation rate (Consumer Price Index) averaged 7.9 percent between 1971–80 and 9.0 percent between 1976–80.

IRAs Cut Your Tax Bills

Basically IRAs are a lot like the retirement plans millions of Americans have at work.

At work your employer contributes money into a plan (and you may be allowed to contribute some too). For all practical purposes, your employer's contribution is some income for you, unless you leave the plan before you have earned any rights to benefits. But you don't pay taxes on this money, which your employer uses to make tax-sheltered investments in a pension fund for all employees. You're not liable for taxes until your employer starts paying you benefits or you take a lump-sum distribution from the plan.

With an IRA, your most immediate benefit will be to lower taxes beginning with the first year in which you make an IRA investment. Money you contribute to your IRA is deducted on your tax return for that year. If you're in a 25 percent tax bracket and contribute $2,000 to an IRA, you'll reduce your tax obligation for that year by 25 percent of $2,000, or $500. If you're in a 40 percent tax bracket, you'll reduce it by $800; if in a 50 percent bracket, by $1,000.

In other words, right at the start, Uncle Sam is giving you that much extra money to play with—provided you invest it in an IRA.

In time, these tax reductions alone can add up to a significant sum. Table 5, which shows these reductions, is actually very conservative because it assumes you'll always be in the same tax bracket. But most people move into higher brackets as their incomes increase. Their total tax reduction with an IRA would be greater than the table indicates.

Table 5: How Tax Bills Are Lowered While You Build Your IRA Total Tax Deferred at Various Tax Brackets

Plan Years Completed	20%	25%	30%	40%	50%
$2,000—Maximum Annual Individual Contribution					
1	$ 400	$ 500	$ 600	$ 800	$ 1,000
5	2,000	2,500	3,000	4,000	5,000
10	4,000	5,000	6,000	8,000	10,000
20	8,000	10,000	12,000	16,000	20,000
30	12,000	15,000	18,000	24,000	30,000
40	16,000	20,000	24,000	32,000	40,000
$2,250—Maximum Annual Spousal Contribution					
1	$ 450	$ 563	$ 675	$ 900	$ 1,125
5	2,250	2,813	3,375	4,500	5,625
10	4,500	5,625	6,750	9,000	11,250
20	9,000	11,250	13,500	18,000	22,500
30	13,500	16,875	20,250	27,000	33,750
40	18,000	22,500	27,000	36,000	45,000
$4,000—Maximum Annual Working Couple Contribution					
1	$ 800	$ 1,000	$ 1,200	$ 1,600	$ 2,000
5	4,000	5,000	6,000	8,000	10,000
10	8,000	10,000	12,000	16,000	20,000
20	16,000	20,000	24,000	32,000	40,000
30	24,000	30,000	36,000	48,000	60,000
40	32,000	40,000	48,000	64,000	80,000

Compare Your Tax-Equivalent Returns

Another way to measure an IRA's value as a good investment is to compare its return with the taxable-equivalent return on investments that are not sheltered from taxation.

The taxable-equivalent return will depend on your

tax bracket. But as Table 6 shows, the equivalent returns on IRA investments are usually far above what you could expect to earn without a tax shelter.

For instance, if your IRA earns 12 percent and you're in a 25 percent bracket, it would be the equivalent of a 16 percent taxable return. If you're in a 30 percent bracket, it would be the equivalent of 17.14 percent; if in a 40 percent bracket, of 20 percent; and if in a 50 percent bracket, of 24 percent.

If your IRA earns 16 percent and you're in a 25 percent bracket, it would be the equivalent of a taxable 21.33 percent; in a 30 percent bracket, of 22.86 percent; in a 40 percent bracket, of 26.67 percent; and in a 50 percent bracket, of 32 percent.

Table 6: Taxable Equivalent IRA Returns at Various Investment Yields

Tax Bracket	Investment Yields				
	8%	10%	12%	14%	16%
20%	10.00%	12.50%	15.00%	17.50%	20.00%
25%	10.67%	13.33%	16.00%	18.67%	21.33%
30%	11.43%	14.29%	17.14%	20.00%	22.86%
35%	12.31%	15.38%	18.46%	21.54%	24.62%
40%	13.33%	16.67%	20.00%	23.33%	26.67%
45%	14.55%	18.18%	21.82%	25.45%	29.09%
50%	16.00%	20.00%	24.00%	28.00%	32.00%

The Power of Tax-Sheltered Compounding

An IRA's greatest fortune-building power is that all interest, dividends, and capital gains are sheltered from taxation too. This gives IRA investments fantastic leverage over investments that are not tax-sheltered.

The longer an IRA is kept going, the more this leverage can work to multiply the value of your investments. Table 7 shows the tax-sheltered gains you'd make with an IRA if you invested $2,000 at the beginning of each year at constant 8, 10, 12, 14, or 16 percent returns.

Let's be conservative and analyze the 12 percent table. At this writing, anyone buying an IRA can earn 12 percent (and more) with complete safety, although this may not always be the case. But if you earned 12 percent each year, after 10 years your total $20,000 investment would already have nearly doubled and be worth $39,308, a $19,308 gain. After 20 years, your $40,000 invested would be worth $161,396, a tax-sheltered gain of $121,396.

From then on, gains are truly spectacular. In 30 years, your $60,000 investment would have grown to $540,584—a gain of $480,580, or nearly a half-million dollars. After 40 years, your $80,000 investment would have built an IRA worth $1,718,284, a gain of $1,638,248. For each dollar invested in your IRA, you'd now have $21.48.

Invested at a constant 14 percent return, you'd build an IRA worth $207,536 in 20 years, a $167,536 gain; $813,474 in 30 years, a $753,474 gain; and $3,059,816—a gain of $2,979,816—in 40 years. For each dollar invested, you'd have $38.25.

Invested at 16 percent, you'd have $267,680 in 20 years, a $227,680 gain; $1,230,322 in 30 years, a $1,117,322 gain; and $5,276,956—a $5,196,956 gain—in 40 years. Each dollar invested would now be worth $65.96.

Of course, those numbers are for maximum $2,000 annual IRA contributions by one person. Maximum spousal IRA contributions of $2,250 per year would produce total fund values and gains 12.5 percent higher than shown in the table, and maximum contributions of $2,000 each by working couples would double the number.

At what today appears a conservative return of 12 percent, a working couple could build a fund worth $322,792 in 20 years, a gain of $242,792; $1,081,168 in 30 years, a gain of $961,168; and $3,436,568 in 40 years, a gain of $3,276,568.

Table 7: Tax-Sheltered IRA Gains at Various Rates of Return
(Assumes $2,000 invested at start of each year)

8%

Plan Years Completed	Total Investment	IRA Value at Year-End	Tax-Sheltered Gain
1	$ 2,000	$ 2,160	$ 160
5	10,000	12,670	2,670
10	20,000	31,290	11,290
15	30,000	58,648	28,648
20	40,000	98,844	58,844
25	50,000	157,908	107,908
30	60,000	244,690	184,690
35	70,000	372,204	302,204
40	80,000	559,560	479,560

10%

Plan Years Completed	Total Investment	IRA Value at Year-End	Tax-Sheltered Gain
1	$ 2,000	$ 2,200	$ 200
5	10,000	13,430	3,430
10	20,000	35,062	15,062
15	30,000	69,898	39,898
20	40,000	126,004	86,004
25	50,000	216,362	166,362

Table 7 Cont.

10%

Plan Years Completed	Total Investment	IRA Value at Year-End	Tax-Sheltered Gain
30	60,000	361,886	301,886
35	70,000	596,252	526,252
40	80,000	973,702	893,702

12%

Plan Years Completed	Total Investment	IRA Value at Year-End	Tax-Sheltered Gain
1	$ 2,000	$ 2,240	$ 240
5	10,000	14,230	4,230
10	20,000	39,308	19,308
15	30,000	83,506	53,506
20	40,000	161,396	121,396
25	50,000	298,666	248,666
30	60,000	540,584	480,584
35	70,000	966,926	896,926
40	80,000	1,718,284	1,638,284

14%

Plan Years Completed	Total Investment	IRA Value at Year-End	Tax-Sheltered Gain
1	$ 2,000	$ 2,280	$ 280
5	10,000	15,070	5,070
10	20,000	44,088	24,088
15	30,000	99,960	69,960
20	40,000	207,536	167,536
25	50,000	414,664	364,664
30	60,000	813,474	753,474
35	70,000	1,581,344	1,511,344
40	80,000	3,059,816	2,979,816

16%

Plan Years Completed	Total Investment	IRA Value at Year-End	Tax-Sheltered Gain
1	$ 2,000	$ 2,320	$ 320
5	10,000	15,954	5,954
10	20,000	49,464	29,464
15	30,000	119,850	89,850
20	40,000	267,680	227,680
25	50,000	578,176	528,176
30	60,000	1,230,322	1,170,322
35	70,000	2,600,054	2,530,054
40	80,000	5,276,956	5,196,956

How Big an IRA Can You Build at Your Age?

Obviously an IRA's fortune-building potential is greatest for younger workers. If they start now, they can easily build six-figure, and in many cases seven-figure, IRAs.

But whatever your age, IRAs are a good investment because they can give you more money for maintaining decent living standards in retirement than you might think. Even workers in middle years can easily build substantial six-figure, and in some cases seven-figure, IRAs if they stick to a program and earn a high enough return.

Table 8 shows the projected growth of an IRA at an annual 12 percent return for contributors at various ages today, assuming a $2,000 contribution is made at the start of each year. Again, the 12 percent rate was selected because it is apparently a conservative one. It can easily be earned with safety today—but that may not always be the case over the next few decades.

At 12 percent, a 25-year-old worker contributing

$2,000 each year could build an IRA worth $915,126 by age 59½, when distributions from the IRA could begin. If today's 25-year-old decided not to tap the IRA until age 65, it would have grown to $1,718,284. And if the IRA wasn't touched until age 70½—when by law, distributions *must* begin—it would have grown to $3,227,100.

If you're 35 years old today, at 12 percent a $2,000 investment each year would grow to more than a quarter-million dollars ($282,665) by age 59½; more than a half-million dollars ($540,584) by age 65; and more than a million ($1,027,061) by age 70½. If you're 45 today, you'd have $79,031 by age 59½, $161,396 by age 65, and $318,705 if you continue contributing through age 70½.

Even if you're 55 years old today, a 12 percent IRA with $2,000 invested each year would grow to $13,406 by age 59½, $39,308 by age 65, and $90,636 by age 70½.

All these figures would be 12½ percent higher if you made the maximum annual $2,250 spousal contribution and doubled if you made the maximum $4,000 working couple contributions.

Results would also be better if you managed to invest at a higher rate of return. At a constant 14 percent, today's 35-year-old investing $2,000 at the start of each year would have $389,202 by age 59½, $813,474 by age 65, and $1,694,178 by age 70½. Starting at age 45, you'd have $93,822 by age 59½, $207,536 by 65, and $445,830 by 70½. A 25-year-old investing at 14 percent would have $1,484,244 by age 59½, $3,059,816 by 65, and $6,322,080 by 70½.

At 16 percent, a 35-year-old could have $538,302 by age 59½, $1,230,322 by 65, and $2,810,218 by 70½. Starting at age 45, you'd have $111,475 by age 59½, $267,680 by 65, and 626,590 by 70½. A 25-year-old at 16 percent would accumulate $2,420,749 by age 59½, $5,276,956 by 65, and $12,443,149 if continuing contributions through age 70½.

Table 8: Projected IRA Growth at Annual 12 Percent Return
for Contributors at Various Ages Today
(Assumes $2,000 invested at start of each year)

Your Age Now	IRA at Age 59½	IRA at Age 65	IRA at Age 70½
25	$915,126	$1,718,284	$3,227,100
30	511,604	966,926	1,823,501
35	282,665	540,584	1,027,061
40	152,750	298,666	575,139
45	79,031	161,396	318,705
50	37,201	83,506	173,199
55	13,466	39,308	90,636
60	——	14,230	43,786

How Much Retirement Income Can Your IRA Buy?

If you have so much other retirement income that you
don't need your IRA for living expenses when you retire,
as you start withdrawing from it, you can reinvest the
distributions, taking advantage of opportunities in your
retirement years that you couldn't have afforded otherwise.

But most people will view IRAs as an additional
source of retirement income. How much income an IRA
can buy will depend on how big the IRA is, the rate of
return, and how long it is to last. The maximum number
of years the IRA can be maintained will be established
by an IRS formula based on your life expectancy or on
the combined life expectancy of you and your spouse.
As an alternative, you can buy an insurance company
annuity.

For an estimate of how much retirement income various-sized IRAs can buy at various rates of return, look at Table 9.

Even a modest $25,000 IRA can be a valuable retirement income supplement. If invested at 12 percent over a 15-year payout period, it would provide an additional annual income of $3,670, or $305 a month. Paid out over 20 years, it would pay $3,347 a year, or $278 a month; over 25 years, $3,187 a year, or $265 a month.

A $50,000 IRA paid out over 15 years at 12 percent would pay $7,341 a year, or $611 a month; over 20 years, $6,933 a year, or $582 a month; and over 25 years, $6,374, or $531 a month.

A $100,000 IRA paid out over 20 years at 12 percent would pay $13,387 a year, or $1,115 a month. A $250,000 IRA invested at that rate for 20 years would pay $33,470 a year, or $2,789 a month; a $500,000 IRA, $66,939 a year, or $5,578 a month; and a $1 million IRA, $133,870 a year, or $11,150 a month.

Higher rates of return, of course, would provide a bigger retirement income.

You can easily estimate how much retirement income any size IRA would buy at various rates by making adjustments in these tables. To learn what a $300,000 IRA would pay, for instance, just triple the numbers in the $100,000 table.

Table 9: Annual Payout Estimate

Years to Exhaust IRA	**$25,000 IRA—** Annual Rate of Return on Fund				
	8%	*10%*	*12%*	*14%*	*16%*
5	$6,261	$6,594	$6,935	$7,282	$7,635
10	3,725	4,068	4,424	4,792	5,172
15	2,920	3,286	3,670	4,070	4,483
20	2,546	2,936	3,347	3,774	4,216
25	2,342	2,754	3,187	3,637	4,100
30	2,220	2,652	3,103	3,570	4,047
Monthly Payout					
5	$521	$549	$577	$606	$636
10	310	339	368	399	431
15	243	273	305	339	373
20	212	244	278	324	351
25	195	229	265	303	341
30	185	221	258	297	337

Years to Exhaust IRA	**$50,000 IRA—** Annual Rate of Return on Fund				
	8%	*10%*	*12%*	*14%*	*16%*
5	$12,522	$13,189	$13,870	$14,564	$15,270
10	7,451	8,137	8,849	9,586	10,345
15	5,841	6,573	7,341	8,140	8,968
20	5,092	5,872	6,993	7,549	8,433
25	4,683	5,508	6,374	7,275	8,201
30	4,441	5,304	6,207	7,140	8,094
Monthly Payout					
5	$1,043	$1,099	$1,155	$1,214	$1,273
10	620	678	737	799	862
15	486	547	611	678	747
20	424	489	582	629	703
25	390	459	531	606	683
30	370	442	517	595	675

$100,000 IRA—

Years to Exhaust IRA	Annual Rate of Return on Fund				
	8%	10%	12%	14%	16%
5	$25,045	$26,379	$27,740	$29,128	$30,541
10	14,902	16,274	17,698	19,171	20,690
15	11,682	13,147	14,682	16,281	17,936
20	10,185	11,745	13,387	15,099	16,867
25	9,367	11,016	12,749	14,550	16,401
30	8,880	10,608	12,414	14,280	16,189
Monthly Payout					
5	$2,087	$2,198	$2,311	$2,427	$2,545
10	1,241	1,356	1,474	1,598	1,724
15	973	1,095	1,223	1,357	1,495
20	848	978	1,115	1,258	1,406
25	780	918	1,062	1,213	1,367
30	740	884	1,035	1,190	1,349

$250,000 IRA—

Years to Exhaust IRA	Annual Rate of Return on Fund				
	8%	10%	12%	14%	16%
5	$62,614	$65,949	$69,352	$72,821	$76,352
10	37,257	40,686	44,246	47,928	51,725
15	29,207	32,868	36,706	40,702	44,839
20	25,463	29,365	33,470	37,747	42,167
25	23,420	27,542	31,875	36,375	41,003
30	22,207	26,520	31,036	35,701	40,471
Monthly Payout					
5	$5,218	$5,496	$5,779	$6,068	$6,363
10	3,105	3,391	3,687	3,994	4,310
15	2,434	2,739	3,059	3,392	3,737
20	2,122	2,447	2,789	3,146	3,514
25	1,952	2,295	2,656	3,031	3,417
30	1,851	2,210	2,586	2,975	3,373

Years to Exhaust IRA	$500,000 IRA— Annual Rate of Return on Fund				
	8%	10%	12%	14%	16%
5	$125,228	$131,899	$138,705	$145,642	$152,705
10	74,515	81,373	88,857	95,857	103,451
15	58,415	65,737	73,412	81,404	89,679
20	50,926	58,730	66,939	75,493	84,334
25	46,839	55,084	63,750	72,749	82,006
30	44,414	53,040	62,072	71,401	80,943
	Monthly Payout				
5	$10,436	$10,992	$11,559	$12,137	$12,725
10	6,210	6,781	7,374	7,988	8,621
15	4,868	5,478	6,118	6,784	7,473
20	4,244	4,894	5,578	6,291	7,028
25	3,903	4,590	5,313	6,062	6,834
30	3,701	4,420	5,173	5,950	6,745

Payout Years Provide the Fortune-Building "Kicker"

An IRA's retirement fortune-building potential is realized to the fullest when its tax-sheltered leverage continues to work as you pay the IRA out to yourself.

Once more, we'll assume a constant 12 percent return. You can't plan on averaging that every year in the future because interest rate levels are sure to fluctuate, perhaps greatly. But the example demonstrates the fortune-building kicker the payout years can provide (see Table 10).

In the example, $2,000 is contributed into an IRA each year until age 65. Then contributions stop, and the IRA is paid out in equal installments over a 25-year period. The example assumes that a couple has a combined life expectancy that would permit a 25-year payout in the IRS life expectancy tables. (The husband would be about 5 years older than his wife.)

With this scenario, even if this couple starts an IRA at a relatively advanced age, they'd reap substantial gains. And if they started at a relatively young age, their gains would be remarkable. For instance:

• Age 55 now: in 10 years your $20,000 investment at 12 percent would have grown to $39,308. For the next 25 years, your IRA would pay an annual income of $5,012 —or $418 a month—for a total payout of $125,300, or $6.27 for each dollar invested. If both spouses began making maximum IRA contributions at age 55, those numbers would double. Their $40,000 investment would provide an annual retirement income of $10,024—or $836 a month—for a total payout of $250,600.

• Age 45: a $40,000 investment would build an IRA worth $161,396 by age 65. For the next 25 years, the IRA would pay $20,578 a year—or $1,715 a month. The total payout would be $514,450, or $12.86 for each dollar invested. If both spouses worked and contributed the limit, they would have an annual 25-year retirement income of $41,156—or $3,430 a month—for a total payout of $1,028,900.

• Age 35: a $60,000 investment over the next 30 years would build an IRA worth $540,584. Over the following 25 years, this would pay a retirement income of $68,925 a year—or $5,744 a month. The total payout would be $1,723,125, or $28.72 for each dollar invested. The payout if both spouses worked and contributed the limit would be $3,446,250.

• Age 25: an $80,000 investment over 40 years would build an IRA worth $1,718,284. For the next 25 years, it would pay $219,082 a year—or $18,257 a month—for a total payout of $5,477,050, or $68.46 for each dollar in-

Table 10: Total Return from IRA Investments of $2,000 Per Year with Fixed 25-Year Payout Plan and Constant 12 Percent Return

(Contributions stop at age 65; entire IRA pays out in 25 years)

| Age Now | Total Invested | Value at Age 65 | 25-Year Payout after Age 65 | | | Dollars Paid Out for Each Dollar Paid In |
			Annual Income	Monthly Income	Total Paid Out	Dollar Paid In
55	$20,000	$ 39,308	$ 5,012	$ 418	$ 125,300	$ 6.27
50	30,000	83,605	10,660	889	266,500	8.88
45	40,000	161,396	20,578	1,715	514,450	12.86
40	50,000	298,666	38,080	3,174	952,000	19.04
35	60,000	540,584	68,925	5,744	1,723,125	28.72
30	70,000	966,926	123,284	10,274	3,082,100	44.03
25	80,000	1,718,284	219,082	18,257	5,477,050	68.46

Note: Assumes couple has husband who works and is 5 years older than his wife.

37

vested. The total payout for a working couple's $160,000 investment would be $10,954,100.

As spectacular as these results are, you could do even better if you were fortunate enough not to have to start withdrawing from your IRA until age 70½ and if you did not require a fixed income and could strictly follow the IRS minimum-withdrawal rules after age 70½. An example of how to do this is in Chapter 11.

3

Ten IRA Fortune-
Building Rules

Congress has given you an unprecedented opportunity
to build a tax-sheltered pool of retirement savings with
an IRA. Unlike Social Security, for which contributions
are mandatory, the benefits you receive from your IRA
will depend on how much money you contribute voluntarily—and how wisely you invest it.

Here are 10 rules to help you maximize your IRA
investment returns.

1. Keep Your Eye on the CPI

In building your retirement fund, your goal should be to
keep your money earning a return that betters the rate at
which prices in general are rising—which is to say, the
inflation rate, as measured by the Consumer Price Index
(CPI). If you can consistently do that, you will always be
ahead of inflation because you have a powerful investment kicker: the fact that your IRA's earnings are compounding tax-sheltered. The larger your IRA becomes,
the more effective this kicker can be in helping to build a
retirement fortune.

In past years, it was difficult for many people to better the inflation rate with their savings because of ceilings on the interest paid at banks and thrift institutions. But now there are no statutory rate ceilings on IRA savings instruments at these institutions. There is also a new option in the marketplace: the money market mutual funds, which grew rapidly because they could pay small investors the money market rates formerly available to big investors.

Consequently, there are now opportunities for beating the inflation rate that did not exist before—opportunities that include federally insured savings instruments that do not hold the risk of capital loss found in the stock market or in bond markets, where investors have been battered by inflation and high interest rates.

In the United States, the rate at which prices of goods and services rise or fall is measured by the Consumer Price Index. The Bureau of Labor Statistics issues these reports every month. If you're not already doing so, start looking for these reports, which are widely carried in newspapers and on radio and television newscasts.

The CPI is by no means a perfect measure of inflation, but at the moment it is the best inflation measurement we have. There can be big swings in the monthly CPI rate for one reason or another. If the CPI rate is occasionally higher than the rate your IRAs are earning, it's nothing to worry about; there may be periods when inflation rises at such a rapid rate that it outpaces all IRA investments comparable with yours month after month.

But if the CPI rate is consistently higher than the return on your IRAs—and higher-yielding IRA investments with equivalent safety and convenience are available—then switch your retirement money into those investments.

For a historical perspective, Table 11 shows what the

Table 11: Consumer Price Index, 1960–81
(Based on Annual Average)

Year	Index	Percent Change	Year	Index	Percent Change
1960	88.7		1971	121.3	4.3
1961	89.6	1.0	1972	125.3	3.3
1962	90.6	1.1	1973	133.1	6.2
1963	91.7	1.2	1974	147.7	11.0
1964	92.9	1.3	1975	161.2	9.1
1965	94.5	1.7	1976	170.5	5.8
1966	97.2	2.9	1977	181.5	6.5
1967	100.0	2.9	1978	195.4	7.8
1968	104.2	4.2	1979	217.4	11.3
1969	109.8	5.4	1980	246.8	13.5
1970	116.3	5.9	1981	272.4	10.4

CPI has been doing since 1960. As you can see, it began rising in the late 1960s and reached new and dangerous heights as the 1970s drew to a close. It would have been difficult for most people to beat the inflation rate in many of those years. But with tax-sheltered IRAs and the new investment options becoming available to savers and investors, it may be easier to do so in the future.

2. Start Soon and Invest Regularly

You've heard this thousands of times before, but it's worth saying again. Whatever your age or income, to make the most of your IRA (or any other investment program), start it right away and keep at it.

Not everyone is fortunate enough to be able to put money aside and not touch it until age 59½, although there would be circumstances where you'd come out ahead paying the penalties for taking the money out earlier anyhow. But if you can manage to spend a little less now and put more money into an IRA, that money can multiply many times over.

Investing now gets compound interest working for you right away. Investing regularly makes the growth of your IRA like a snowball rolling downhill. It may not be big at the start, but by the time it nears the bottom of the hill, it is many times its original size.

Table 12, a 40-year 12 percent table, demonstrates this principle. In the first year, your IRA would earn only $240. By the seventh year, it would earn $2,420, or $420 more than your annual contribution. In 10 years, it would earn $4,212, or more than double your maximum contribution. The IRA's earnings would be triple the size of your contribution in the thirteenth year, quadruple it in the fifteenth year, and quintuple it in the sixteenth year.

These regular contributions can produce astounding results. After 20 years, your IRA would earn more than 8 times your $2,000 contribution. After 30 years, it would earn nearly 29 times your contribution. And after 40 years, it would earn $184,102, or 92 times your contribution.

Table 12: IRA Growth at Constant 12 Percent Return
(*Assumes $2,000 invested at start of each year*)

Year	Total Investment	IRA Value at Year-End	IRA Earnings During the Year
1	$ 2,000	$ 2,240	$ 240
2	4,000	4,748	508
3	6,000	7,558	810
4	8,000	10,704	1,146
5	10,000	14,230	1,526

6	12,000	18,178	1,948
7	14,000	22,598	2,420
8	16,000	27,550	2,952
9	18,000	33,096	3,546
10	20,000	39,308	4,212
11	22,000	46,266	4,958
12	24,000	54,058	5,792
13	26,000	62,784	6,726
14	28,000	72,558	7,774
15	30,000	83,506	8,948
16	32,000	95,766	10,260
17	34,000	109,498	11,732
18	36,000	124,878	13,380
19	38,000	142,104	15,226
20	40,000	161,396	17,292
21	42,000	183,004	19,608
22	44,000	207,204	22,200
23	46,000	234,310	25,106
24	48,000	264,666	28,356
25	50,000	298,666	32,000
26	52,000	336,748	36,082
27	54,000	379,396	40,648
28	56,000	427,164	45,768
29	58,000	480,664	51,500
30	60,000	540,584	57,920
31	62,000	607,694	65,110
32	64,000	682,858	73,164
33	66,000	767,040	82,182
34	68,000	861,326	92,286
35	70,000	966,926	103,600
36	72,000	1,085,196	116,270
37	74,000	1,217,660	130,464
38	76,000	1,366,020	146,360
39	78,000	1,532,182	164,162
40	80,000	1,718,284	184,102

3. Invest as Early in the Year as You Can

You may have noticed that until now all tables in this book that estimate an IRA's growth have assumed that investments are made at the start of each year. That's because the sooner you invest in your IRA each year, the faster it will grow.

Obviously it's not always possible to make your entire IRA investment each January. At that time, many people are more concerned with paying Christmas bills than with putting money where it can't be touched until age 59½—assuming they have any cash on hand at all.

In that sense, *all* IRA growth tables in this book are unattainable for most people because they are idealized examples. Most people could never live up to them.

Nevertheless, to make the most of your IRA try to bunch your investments close to the start of each year rather than waiting until later in the year—or until just before you file your tax return in the following year, as so many people do. That way, your contributions for the year will be compounding tax-sheltered for as long as possible. And you gain an added benefit if you make part or all of your contribution by transferring funds from a taxable investment or savings account, reducing that tax accordingly.

Concentrating investments at the start of each year won't make much difference in the size of your IRA in the beginning. But the bigger your IRA becomes, the bigger the difference it will make.

Assume you contribute $2,000 to an IRA earning 12 percent at the start of each year and someone else contributes $2,000 at the very end of the year. After the first year, your IRA will have earned $240 and will be worth $2,240, while the other IRA hasn't had time to earn anything. Thereafter, at the end of each year, your IRA's value will always exceed that of the other IRA by that year's earnings (see Table 13).

After the second year, your IRA will be worth $4,748 and the other IRA will be worth $4,240—a $508 difference in your favor—and so on. In 10 years, your IRA will be worth $4,212 more than the other; in 20 years, $17,292 more; in 30 years, $57,920 more, and in 40 years, $184,102 more.

Table 13: How Money Grows Faster When Invested at the Start of the Year Instead of at the End of the Year

(Assumes $2,000 invested per year at a constant 12 percent return)

Plan Year Completed	IRA Value If Invested at Start of Year	IRA Value If Invested at End of Year	Difference
1	$ 2,240	$ 2,000	$ 240
2	4,748	4,240	508
3	7,558	6,748	810
4	10,704	9,558	1,146
5	14,230	12,704	1,526
6	18,178	16,230	1,948
7	22,598	20,178	2,420
8	27,550	24,598	2,952
9	33,096	29,550	3,546
10	39,308	35,096	4,212
11	46,266	41,308	4,958
12	54,058	48,266	5,792
13	62,784	56,058	6,726
14	72,558	64,784	7,774
15	83,506	74,558	8,948

Table 13 Cont.

Plan Year Completed	IRA Value If Invested at Start of Year	IRA Value If Invested at End of Year	Difference
16	95,766	85,506	10,260
17	109,498	97,766	11,732
18	124,878	111,498	13,380
19	142,104	126,878	15,226
20	161,396	144,104	17,292
21	183,004	163,396	19,608
22	207,204	185,004	22,200
23	234,310	209,204	25,106
24	264,666	236,310	28,356
25	298,666	266,666	32,000
26	336,748	300,666	36,082
27	379,396	338,748	40,648
28	427,164	381,396	45,768
29	480,664	429,164	51,500
30	540,584	482,664	57,920
31	607,694	542,584	65,110
32	682,858	609,694	73,164
33	767,040	684,858	82,182
34	921,326	769,040	92,286
35	966,926	863,326	103,600
36	1,085,196	968,926	116,270
37	1,217,660	1,087,196	130,464
38	1,366,020	1,219,660	146,360
39	1,532,182	1,368,020	164,162
40	1,718,284	1,534,182	184,102

4. Don't Settle for Less Than a Fair Return

In 1980, some people were buying IRA savings certificates at banks and savings and loan associations
that paid a mere 8 percent return—and were tying up
their money for 3 or more years to get that return. Yet
other banks and savings associations were paying IRA
buyers 12 percent on 2½-year certificates. And some institutions were marketing 6-month money market certificates, which paid up to 15 percent or so, as IRAs.
(To qualify for those, of course, you had to have at least
$10,000.)

Over a period of years, the effect of a big difference
in rate on your IRA is substantial. A 12 percent IRA will
be more than double the size of an 8 percent IRA in 27
years—$379,396 versus $188,676 if $2,000 contributions
are made at the start of each year. In 40 years it will be
more than triple an 8 percent IRA—$1,718,284 versus
$559,560. So don't allow even a few years to go by with
an IRA earning a below-market rate.

Remember those numbers if you're ever tempted to
accept a below-market return on your IRA as a favor for
a friend or business associate who has an interest in selling you the IRA, or you're reluctant to take the time to
carry or mail an IRA contribution to some other sponsor
if the sponsor you're dealing with is paying far below the
market.

Table 14 illustrates how substantial differences in return can affect the IRA money you will have available to
you when you retire. After 40 years, the value of a 10
percent IRA is not double that of a 5 percent IRA; it is
nearly 4 times as great. And the value of a 15 percent
IRA is not 3 times that of a 5 percent IRA; it is 16 times
as great.

Table 14: What a Difference a Rate Makes

Rate of Return (%)	After 10 Years	After 20 Years	After 30 Years	After 40 Years
5	$26,412	$ 69,438	$ 139,520	$ 253,678
6	27,942	77,984	167,602	328,094
7	29,566	87,730	202,144	427,218
8	31,290	98,844	244,690	559,560
9	33,120	111,528	297,150	736,582
10	35,052	126,004	361,886	973,702
11	37,122	142,530	441,826	1,291,652
12	39,308	161,396	540,584	1,718,284
13	41,628	182,938	662,630	2,290,970
14	44,088	207,536	813,474	3,059,816
15	46,698	235,620	999,912	4,091,906
16	49,464	267,680	1,230,322	5,276,956
17	52,398	304,276	1,515,006	7,334,780
18	55,510	346,042	1,866,636	9,827,182
19	58,806	393,604	2,300,774	13,160,992
20	62,300	448,050	2,836,514	17,625,258

5. Understand How "Little" Differences Affect Total Return

Even very small differences in the rate of return on your IRA—or on how your rate of return is compounded if it is an investment that pays interest—can make a big difference in total return over a long period of time.

All things being equal, if you can get a fraction of a percent higher in one investment as compared with another, take it.

The qualification is that all things be equal. It wouldn't make sense to make a much riskier investment for a slightly higher rate if you can't afford the risk. But when all conditions are virtually the same, select the investment that pays the most, no matter how slight the difference—and especially if you're investing for the long haul.

Let's look at 3 fixed-rate IRAs that are the same in all particulars except for the annual rate of return. One sponsor offers 12 percent, the next 12¼ percent, and the third 12½ percent (Table 15).

Investing $2,000 a year at those constant rates of return, after 5 years, you'd be only $102 ahead in the 12¼ percent plan and $206 ahead in the 12½ percent plan. After 10 years, the difference would be only $568 in the 12¼ percent plan and $1,142 at 12½ percent.

But in 20 years, the differences would be more significant. You'd be $5,122 ahead at 12¼ percent and $10,414 ahead at 12½ percent. In 30 years, you'd be $28,132 ahead at 12¼ percent and $57,794 ahead at 12½ percent; after 40 years, your 12¼ percent IRA would be worth $127,768 more and the 12½ percent IRA, $265,298 more.

Of course, with many IRAs, you won't know the future rate of return. You must base your estimate on past performance and future projections. Even under those circumstances, if it appears one IRA investment has been consistently doing a little better than another with the same characteristics, weigh the odds in your favor and select the one that has been doing the best.

Table 15: Over a Long Period, Even a Little Change in the
Rate of Return Can Make a Big Difference
(Assumes $2,000 invested at the start of each year)

Plan Years	12%	12¼%	Difference Between 12% and 12¼%	12½%	Difference Between 12% and 12½%
1	$ 2,240	$ 2,244	$ 4	$ 2,250	$ 10
2	4,748	4,764	16	4,780	32
3	7,558	7,592	34	7,628	70
4	10,704	10,768	64	10,832	128
5	14,230	14,332	102	14,436	206
6	18,178	18,332	154	18,490	312
7	22,598	22,824	226	23,052	454
8	27,550	27,864	314	28,184	634
9	33,096	33,524	418	33,956	860
10	39,308	39,876	568	40,450	1,142
11	46,266	47,006	740	47,758	1,492
12	54,058	55,008	950	55,978	1,920
13	62,784	63,992	1,208	65,224	2,440
14	72,558	70,076	1,518	75,628	3,070
15	83,506	85,396	1,892	87,332	3,826
16	95,766	98,102	2,336	100,498	4,732
17	109,498	112,364	2,866	115,310	5,812
18	124,878	128,374	3,496	131,974	7,096
19	142,104	146,344	4,240	150,720	8,616
20	161,396	166,518	5,122	171,810	10,414
21	183,004	189,160	6,156	195,538	12,534
22	207,204	214,578	7,374	222,230	15,026
23	234,310	243,110	8,800	252,258	17,948
24	264,666	275,134	10,468	286,040	21,374
25	298,666	311,084	12,418	324,046	25,380

26	336,748	351,438	14,690	366,802	30,054
27	379,396	396,734	17,338	414,902	35,506
28	427,164	447,578	20,414	469,014	41,850
29	480,664	504,652	23,988	529,892	49,228
30	540,584	568,716	28,132	598,378	57,794
31	607,694	640,630	32,936	675,426	67,720
32	682,858	721,352	38,494	762,104	79,246
33	767,040	811,962	44,922	859,618	92,578
34	861,326	915,672	52,346	969,320	107,994
35	966,926	1,007,844	60,918	1,092,734	125,808
36	1,085,196	1,115,798	70,602	1,231,576	146,380
37	1,217,660	1,299,854	82,194	1,387,774	170,114
38	1,366,020	1,461,332	95,312	1,563,496	197,476
39	1,532,182	1,642,590	110,408	1,761,184	229,002
40	1,718,284	1,845,052	127,768	1,983,582	265,298

6. Understand How Commissions Affect Investment Returns

In many circumstances it may be worthwhile to pay a fee or commission to make an IRA investment. If you can afford and understand the risk in a self-directed IRA in which you buy and sell stocks, you must pay brokerage commissions for each purchase or sale. But if you know what you're doing and make good investments, you may outpace more conservative investments. Or your research may lead you to a "load" mutual fund that will provide above-average returns even after deducting the front-end sales charge, often 8½ percent.

On the whole though, most people lack the financial sophistication and resources needed for self-directed plans and other more esoteric IRAs and are better off investing 100 percent of their money rather than having the retirement fortune-building power of their IRA contributions reduced by fees or commissions. Dollars you pay in commissions can't work for you.

This is especially true if you're not going to contribute to your IRA for a long period. The shorter the time you expect to keep your IRA, the higher the rate of return you must earn just to match the return without a fee or commission. On the other hand, the longer you continue contributing to the IRA with a fixed fee or commission, the less impact the fees have on overall investment results.

If you pay an 8½ percent commission when you contribute $2,000 to an IRA instead of investing $2,000 in the first year, you're investing only $1,830, or $170 less. If both IRAs rise 12 percent in value during the first year, the $2,000 IRA would be worth $2,240 at year-end, but the $1,830 IRA would be worth only $2,049 (see Table 16). For the $1,830 IRA to be worth as much as the $2,000 IRA by the end of the year, the $1,830 IRA would have to increase in value by a hefty 22.4 percent—nearly double the rate of return on the IRA without commissions.

In time, though, this gap would narrow. Assuming the same level of annual contributions, after 5 years the IRA with the 8½ percent commission deducted each year would have had to be earning at a constant 15.1 percent rate to be as valuable as the non-commission IRA earning 12 percent—still a significant difference. But after 10 years, it would drop to 13.5 percent, after 15 years to 13.0 percent, and after 20 years to 12.7 percent.

This means that if you're thinking of making an IRA investment that charges a fixed commission when you make contributions—a load mutual fund, for instance—you should plan on maintaining that fund's investment program for many years to offset the impact of the commissions on your return.

(Assumes $2,000 invested at start of each year, 8½ percent commission, and constant 12 percent rate of return)

Plan Years Completed	IRA with 8½% Commission	IRA with No Commission	Difference	Return with Commission Needed to Match 12% IRA with No Commission
1	$ 2,049	$ 2,240	$ 191	22.4%
2	4,344	4,748	404	18.7%
3	6,915	7,558	643	16.9%
4	9,794	10,704	910	15.8%
5	13,020	14,230	1,210	15.1%
6	16,632	18,178	1,546	14.6%
7	20,677	22,598	1,921	14.2%
8	25,208	27,550	2,342	14.0%
9	30,282	33,096	2,814	13.7%
10	35,966	39,308	3,342	13.5%
15	76,407	83,506	7,099	13.0%
20	147,677	161,396	13,719	12.7%
25	273,279	298,666	25,387	12.5%
30	494,634	540,584	45,950	12.4%
35	884,737	966,926	82,189	12.3%
40	1,572,229	1,718,284	146,055	12.3%

It also means you should have some reason to anticipate a higher return on the IRA with the commission as opposed to the non-commission IRA. Otherwise, there would be no point in selecting an IRA that charged a commission. If both earned 12 percent and you contributed $2,000 each year, the IRA on which you paid an 8½ percent commission would be worth $3,342 less than the no-fee IRA in 10 years, $13,719 less in 20 years, $45,950 less in 30 years, and $146,055 less in 40 years.

---

7. Diversify Your IRA Investments

Diversification is a basic rule of investment. You don't want all of your IRA eggs in one basket. If the bottom fell out of that basket, you'd be wiped out—or at least hurt seriously.

There's no need to diversify right away, although that would be a good habit to get into. But when your IRA begins to grow, consider alternative investments. You could either roll over or transfer assets into the new IRA or IRAs, or stop making contributions to the old IRA and begin contributing to the new IRA or IRAs.

In addition to the usual reasons, another good reason for diversifying where IRAs are concerned is that, unlike regular investments, IRAs are subject to a host of IRS rules and regulations. Some penalties for breaking these rules, intentionally or unintentionally, are vexing but tolerable. But other penalties are severe and could result in disqualification of the entire IRA. This would throw it into your ordinary income for that year and might also subject you to additional tax penalties.

To protect yourself if you have a substantial amount of IRA money—either through investments you have built up over the years or through a rollover into an IRA from an employer pension plan—split it up into 2 or more IRAs. That way if a serious technical error is made in the handling or movement of one of your IRAs, the others will not be affected.

---

8. Don't Hesitate to Move Your IRAs Around

One of the great retirement fortune-building characteristics of an IRA is that you are not locked into it forever. If you're not satisfied with its performance (or if you're dissatisfied for any other reason), you may move your money out of that IRA and into another one. You can change your investment policies quickly to adapt to changes in financial markets or in your own circumstances.

Take care to follow IRS rules when rolling over or transferring money from one IRA to another. These rules are discussed in Chapter 9, and you should read them before proceeding with any IRA move. But you have a great deal of flexibility operating within those rules.

There's always a danger of overreacting to market ups and downs and moving money from one IRA to another too often. A mutual fund's performance may vary considerably from quarter to quarter or even year to year, for instance. But if you're investing for the long-term and the fund is oriented to the long-term and has a good overall record, this should not worry you.

There's also a risk of falling into the habit of switching IRA money into each hot new investment or investment fad that comes along. Many of these new investments have unproven track records—or may cause your IRA to be nibbled away by fees and commissions when the new investments do no better than the ones you abandoned.

Every IRA investment should be made with the hope that it is for the long term and will work out well. But any time an investment clearly begins to demonstrate that it is not living up to the promise you thought it had —or after a thorough analysis you conclude you could do much better with some other investment—don't hesitate to switch, perhaps seeking professional advice if the sum involved is large.

Under some circumstances, it pays to take a sponsor penalty for pulling out of an IRA investment. IRA savings certificates at banks and thrift institutions usually require a penalty if money is withdrawn before maturity. However, if the return you can get by switching to a different certificate or investment is high enough, you would come out ahead.

Make this calculation by determining what the original investment would be worth if you held it to maturity. Then go back and subtract the penalty and determine how much you would have to put in the new investment if you made the switch, and estimate what the new investment would be worth on the old investment's maturity date. If the new investment will be worth much more, then making the switch is worth the penalty.

Moving an IRA or IRAs could also be part of a long-term investment strategy. It hardly pays to open a self-directed IRA that invests in stocks unless you have a fairly large sum, otherwise your IRA would be eaten up by broker fees and commissions and odd-lot differentials for buying small amounts of stock. But you may decide to first build an IRA worth $10,000 or $20,000 in bank or thrift institution certificates or a money market fund, and then switch to a self-directed plan when the sum is large enough to make it worthwhile.

Changes in your own circumstances could also dictate moving IRAs around. If you came into a windfall inheritance that assured a comfortable retirement, you may be willing to take more chances with your IRAs. But if you lost other assets and your IRAs became a substantial part of your holdings, you may wish to begin making more conservative IRA investments. And on the whole, the older you get and the closer you are to retirement, the more careful you may want to be with your IRA funds.

By all means take advantage of opportunities to move IRA money that do not require a rollover or transfer from one sponsor to another. If you have an IRA with a family of mutual funds, you can switch assets from one type to another at a minimal expense without worrying about breaking IRS rollover and transfer rules.

---

9. Don't Put Your IRA Money Away and Forget It

As time goes on, keep an eye on alternative IRA investments. Not too long ago, stock market gurus were talking about "one-decision stocks." Supposedly these stocks were such good investments that you could buy them, put them away, and forget them.

People who bought those stocks got burned. Investment fashions changed—and many "one-decision stocks" became financial disasters for the people who believed the stock market gurus and held on to them.

The point is *never* put your IRA money away and forget it. Monitor your IRAs constantly. Are they doing as well as other IRA investments? Or are they lagging? And since you opened your IRA or IRAs, have new investment vehicles been put on the market that are better suited to your circumstances?

The universal IRA stimulated a lot of creative thinking on the part of IRA sponsors. Many new approaches to IRAs were brought to the marketplace early in 1982 when IRAs became universal and everyone who worked could have one, and you can expect more innovations in the future.

There's also a major deregulation of savings rates taking place at banks, savings and loan institutions, and credit unions. This will result in the creation of new types of savings accounts and certificates, some of which may also be better suited for you than the IRA investments you have now.

Profound changes are taking place in financial markets catering to the smallest as well as to the largest investors. To maximize your IRA investment returns, keep abreast of them and adjust your IRA investments accordingly.

---

10. Use Your Tax Shelter as Long as You Can

When you retire, you may have several sources of savings or other assets available to you in addition to your IRA or IRAs.

You'll usually come out ahead by maintaining your IRAs—and their tax-sheltered earning power—as long as you can. If you must supplement your retirement income from Social Security, other pension plans, and your other investments, consider drawing funds from other sources first.

As long as you are paying income tax, all things being equal, the tax-sheltered IRA will give you a better return than you could enjoy on taxable investments. Liquidate the taxable investments first, while the assets in the IRA continue to grow at the faster tax-sheltered rate.

After age 70½ you *must* begin withdrawing from your

IRA according to life expectancy formulas prepared by the IRS (or through insurance annuities based on the insurance company's own mortality tables). Basically what's involved at this point is reversing some IRA-building procedures to stretch your retirement income out to the maximum: i.e., bunching withdrawals at the end of the year, just as you bunched contributions at the beginning of the year while building your IRAs.

An explanation of the IRS withdrawal rules and an example of how to maximize an IRA's earning power is in Chapter 11.

4

Figuring It Out for Yourself

This is a "chapter of numbers." Its purpose is to enable you to make your own estimates of what IRAs would grow to at various rates of return.

If your main concern at the moment is learning more about how IRAs work and how to set up an IRA, skip this chapter. Move on to Part II.

But don't forget that the chapter is here and that by using the tables in it you can project the future growth of any IRA whether or not you're making regular additional contributions each year. These tables can be used for many purposes, including projecting the growth of IRAs you already own, comparing the growth of your IRAs with other IRAs, and helping to decide whether to roll a lump-sum distribution from an employer plan into an IRA.

What You Can Do with These Tables

This chapter has 2 sets of tables. Both allow year-by-year IRA growth estimates for up to 40 years at annual rates of return ranging from 6 percent to 20 percent (whole numbers only).

The first set—the A tables—is for estimating how

IRAs would grow with fixed annual contributions. It also has examples showing how IRAs with annual contributions of $1,000, $2,000, $2,250, and $4,000 would grow.

The second set—the B tables—allows you to estimate how IRAs would grow if you discontinue contributions.

You could stop making contributions to an IRA for many reasons. It could be because you couldn't afford more contributions or because you decided to start contributing to another IRA or IRAs instead. Or you could drop out of the work force or roll over a large sum from an employer retirement plan and never contribute more to it.

In addition, by using the A and B tables in combination, you can estimate:

• What your IRA would grow to if you changed the fixed amount you contributed each year or began contributing a fixed amount for the first time.

• What your IRA would grow to with fixed contributions if the rate of return changes.

These estimates can also be made with calculators by various methods. Most people will find that using the multiples on these tables in combination with a calculator will be quicker, especially if you are trying to project an IRA's growth far into the future.

These Results Are Estimates Only

The results you'll achieve with these tables are *estimates only*, as are all other examples in this book.

The key numbers in both sets of tables are *basic multipliers* for terms ranging from one to 40 years. To simplify your calculations, these basic multipliers have been reduced to 3 digits after the decimal point.

Consequently, results of calculations made with

these basic multipliers will differ slightly from those made by computers or calculators that base calculations on more than 3 digits. However, even with a large sum over a long period of years, the differences would be relatively minor.

Moreover, even calculations made with more precise calculating methods are at best only rough estimates of the results you would actually achieve by investing in an IRA.

One reason is that the longer the period of time involved, the greater the likelihood that there will be changes in interest rate levels and IRA contribution limits that will tend to make today's estimates of IRA growth obsolete. If inflation rates move to still higher levels, for instance, IRA contribution limits would probably increase accordingly to keep pace with higher salary levels.

Another reason is that all of these projections—those in the tables in this book, as well as those made by IRA sponsors in advertisements and promotional literature—are based on idealized conditions almost never achieved in real life.

The tables in this chapter assume that to achieve the stated results, all contributions will be made at exactly the start of the year. Tables in promotional literature and advertisements of most IRA sponsors usually make the same assumption. Although many IRA investors may concentrate their investments near the beginning of the year, it is unlikely—and in many cases impossible—that they will make their total IRA investments at *exactly* the start of the year. January 1 is a legal holiday (New Year's Day), and if it falls on a weekend, there may be another day when financial institutions are closed and financial markets are not operating.

For most of us, IRA investments will be spread out

over the year or even into the following year. Many people wait until the last minute to make their IRA contributions; others make regular payroll contributions during the year and into the following year, complicating their actual rate of return with compounding.

Consequently, although the calculating methods used to estimate IRA growth in this book are slightly less precise than those used by the computers that create many of the growth tables in IRA promotional literature, no method can pinpoint exactly how an IRA will grow for most people. But all of these methods do give a reasonable estimate of what your IRA would grow to over any period of time at any given approximate rate of return.

Using the A Tables: IRAs with Fixed Annual Contributions

Each of the A tables, which are for calculating the future worth of IRAs with fixed annual contributions, has 6 columns.

The first indicates the plan years completed.

The second and most important column lists the basic multiplier for each of the 40 plan years.

The multiplier is what $1 would grow to at that rate of return and for that period of time. If you multiply any other number by it, it will show what the other number would grow to at that rate of return for that period of time.

The other 4 columns show how $1,000, $2,000 (the maximum individual contribution), $2,250 (the maximum spousal contribution), or $4,000 (the maximum a working couple could contribute) would grow at the designated rate of return.

These last 4 columns can be used to make quick at-a-glance estimates of how an IRA would grow with those fixed contributions, and in many cases, this may be all the information you'll need.

If you were contributing the maximum $2,250 to a spousal IRA earning 12 percent and planned to retire in 20 years, for instance, you could quickly see on the 12 percent A table that in 20 years your IRA would grow to about $181,000 ($181,571). Or if you and your spouse were contributing $2,000 each at a 14 percent return and wanted to estimate what your IRAs would grow to in 9 years, the 14 percent A table would show the answer to be about $73,000 ($73,348).

For other than the numbers in the last 4 columns on the tables, use the basic multiplier, which shows the growth of $1. Here are some examples:

Problem: What would an IRA grow to if you contributed $1,250 a year for 17 years at an average 12 percent return?

Answer: Turn to the 12 percent A table and find the multiplier for 17 years, which is 54.749. Then multiply that by the amount contributed each year: 54.749 × $1,250 = $68,436.

Problem: What would an IRA grow to if you contributed $1,600 a year for 9 years at a 14 percent return?

Answer: Turn to the 14 percent A table. The multiplier for 9 years is 18.337 × $1,600 = $29,339.

NOTE: If you are making investment estimates in round numbers, you may be able to take mathematical shortcuts by using one of the numbers in the tables of examples rather than finding the multiplier and multiplying the estimates out.

For instance, to estimate how regular contributions

of $500 would grow, just divide the $1,000 examples in half. Or to estimate how a working couple's combined contributions of $3,000 would grow, multiply the $1,000 example by 3, and so on.

The $1,000 column is especially useful in making shortcuts. Dividing those numbers by 10, which simply involves putting a decimal point in front of the last digit, shows how $100 would grow.

Using the B Tables: IRA Growth with No Additions

Each of the B tables, which are for estimating the future worth of an IRA if contributions are discontinued, has 5 columns.

The first shows the plan years completed; the second gives the basic multiplier for each year.

The other 3 columns show how $1,000, $10,000, or $100,000 would grow at the designated rate of return.

As with the A tables, to estimate what any sum would grow to at that rate, multiply the sum by the basic multiplier for the desired period of years.

Problem: You build an IRA up to $16,320 and then stop making contributions at age 38 because you prefer contributing to a company plan at work. At a 10 percent return, what will it be worth in 27 years when you are age 65?

Answer: Turn to the 10 percent B table. The multiplier for 27 years is 13.109 × $16,320 = $213,939.

Problem· You receive a $126,580 rollover from an employer plan at age 59. If invested at an average 12 percent return, what will it be worth in 6 years when you are 65?

Answer: Turn to the 12 percent B table. The multiplier for 6 years is 1.973 × $126,580 = $249,742.

Problem: You build an IRA worth $2,650 and then quit work at age 26 to marry and have a family. Invested at an average 12 percent return, what will it be worth in 39 years when you are age 65?

Answer: Turn to the 12 percent B table. The 39-year multiplier is 83.081 × $2,650 = $220,165.

NOTE: As with the A tables, you may be able to take mathematical shortcuts by using the examples. For instance, to estimate what $50,000 would grow to for any number of years, you could either divide what $100,000 would grow to by 2 or multiply what $10,000 would grow to by 5, and so on.

How to Estimate Growth If the Amount Contributed Changes

By using both sets of tables, you can make a 2-step estimate of what your IRA would grow to if you changed the fixed amount contributed each year (or began making fixed contributions each year).

To do this, first go to the appropriate B table (the table showing what an IRA would grow to with no further additions). Use the multiplier on this table to estimate what the total in the IRA at the time you changed the amount contributed regularly (or began contributing the same amount regularly) would grow to with no further additions.

Then turn to the appropriate A table. Use that multiplier to estimate what the new fixed contributions would grow to over the same time period.

Then add the 2 results together.

Problem: After you've built an IRA worth $204,760, Congress changes the law and increases the maximum annual contribution to $3,000. You plan to retire in 6 years. What will your IRA be worth if you can invest it at an 8 percent return while contributing the new limit to $3,000 each year?

Answer: First turn to the 8 percent B table. The multiplier for 6 years is 1.586 × $204,760 = $324,749.

Then turn to the 8 percent A table. The 6-year multiplier is 7.922 × $3,000 = $23,766.

$324,749 + $23,766 = $348,515.

Problem: Contributing to an IRA on an irregular basis, you have accumulated $73,525. You can now afford to contribute $2,000 each year for 10 years until you retire. If you can invest it at 12 percent, what will it be worth then?

Answer: Turn to the 12 percent B table. The 10-year multiplier is 3.105 × $73,525 = $228,295.

Then turn to the 12 percent A table. The 10-year multiplier is 19.654 × $2,000 = $39,308.

$228,295 + $39,308 = $267,603.

How to Estimate IRA Growth If the Rate of Return Changes

The same 2-step procedure can be used if you're making fixed contributions and the rate of return changes.

In this case you'd first turn to the appropriate B table to estimate what the IRA would grow to at the new rate with no more additions. Then turn to the A table to see what the regular additions would grow to at the new rate.

Problem: You have accumulated $130,678 in an IRA and reinvest it at a new return of 14 percent. If you are contributing $2,000 each year, what will the IRA be worth in 8 years?

Answer: First turn to the 14 percent B table. The 8-year multiplier is 2.852 × $130,678 = $372,694.

Then turn to the 14 percent A table. The 8-year multiplier is 15.085 × $2,000 = $30,170.

$372,694 + $30,170 = $402,864.

A TABLES
IRA Growth with Regular Annual Contributions*

Estimates of IRA growth at constant rates of return of 6 percent to 20 percent for annual contributions of $1,000, $2,000 (single IRA maximum), $2,250 (spousal IRA maximum), and $4,000 (joint return maximum). Tables also show *basic multipliers* for growth of $1.

---

* These are annual rates of return assuming IRA contributions are made at the start of each year. In practice, differing contribution dates and longer or shorter multipliers would produce different results. Also, results may differ slightly from other tables based on the same rates of return because of differences in rounding out and compounding.

A–6%

To estimate what any sum invested *regularly* at this return would grow to at a constant 6 percent rate of return for any period of from one to 40 years, multiply that sum by the basic multiplier, which shows what $1 would grow to. (The table assumes that each investment is made at the *start* of each year.)

Examples

Plan Years Completed	Basic Multiplier ($1)	$1,000	(Single IRA Maximum) $2,000	(Spousal IRA Maximum) $2,250	(Joint Return Maximum) $4,000
1	1.060	$ 1,060	$ 2,120	$ 2,385	$ 4,240
2	2.183	2,183	4,366	4,912	8,732
3	3.374	3,374	6,748	7,592	13,496
4	4.637	4,637	9,274	10,433	18,584
5	5.975	5,975	11,950	13,444	23,900
6	7.393	7,393	14,786	16,634	29,572
7	8.897	8,897	17,794	20,018	35,588
8	10.491	10,491	20,982	23,605	41,964
9	12.180	12,180	24,360	27,405	48,720
10	13.971	13,971	27,942	31,435	55,884
11	15.869	15,869	31,738	35,705	63,476
12	17.882	17,882	35,764	40,235	71,528
13	20.015	20,015	40,030	45,034	80,060
14	22.276	22,276	44,552	50,121	89,104
15	24.672	24,672	49,344	55,512	98,688

70

16	27.212	27.212	54,424	61,227	108,848
17	29.905	29,905	59,810	67,286	119,620
18	32.760	32,760	65,520	73,710	131,040
19	35.785	35,785	71,570	80,516	143,140
20	38.992	38,992	77,984	87,732	155,968
21	42.392	42,392	84,784	95,382	169,568
22	45.995	45,995	91,990	103,489	183,980
23	49.815	49,815	99,630	112,084	199,260
24	53,864	53,864	107,728	121,194	215,456
25	58.156	58,156	116,312	130,851	232,634
26	62,705	62,705	125,410	141,086	250,820
27	67,528	67,528	135,056	151,938	270,112
28	72,639	72,639	145,278	163,438	290,556
29	78,058	78,058	156,116	175,631	312,232
30	83,801	83,801	167,602	188,552	335,204
31	89,889	89,889	179,778	202,250	359,556
32	96,343	96,343	192,686	216,772	385,372
33	103,183	103,183	206,366	232,162	412,732
34	110,434	110,434	220,868	248,477	441,736
35	118,120	118,120	236,240	265,770	472,480
36	126,268	126,268	252,536	284,103	505,072
37	134,904	134,904	269,808	303,534	539,616
38	144,058	144,058	288,116	324,131	576,232
39	153,762	153,762	307,524	345,965	615,048
40	164,047	164,047	328,094	369,106	656,188

A–8%

To estimate what any sum invested *regularly* at this return would grow to at a constant 8 percent rate of return for any period of from one to 40 years, multiply that sum by the basic multiplier, which shows what $1 would grow to. (The table assumes that each investment is made at the *start* of each year.)

		Examples			
Plan Years Completed	Basic Multiplier ($1)	$1,000	(Single IRA Maximum) $2,000	(Spousal IRA Maximum) $2,250	(Joint Return Maximum) $4,000
1	1.080	$ 1,080	$ 2,160	$ 2,430	$ 4,320
2	2.246	2,246	4,492	5,054	8,984
3	3.506	3,506	7,012	7,889	14,024
4	4.866	4,866	9,732	10,949	19,464
5	6.335	6,335	12,670	14,254	25,340
6	7.922	7,922	15,844	17,825	31,688
7	9.636	9,636	19,272	21,681	38,544
8	11.487	11,487	22,974	25,846	45,948
9	13.846	13,846	26,972	30,344	53,944
10	15.645	15,645	31,290	35,201	62,580
11	17.977	17,977	35,954	40,448	71,908
12	20.495	20,495	40,990	46,114	81,980
13	23.214	23,214	46,428	52,232	92,856
14	26.152	26,152	52,304	58,842	104,608
15	29.324	29,324	58,648	65,979	117,296

16	131,000	73,688	65,500	32,750	32,750
17	145,800	82,013	72,900	36,450	36,450
18	161,784	91,004	80,892	40,446	40,446
19	179,044	100,712	89,522	44,761	44,761
20	197,688	111,200	98,844	49,422	49,422
21	217,824	122,526	108,912	54,456	54,456
22	239,572	134,759	119,786	59,893	59,893
23	263,056	147,969	131,528	65,764	65,764
24	288,420	162,236	144,210	72,105	72,105
25	315,816	177,647	157,908	78,954	78,954
26	345,400	194,288	172,700	86,350	86,350
27	377,352	212,261	188,676	94,388	94,388
28	411,860	231,671	205,930	102,965	102,965
29	449,132	252,637	224,566	112,283	112,283
30	489,380	275,276	244,690	122,345	122,345
31	532,852	299,729	266,426	133,213	133,213
32	579,800	326,128	289,900	144,950	144,950
33	630,504	354,659	315,252	157,626	157,626
34	685,264	385,461	342,632	171,316	171,316
35	744,408	418,730	372,204	186,102	186,102
36	808,280	454,658	404,140	202,070	202,070
37	877,260	493,459	438,630	219,315	219,315
38	951,764	535,367	475,882	237,941	237,941
39	1,032,224	580,626	516,112	258,056	258,056
40	1,119,120	629,505	559,560	279,780	279,780

A–10%

To estimate what any sum invested *regularly* at this return would grow to at a constant 10 percent rate of return for any period of from one to 40 years, multiply that sum by the basic multiplier, which shows what $1 would grow to. (The table assumes that each investment is made at the *start* of each year.)

Examples

Plan Years Completed	Basic Multiplier ($1)	(Single IRA Maximum) $2,000	(Spousal IRA Maximum) $2,250	(Joint Return Maximum) $4,000
1	1.100	$ 2,200	$ 2,475	$ 4,400
2	2.310	4,620	5,198	9,240
3	3.641	7,282	8,192	14,564
4	5.105	10,210	11,486	20,420
5	6.715	13,430	15,109	26,860
6	8.487	16,974	19,096	33,948
7	10.435	20,870	23,479	41,740
8	12.579	25,158	28,303	50,316
9	14.937	29,874	33,608	59,748
10	17.531	35,062	39,445	70,124
11	20.384	40,768	45,864	81,536
12	23.522	47,044	52,925	94,088
13	26.974	53,948	60,692	107,896
14	30.772	61,544	69,237	123,088
15				

16	39.544	39,544	79,088	88,974	158,176
17	44,599	44,599	89,198	100,348	178,396
18	50,159	50,159	100,318	112,858	200,636
19	56,275	56,275	112,550	126,619	225,100
20	63,002	63,002	126,004	141,755	252,008
21	70,402	70,402	140,804	158,405	281,608
22	78,543	78,543	157,086	176,722	314,172
23	87,497	87,497	174,994	196,868	349,988
24	97,347	97,347	194,694	219,031	389,388
25	108,181	108,181	216,362	243,407	432,724
26	120,099	120,099	240,198	270,223	480,396
27	133,209	133,209	266,418	299,720	532,836
28	147,630	147,630	295,260	332,168	590,520
29	163,494	163,494	326,988	367,862	653,976
30	180,943	180,943	361,886	407,122	723,772
31	200.137	200,137	400,274	450,308	800,548
32	221,251	221,251	442,502	497,815	885,004
33	244,476	244,476	488,952	550,071	977,904
34	270,024	270,024	540,048	607,554	1,080,096
35	298,126	298,126	596,252	670,784	1,192,504
36	329,039	329,039	658,078	740,338	1,316,156
37	363,043	363,043	726,086	816,847	1,452,172
38	400,447	400,447	800,894	901,006	1,601,788
39	441,592	441,592	883,184	993,582	1,766,368
40	486,851	486,851	973,702	1,095,415	1,947,404

A–12%

To estimate what any sum invested *regularly* at this return would grow to at a constant 12 percent rate of return for any period of from one to 40 years, multiply that sum by the basic multiplier, which shows what $1 would grow to. (The table assumes that each investment is made at the *start* of each year.)

Examples

Plan Years Completed	Basic Multiplier ($1)	$1,000	(Single IRA Maximum) $2,000	(Spousal IRA Maximum) $2,250	(Joint Return Maximum) $4,000
1	1.120	$ 1,120	$ 2,240	$ 2,520	$ 4,480
2	2.374	2,374	4,748	5,342	9,496
3	3.779	3,779	7,558	8,503	15,116
4	5.352	5,352	10,704	12,042	21,408
5	7.115	7,115	14,230	16,009	28,460
6	9.089	9,089	18,178	20,450	36,356
7	11.299	11,299	22,598	25,423	45,196
8	13.775	13,775	27,550	30,993	55,100
9	16.548	16,548	33,096	37,233	66,192
10	19.654	19,654	39,308	44,222	78,616
11	23.133	23,133	46,266	52,049	92,532
12	27.029	27,029	54,058	60,815	108,116
13	31.392	31,392	62,748	70,632	125,568
14	36.279	36,279	72,558	81,628	145,116
15	41.753	41,753	83,506	93,944	167,012

16	47.883	47.883	95,766	107,737	191,532
17	54.749	54.749	109,498	123,185	218,996
18	62.439	62.439	124,878	140,488	249,756
19	71.052	71.052	142,104	159,867	284,208
20	80.698	80.698	161,396	181,571	322,792
21	91.502	91.502	183,004	205,880	366,008
22	103.602	103.602	207,204	233,105	414,408
23	117.115	117.115	234,310	263,599	468,620
24	132.333	132.333	264,666	297,749	529,332
25	149.333	149.333	298,666	335,999	597,332
26	168.374	168.374	336,748	378,842	673,496
27	189.698	189.698	379,396	426,821	758,792
28	213.582	213.582	427,164	480,560	854,328
29	240.332	240.332	480,664	540,747	961,328
30	270.292	270.292	540,584	608,157	1,081,168
31	303.847	303.847	607,694	683,656	1,215,338
32	341.429	341.429	682,858	768,215	1,365,716
33	383.520	383.520	767,040	862,920	1,534,080
34	430.663	430.663	861,326	968,992	1,722,652
35	483.463	483.463	966,926	1,087,792	1,933,852
36	542.598	542.598	1,085,196	1,220,846	2,170,392
37	608.830	608.830	1,217,660	1,369,868	2,435,320
38	683.010	683.010	1,366,020	1,536,773	2,732,040
39	766.091	766.091	1,532,182	1,723,705	3,064,364
40	859.142	859.142	1,718,284	1,933,070	3,436,568

A–14%

To estimate what any sum invested *regularly* at this return would grow to at a constant 14 percent rate of return for any period of from one to 40 years, multiply that sum by the basic multiplier, which shows what $1 would grow to. (The table assumes that each investment is made at the *start* of each year.)

Examples

Plan Years Completed	Basic Multiplier ($1)	(Single IRA Maximum) $2,000	(Spousal IRA Maximum) $2,250	(Joint Return Maximum) $4,000
1	1.140	$ 2,280	$ 2,565	$ 4,560
2	2.439	4,878	5,488	9,756
3	3.921	7,842	8,822	15,684
4	5.610	11,220	12,623	22,440
5	7.535	15,070	16,954	30,140
6	9.730	19,460	21,893	38,920
7	12.232	24,464	27,522	48,928
8	15.085	30,170	33,941	60,340
9	18.337	36,674	41,258	73,348
10	22.044	44,088	49,599	88,176
11	26.270	52,540	59,108	105,080
12	31.088	62,176	69,948	124,352
13	36.581	73,162	82,307	146,324
14	42.842	85,684	96,395	171,368
15	49.980	99,960	112,455	199,920

#					
16	58.117	58,117	116,234	130,763	232,468
17	67.394	57,394	134,788	151,637	269,576
18	77.969	77,969	155,938	175,430	311,876
19	90.024	90,024	180,048	202,554	360,096
20	103.768	103,768	207,536	233,478	415,072
21	119.435	119,435	238,870	268,729	477,740
22	137.297	137,297	274,594	308,918	549,188
23	157.658	157,658	315,316	354,731	630,632
24	180.870	180,870	361,740	406,958	723,480
25	207.332	207,332	414,664	466,497	829,328
26	237.499	237,499	474,998	534,373	949,996
27	271.889	271,889	543,778	611,750	1,087,556
28	311.093	311,093	622,186	699,959	1,244,372
29	355.786	355,786	711,572	800,519	1,423,144
30	406.737	406,737	813,474	915,158	1,626,948
31	464.820	464,820	929,640	1,045,845	1,859,280
32	531.035	531,035	1,062,070	1,194,829	2,124,140
33	606.519	606,519	1,213,038	1,364,668	2,426,076
34	692.572	692,572	1,385,144	1,558,287	2,770,288
35	790.672	790,672	1,581,344	1,779,012	3,162,688
36	902.507	902,507	1,805,014	2,030,641	3,610,028
37	1029.998	1,029,998	2,059,996	2,317,496	4,119,992
38	1175.337	1,175,337	2,350,675	2,644,508	4,701,348
39	1341.025	1,341,025	2,682,050	3,017,306	5,364,100
40	1529.908	1,529,908	3,059,816	3,442,293	6,119,632

A–16%

To estimate what any sum invested *regularly* at this return would grow to at a constant 16 percent rate of return for any period of from one to 40 years, multiply that sum by the basic multiplier, which shows what $1 would grow to. (The table assumes that each investment is made at the *start* of each year.)

Examples

Plan Years Completed	Basic Multiplier ($1)	$1,000	(Single IRA Maximum) $2,000	(Spousal IRA Maximum) $2,250	(Joint Return Maximum) $4,000
1	1.160	$ 1,160	$ 2,320	$ 2,610	$ 4,640
2	2.505	2,505	5,010	5,636	10,020
3	4.066	4,066	8,132	9,149	12,264
4	5.877	5,877	11,754	13,223	23,508
5	7.977	7,977	15,954	17,948	31,908
6	10.413	10,413	20,826	23,429	41,652
7	13.240	13,240	26,480	29,790	52,960
8	16.518	16,518	33,036	37,166	66,072
9	20.321	20,321	40,642	45,722	81,284
10	24.732	24,732	49,464	55,647	98,928
11	29.850	29,850	59,700	67,173	119,400
12	35.786	35,786	71,572	80,519	143,144
13	42.671	42,671	85,342	96,010	170,684
14	50.659	50,659	101,318	113,983	202,636
15	59.925	59,925	119,850	134,831	239,700

16	70.673	70,673	141,346	159,014	282,692
17	83.140	83,140	166,280	187,065	332,560
18	97.603	97,603	195,206	219,607	390,412
19	114.379	114,379	228,758	257,353	457,516
20	133.840	133,840	267,680	301,140	535,360
21	156.414	156,414	312,828	351,932	625,656
22	182.601	182,601	365,202	410,852	730,404
23	212.977	212,977	425,954	479,198	851,908
24	248.214	248,214	496,428	558,482	992,856
25	289.088	289,088	578,176	650,448	1,156,352
26	336.502	336,502	673,004	757,130	1,346,008
27	391.502	391,502	783,004	880,880	1,566,008
28	455.303	455,303	910,606	1,024,432	1,821,212
29	529.311	529,311	1,058,622	1,190,950	2,117,244
30	615.161	615,161	1,230,322	1,384,112	2,460,644
31	714.747	714,747	1,429,494	1,608,181	2,858,988
32	830.267	830,267	1,660,534	1,868,101	3,321,068
33	964.269	964,269	1,928,538	2,169,605	3,857,076
34	1119.712	1,119,712	2,239,434	2,519,352	4,478,848
35	1300.027	1,300,027	2,600,054	2,925,061	5,200,108
36	1509.191	1,509,191	3,018,382	3,395,680	6,036,764
37	1751.821	1,751,821	3,503,642	4,379,553	7,007,284
38	2033.273	2,033,273	4,066,546	4,574,864	8,133,092
39	2359.757	2,359,757	4,719,514	5,899,393	9,439,028
40	2638.478	2,638,478	5,276,956	6,596,195	10,553,912

A—18%

To estimate what any sum invested *regularly* at this return would grow to at a constant 18 percent rate of return for any period of return from one to 40 years, multiply that sum by the basic multiplier, which shows what $1 would grow to. (The table assumes that each investment is made at the *start* of each year.)

Examples

Plan Years Completed	Basic Multiplier ($1)	(Single IRA Maximum) $2,000	(Spousal IRA Maximum) $2,250	(Joint Return Maximum) $4,000
1	1.180	$ 2,360	$ 2,655	$ 4,720
2	2.572	5,144	5,787	10,288
3	4.214	8,430	9,484	16,860
4	6.154	12,308	13,847	24,616
5	8.441	16,882	18,992	33,764
6	11.141	22,282	25,067	44,564
7	14.326	28,652	32,234	57,304
8	18.085	36,170	40,691	72,340
9	22.521	45,042	50,672	90,084
10	27.755	55,510	62,449	111,020
11	33.931	67,862	76,345	135,724
12	41.218	82,436	92,741	164,872
13	49.818	99,636	112,091	199,272
14	59.965	119,930	134,921	239,860
15	71.939	143,878	161,863	287,756

16	344,272	193,653	172,136	86,068	86.068
17	410,960	231,165	205,480	102,740	102.740
18	489,652	275,429	244,826	122,413	122.413
19	582,508	327,661	291,254	145,627	145.627
20	692,084	389,297	346,042	173,021	173.021
21	821,376	462,024	410,688	205,344	205.344
22	973,944	547,844	486,972	243,486	243.486
23	1,153,976	649,112	576,988	288,494	288.494
24	1,366,412	768,607	683,206	341,603	341.603
25	1,617,088	909,612	808,544	404,272	404.272
26	1,912,884	1,075,997	956,442	478,221	478.221
27	2,261,920	1,272,330	1,130,960	565,480	565.480
28	2,673,788	1,504,006	1,336,894	668,447	668.447
29	3,159,788	1,777,381	1,579,894	789,947	789.947
30	3,733,272	2,099,966	1,866,636	933,318	933.318
31	4,409,980	2,480,614	2,204,990	1,102,495	1102.495
32	5,208,500	2,929,781	2,604,250	1,302,125	1302.125
33	6,150,748	3,459,796	3,075,374	1,537,687	1537.687
34	7,262,604	4,085,215	3,631,302	1,815,651	1815.651
35	8,574,592	4,823,208	4,287,296	2,143,648	2143.648
36	10,122,740	5,694,041	5,061,370	2,530,685	2530.685
37	11,949,556	6,721,625	5,974,778	2,987,389	2987.389
38	14,105,196	7,934,173	7,052,598	3,526,299	3526.299
39	16,648,852	9,364,979	8,324,426	4,162,213	4162.213
40	19,654,364	11,055,580	9,827,182	4,913,591	4913.591

A–20%

To estimate what any sum invested *regularly* at this return would grow to at a constant 20 percent rate of return for any period of from one to 40 years, multiply that sum by the basic multiplier, which shows what $1 would grow to. (The table assumes that each investment is made at the *start* of each year.)

Examples

Plan Years Completed	Basic Multiplier ($1)	$1,000	(Single IRA Maximum) $2,000	(Spousal IRA Maximum) $2,250	(Joint Return Maximum) $4,000
1	1.200	$ 1,200	$ 2,400	$ 2,700	$ 4,800
2	2.640	2,640	5,280	5,940	10,560
3	4.368	4,368	8,736	9,828	17,472
4	6.441	6,441	12,882	14,492	25,764
5	8.929	8,929	17,858	20,090	35,716
6	11.915	11,915	23,830	26,808	47,660
7	15.499	15,499	30,998	34,872	61,996
8	19.798	19,798	35,596	44,545	79,192
9	24.958	24,958	49,916	56,155	99,832
10	31.150	31,150	62,300	70,087	124,600
11	38.580	38,580	77,160	86,805	154,320
12	47.496	47,496	94,992	106,860	189,984
13	58.195	58,195	116,390	130,936	232,780
14	71.035	71,035	142,070	159,828	284,140
15	86.442	86,442	172,884	194,494	345,768

16	104.930	104,930	209,860	236,092	419,720
17	127.116	127,116	254,232	286,011	508,464
18	153.739	153,739	307,478	345,912	614,956
19	185.687	185,687	371,374	417,795	742,748
20	224.025	224,025	448,050	504,056	896,100
21	270.030	270,030	540,060	607,657	1,080,120
22	325.236	325,236	650,472	731,781	1,300,944
23	391.484	391,484	782,968	880,839	1,565,936
24	470.981	470,981	941,962	1,059,707	1,883,924
25	566.377	566,377	1,132,754	1,274,348	2,265,508
26	680.852	680,852	1,361,704	1,531,917	2,723,408
27	818.223	818,223	1,636,446	1,841,001	3,272,892
28	983.067	983,067	1,966,134	2,211,900	3,932,268
29	1180.881	1,180,881	2,361,762	2,656,982	4,723,524
30	1418.257	1,418,257	2,836,514	3,191,078	5,673,028
31	1703.109	1,703,109	3,406,218	3,831,995	6,812,436
32	2044.931	2,044,931	4,089,862	4,601,094	8,179,724
33	2455.117	2,455,117	4,910,234	5,524,013	9,820,468
34	2947.341	2,947,341	5,894,682	6,631,517	11,789,364
35	3538.009	3,538,009	7,076,018	7,960,520	14,152,036
36	4246.811	4,246,811	8,493,622	9,555,324	16,987,244
37	5097.373	5,097,333	10,194,746	11,469,089	20,389,492
38	6118.048	6,118,048	12,236,096	13,765,608	24,472,192
39	7342.857	7,342,857	14,685,714	16,521,428	29,371,428
40	8812.629	8,812,629	17,625,258	19,828,415	35,250,516

IRA Growth with No More Contributions

IRA growth at constant rates of return of 6 percent to 20 percent for basic $1 multiplier and for $1,000, $10,000, and $100,000 if no more contributions are made.

B–6%

To estimate what any sum would grow to at a constant 6 percent rate of return if left untouched for from one to 40 years, multiply that sum by the basic multiplier, which is the growth of $1. (The table assumes that the original investment was made at the *start* of the first year.)

Plan Years Completed	Basic Multiplier ($1)	Examples		
		$1,000	$10,000	$100,000
1	1.060	$ 1,060	$ 10,600	$ 106,000
2	1.123	1,123	11,230	112,300
3	1.191	1,191	11,910	119,100
4	1.262	1,262	12,620	126,200
5	1.338	1,338	13,380	133,800
6	1.418	1,418	14,180	141,800
7	1.503	1,503	15,030	150,300
8	1.593	1,593	15,930	159,300
9	1.689	1,689	16,890	168,900

14	226,000	22,600	2.260	2.260
15	239,600	23,960	2.396	2.396
16	254,000	25,400	2.540	2.540
17	269,200	26,920	2.692	2.692
18	285,400	28,540	2.854	2.854
19	302,500	30,250	3.025	3.025
20	320,700	32,070	3.207	3.207
21	339,900	33,990	3.399	3.399
22	360,300	36,030	3.603	3.603
23	381,900	38,190	3.819	3.819
24	404,800	40,480	4.048	4.048
25	429,100	42,910	4.291	4.291
26	454,900	45,490	4.549	4.549
27	482,200	48,220	4.822	4.822
28	511,100	51,110	5.111	5.111
29	541,800	54,180	5.418	5.418
30	574,300	57,430	5.743	5.743
31	608,800	60,880	6.088	6.088
32	645,300	64,530	6.453	6.453
33	684,000	68,400	6.840	6.840
34	725,100	72,510	7.251	7.251
35	768,600	76,860	7.686	7.686
36	814,700	81,470	8.147	8.147
37	863,600	86,360	8.636	8.636
38	915,400	91,540	9.154	9.154

B–8%

To estimate what any sum would grow to at a constant 8 percent rate of return if left untouched for from one to 40 years, multiply that sum by the basic multiplier, which is the growth of $1. (The table assumes that the original investment was made at the *start* of the first year.)

Plan Years Completed	Basic Multiplier ($1)	Examples			
		$1,000	*$10,000*	*$100,000*	
1	1.080	$ 1,080	$ 10,800	$ 108,000	
2	1.166	1,166	11,660	116,660	
3	1.259	1,259	12,590	125,900	
4	1.360	1,360	13,600	136,000	
5	1.469	1,469	14,690	146,900	
6	1.586	1,586	15,860	158,600	
7	1.713	1,713	17,130	171,300	
8	1.850	1,850	18,500	185,000	
9	1.999	1,999	19,990	199,900	
10	2.158	2,158	21,580	215,800	
11	2.331	2,331	23,310	233,100	
12	2.518	2,518	25,180	251,800	
13	2.719	2,719	27,190	271,900	
14	2.937	2,937	29,370	293,700	
15	3.172	3,172	31,720	317,200	

16	3,425	3,425	34,250	342,500
17	3,700	3,700	37,000	370,000
18	3,996	3,996	39,960	399,600
19	4,315	4,315	43,150	431,500
20	4,660	4,660	46,600	466,000
21	5,033	5,033	50,330	503,300
22	5,436	5,136	54,360	543,600
23	5,871	5,871	58,710	587,100
24	6,341	6,341	63,410	634,100
25	6,848	6,848	68,480	684,800
26	7,396	7,396	73,960	739,600
27	7,988	7,988	79,880	798,800
28	8,627	8,627	86,270	862,700
29	9,317	9,317	93,170	931,700
30	10,062	10,062	100,620	1,006,200
31	10,867	10,867	108,670	1,086,700
32	11,737	11,737	117,370	1,173,700
33	12,676	12,676	126,760	1,267,600
34	13,690	13,690	136,900	1,369,000
35	14,785	14,785	147,850	1,478,500
36	15,968	15,968	159,680	1,596,800
37	17,245	17,245	172,450	1,724,500
38	18,625	18,625	186,250	1,862,500
39	20,115	20,115	201,150	2,011,500
40	21,724	21,724	217,240	2,172,400

B–10%

To estimate what any sum would grow to at a constant 10 percent rate of return if left untouched for from one to 40 years, multiply that sum by the basic multiplier, which is the growth of $1. (The table assumes that the original investment was made at the *start* of the first year.)

Plan Years Completed	Basic Multiplier ($1)	Examples			
		$1,000	$10,000	$100,000
1	1.100	$ 1,100	$ 11,000	$ 110,000
2	1.210	1,210	12,100	121,000
3	1.331	1,331	13,310	133,100
4	1.464	1,464	14,640	146,400
5	1.610	1,610	16,100	161,000
6	1.771	1,771	17,710	177,100
7	1.948	1,948	19,480	194,800
8	2.143	2,143	21,430	214,300
9	2.357	2,357	23,570	235,700
10	2.593	2,593	25,930	259,300
11	2.853	2,852	28,530	285,300
12	3.138	3,138	31,380	313,800
13	3.452	3,452	34,520	345,200
14	3.797	3,797	37,970	379,700
15	4.177	4,177	41,770	417,700

16	4.594	4.594	45,940	459,400
17	5.054	5.054	50,540	505,400
18	5.559	5.559	55,590	555,900
19	6.115	6.115	61,150	611,500
20	6.727	6.727	67,270	672,700
21	7.400	7.400	74,000	740,000
22	8.140	8.140	81,400	814,000
23	8.954	8.954	89,540	895,400
24	9.849	9.849	98,490	984,900
25	10.834	10.834	108,340	1,083,400
26	11.918	11.918	119,180	1,191,800
27	13.109	13.109	131,090	1,310,900
28	14.420	14.420	144,200	1,442,000
29	15.863	15.863	158,630	1,586,300
30	17.449	17.449	174,490	1,744,900
31	19.194	19.194	191,940	1,919,400
32	21.113	21.113	211,130	2,111,300
33	23.225	23.225	232,250	2,322,500
34	25.547	25.547	255,470	2,554,700
35	28.102	28.102	281,020	2,810,200
36	30.912	30.912	309,120	3,091,200
37	34.003	34.003	340,030	3,400,300
38	37.404	37.404	374,040	3,740,400
39	41.144	41.144	411,440	4,114,400
40	45.259	45.259	452,590	4,525,900

B–12%

To estimate what any sum would grow to at a constant 12 percent rate of return if left untouched for from one to 40 years, multiply that sum by the basic multiplier, which is the growth of $1. (The table assumes that the original investment was made at the *start* of the first year.)

Plan Years Completed	Basic Multiplier ($1)	Examples $1,000	$10,000	$100,000
1	1.120	$ 1,120	$ 11,200	$ 112,000
2	1.254	1,254	12,540	125,400
3	1.404	1,404	14,040	140,400
4	1.573	1,573	15,730	157,300
5	1.762	1,762	17,620	176,200
6	1.973	1,973	19,730	197,300
7	2.210	2,210	22,100	221,000
8	2.475	2,475	24,750	247,500
9	2.773	2,773	27,730	277,300
10	3.105	3,105	31,050	310,500
11	3.478	3,478	34,780	347,800
12	3.895	3,895	38,950	389,500
13	4.363	4,363	43,630	436,300
14	4.887	4,887	48,870	488,700
15	5.473	5,473	54,730	547,300

16	6.130	6,130	61,300	613,000
17	6.866	6,866	68,660	686,600
18	7.689	7,689	76,890	768,900
19	8.612	8,612	86,120	861,200
20	9.646	9,646	96,460	964,600
21	10.803	10,803	108,030	1,080,300
22	12.100	12,100	121,000	1,210,000
23	13.552	13,552	135,520	1,355,200
24	15.178	15,178	151,780	1,517,800
25	17.000	17,000	170,000	1,700,000
26	19.040	19,040	190,400	1,904,000
27	21.324	21,324	213,240	2,132,400
28	23.883	23,883	238,830	2,388,300
29	26.749	26,749	267,490	2,674,900
30	29.959	29,959	299,590	2,995,900
31	33.555	33,555	335,550	3,355,500
32	37.581	37,581	375,810	3,758,100
33	42.091	42,091	420,910	4,209,100
34	47.142	47,142	471,420	4,714,200
35	52.799	52,799	527,990	5,279,900
36	59.135	59,135	591,350	5,913,500
37	66.231	66,231	662,310	6,623,100
38	74.179	74,179	741,790	7,417,900
39	83.081	83,081	830,810	8,308,100
40	93.050	93,050	930,500	9,305,000

B—14%

To estimate what any sum would grow to at a constant 14 percent rate of return if left untouched for from one to 40 years, multiply that sum by the basic multiplier, which is the growth of $1. (The table assumes that the original investment was made at the *start* of the first year.)

Plan Years Completed	Basic Multiplier ($1)	Examples			
		$1,000	$10,000	$100,000	
1	1.140	$ 1,140	$ 11,400	$ 114,000	
2	1.299	1,299	12,990	129,900	
3	1.481	1,481	14,810	148,100	
4	1.688	1,688	16,880	168,800	
5	1.925	1,925	19,250	192,500	
6	2.194	2,194	21,940	219,400	
7	2.502	2,502	25,020	250,200	
8	2.852	2,852	28,520	285,200	
9	3.251	3,251	32,510	325,100	
10	3.707	3,707	37,070	370,700	
11	4.226	4,226	42,260	422,600	
12	4.817	4,817	48,170	481,700	
13	5.492	5,492	54,920	549,200	
14	6.261	6,261	62,610	626,100	
15	7.137	7,137	71,370	713,700	

16	8.137	8,137	81,370	813,700
17	9.276	9,276	92,760	927,600
18	10.575	10,575	105,750	1,057,500
19	12.055	12,055	120,550	1,205,500
20	13.743	13,743	137,430	1,374,300
21	15.667	15,667	156,670	1,566,700
22	17.861	17,861	178,610	1,786,100
23	20.361	20,361	203,610	2,036,100
24	23.212	23,212	232,120	2,321,200
25	26.461	26,461	264,610	2,646,100
26	30.166	30,166	301,660	3,016,600
27	34.389	34,389	343,890	3,438,900
28	39.204	39,204	392,040	3,920,400
29	44.693	44,693	446,930	4,469,300
30	50.950	50,950	509,500	5,095,000
31	58.083	58,083	580,830	5,808,300
32	66.214	66,214	662,140	6,621,400
33	75.484	75,484	754,840	7,548,400
34	86.052	86,052	860,520	8,605,200
35	98.100	98,100	981,000	9,810,000
36	111.834	111,834	1,118,340	11,183,400
37	127.490	127,490	1,274,900	12,749,000
38	145.339	145,339	1,453,390	14,533,900
39	165.687	165,687	1,656,870	16,568,700
40	188.883	188,883	1,888,830	18,888,300

B–16%

To estimate what any sum would grow to at a constant 16 percent rate of return if left untouched for from one to 40 years, multiply that sum by the basic multiplier, which is the growth of $1. (The table assumes that the original investment was made at the *start* of the first year.)

Plan Years Completed	Basic Multiplier ($1)	Examples		
		$1,000	$10,000	$100,000
1	1.160	$ 1,160	$ 11,600	$ 116,000
2	1.345	1,345	13,450	134,500
3	1.560	1,560	15,600	156,000
4	1.810	1,810	18,100	181,000
5	2.100	2,100	21,000	210,000
6	2.436	2,436	24,360	243,600
7	2.826	2,826	28,260	282,600
8	3.278	3,278	32,780	327,800
9	3.802	3,802	38,020	380,200
10	4.411	4,411	44,110	441,100
11	5.117	5,117	51,170	511,700
12	5.936	5,936	59,360	593,600
13	6.885	6,885	68,850	688,500
14	7.987	7,987	79,870	798,700
15	9.265	9,265	92,650	926,500

16	10.748	10.748	107,480	1,074,800
17	12.467	12.467	124,670	1,246,700
18	14.462	14.462	144,620	1,446,200
19	16.776	16.776	167,760	1,677,600
20	19.460	19.460	194,600	1,946,000
21	22.574	22.574	225,740	2,257,400
22	26.186	26.186	261,860	2,618,600
23	30.376	30.376	303,760	3,037,600
24	35.236	35.236	352,360	3,523,600
25	40.874	40.874	408,740	4,087,400
26	47.414	47.414	474,140	4,741,400
27	55.000	55.000	550,000	5,500,000
28	63.800	63.800	638,000	6,380,000
29	74.008	74.008	740,080	7,400,800
30	85.849	85.849	858,490	8,584,900
31	99.585	99.585	995,850	9,958,500
32	115.519	115.519	1,155,190	11,551,900
33	134.002	134.002	1,340,020	13,400,200
34	155.443	155.443	1,554,430	15,544,300
35	180.314	180.314	1,803,140	18,031,400
36	209.164	209.164	2,091,640	20,916,400
37	242.630	242.630	2,426,630	24,263,000
38	281.451	281.451	2,814,510	28,145,100
39	326.483	326.483	3,264,830	32,648,300
40	378.721	378.721	3,787,210	37,872,100

B–18%

To estimate what any sum would grow to at a constant 18 percent rate of return if left untouched for from one to 40 years, multiply that sum by the basic multiplier, which is the growth of $1. (The table assumes that the original investment was made at the *start* of the first year.)

Plan Years Completed	Basic Multiplier ($1)	Examples			
		$1,000	*$10,000*	*$100,000*	
1	1.180	$ 1,180	$ 11,800	$ 118,000	
2	1.392	1,392	13,920	139,200	
3	1.643	1,643	16,430	164,300	
4	1.938	1,938	19,380	193,800	
5	2.287	2,287	22,870	228,700	
6	2.699	2,699	26,990	269,900	
7	3.185	3,185	31,850	318,500	
8	3.758	3,758	37,580	375,800	
9	4.435	4,435	44,350	443,500	
10	5.233	5,233	52,330	523,300	
11	6.175	6,175	61,750	617,500	
12	7.287	7,287	72,870	728,700	
13	8.599	8,599	85,990	859,900	
14	10.147	10,147	101,470	1,014,700	
15	11.973	11,973	119,730	1,197,300	

98

n				
16	14.129	14,129	141,290	1,412,900
17	16.672	16,672	166,720	1,667,200
18	19.673	19,673	196,730	1,967,300
19	23.214	23,214	232,140	2,321,400
20	27.393	27,393	273,930	2,739,300
21	32.323	32,323	323,230	3,232,300
22	38.142	38,142	381,470	3,814,200
23	45.007	45,007	450,070	4,500,700
24	53.109	53,109	531,090	5,310,900
25	62.668	62,668	626,680	6,266,800
26	73.948	73,948	739,480	7,394,800
27	87.259	87,259	872,590	8,725,900
28	102.966	102,966	1,029,660	10,296,600
29	121.500	121,500	1,215,000	12,150,000
30	143.370	143,370	1,433,700	14,377,000
31	169.177	169,177	1,691,770	16,917,700
32	199.629	199,629	1,996,290	19,962,900
33	235.562	235,562	2,355,620	23,556,200
34	277.963	277,963	2,779,630	27,796,300
35	327.997	327,997	3,279,970	32,799,700
36	387.036	387,036	3,870,360	38,703,600
37	456.703	456,703	4,567,030	45,670,300
38	538.910	538,910	5,389,100	53,891,000
39	635.913	635,913	6,359,130	63,591,300
40	750.378	750,378	7,503,780	75,037,800

B-20%

To estimate what any sum would grow to at a constant 20 percent rate of return if left untouched for from one to 40 years, multiply that sum by the basic multiplier, which is the growth of $1. (The table assumes that the original investment was made at the *start* of the first year.)

Plan Years Completed	Basic Multiplier ($1)	Examples		
		$1,000	$10,000	$100,000
1	1.200	$ 1,200	$ 12,000	$ 120,000
2	1.440	1,440	14,400	144,000
3	1.728	1,728	17,280	172,800
4	2.073	2,073	20,730	207,300
5	2.488	2,488	24,880	248,800
6	2.985	2,985	29,850	298,500
7	3.583	3,583	35,830	358,300
8	4.299	4,299	42,990	429,900
9	5.159	5,159	51,590	515,900
10	6.191	6,191	61,910	619,100
11	7.430	7,430	74,300	743,000
12	8.916	8,916	89,160	891,600
13	10.699	10,699	106,990	1,069,900
14	12.839	12,839	128,390	1,293,900
15	15.407	15,407	154,070	1,540,700

16	18.488	18,488	184,880	1,848,800
17	22.186	22,186	221,860	2,218,600
18	26.623	26,623	266,230	2,662,300
19	31.947	31,947	319,470	3,194,700
20	38.337	38,337	383,370	3,833,700
21	46.005	46,005	460,050	4,600,500
22	55.206	55,206	552,060	5,520,600
23	66.247	66,247	662,470	6,624,700
24	79.496	79,496	794,960	7,949,600
25	95.396	95,396	953,960	9,539,600
26	114.475	114,475	1,144,750	11,447,500
27	137.370	137,370	1,373,700	13,737,000
28	164.844	164,844	1,648,440	16,484,400
29	197.813	197,813	1,978,130	19,781,300
30	237.376	237,376	2,373,760	23,737,600
31	284.851	284,851	2,848,510	28,485,100
32	341.821	341,821	3,418,210	34,182,100
33	410.186	410,186	4,101,860	41,018,600
34	492.223	492,223	4,922,230	49,222,300
35	590.668	590,668	5,906,680	59,066,800
36	708.801	708,801	7,088,010	70,880,100
37	850.562	850,562	8,505,620	85,056,200
38	1020.674	1,020,674	10,206,740	102,067,400
39	1224.809	1,224,809	12,248,090	122,480,900
40	1469.771	1,469,771	14,697,710	146,977,100

PART II

How IRAs Work

You can open your first IRA in as much time as it takes to sign a piece of paper, but the tax laws relating to IRAs are not simple—and IRAs should not be entered into lightly.

When you open an IRA, you're making a long-term commitment and assuming serious obligations. There are major tax penalties if you break the rules, whether through ignorance or design. Consequently, it's in your own best interest to have a working knowledge of the laws, rules, and regulations covering IRAs, especially those covering your special circumstances.

As noted, in the beginning IRAs were a red-tape nightmare. Everyone with an IRA had to file a special form at tax time, and some people were trapped in Catch-22 situations simply because changes in their job status during the year made them ineligible for IRAs they had already started.

The rules have been simplified since then, and the 1981 Tax Act cleared up many problems when it authorized the universal IRA. But the tax laws on IRAs are still complicated in many respects.

Congress intended IRAs to be a simple form of retirement plan for the unsophisticated taxpayer. But since the authorization of IRAs in 1974, the technical literature about IRAs has expanded continuously. As with almost all sections of the Internal Revenue Code, the questions, explanations, and controversies over this section, together with regulations, pronouncements, and decisions, proliferate endlessly.

The Commerce Clearing House, in its widely used tax services, takes more than 70 pages to describe this "simple" retirement program. The Research Institute of America describes IRAs, including the regulations, in about 37 pages of rather fine print. The Bureau of National Affairs in its "Tax Management" portfolio on

104

IRAs, used mostly by tax lawyers and accountants, devotes more than 150 pages, many in small print, to this subject. Other widely known services have also published extensively on IRAs.

Despite all this analysis by professional technical writers, there are so many gray areas in the rules and regulations on IRAs that individual problems and cases still find their way into the upper levels of the IRS and the courts for interpretation and guidelines.

Nobody knows the answers to every question related to IRAs—and new questions are being asked every day. There are always areas of tax law where there is no clear understanding of what the law means until definitive decisions or rulings are made. Moreover, tax laws themselves are constantly being revised by Congress, as witness the monumental 1981 Act authorizing the universal IRA. Each time a new law is passed, many old questions are no longer of concern, but many new questions are raised.

For these reasons, this section cannot attempt to clear up every tax question related to IRAs. It will, however, give everyone who has an IRA or is thinking of setting one up a good working understanding of the basic rules covering IRAs. It will also be a good general working reference to some of the more complicated points of tax law that bear on IRAs.

For most readers, this will be enough. But if you venture into areas of IRA law where the answers to your questions are not clearly set forth in this book (and in the IRS publications cited in this book), you should seek professional advice. We will also try to point out circumstances where it would be a good idea to get professional advice before taking any actions.

5

IRA ABCs

Some general rules apply to Individual Retirement Arrangements no matter how or where they are set up.

This chapter provides a broad overview of how IRAs work and refers you to more detailed discussions of key points later in the book. Even if you're not concerned with the finer points of IRA law at the moment, read this chapter before setting up an IRA so you understand the fundamentals. It also tells you what you must do—and don't have to do—when you file your tax return.

How IRAs Must Be Set Up

All IRAs must be set up in the United States. The U.S. government would not even deliver its retirement bonds, one of the 3 IRA investment options until their sale was stopped in May 1982, to a foreign address. You may, however, make contributions to the offices of qualified IRA sponsors, even though those offices are located outside the United States.

If you work outside the U.S. during part or all of the year, you may contribute to an IRA only for that portion of your compensation on which you pay U.S. income tax. This effectively excludes many people who work abroad for private companies, as compared with members of the armed forces, the diplomatic corps, and other government employees.

The tax law that made IRAs universal also allowed employees of private companies to exclude up to $75,000 of overseas pay from U.S. taxable income, but none of this can go into an IRA. If you could put it in an IRA, you would be deducting it from your income for a second time.

IRAs must be set up for your exclusive benefit or for the benefit of your beneficiaries and must have a trustee or custodian. The trustee or custodian must be a bank, a federally insured credit union, a savings and loan association, or a person found eligible to act as a trustee or custodian by the IRS. In practice, this will be taken care of automatically by the IRA sponsor. You are not allowed to be your own trustee or custodian.

Except in the case of rollovers, all contributions must be made in cash (which can include checks, money orders, money market fund withdrawal orders, etc.). Rollover contributions can be made in property other than cash, but *only* if this is exactly the property rolled over. Often it is stock in the company sponsoring the plan.

The money or other assets in your IRA must be fully vested at all times. This means that if it is in a plan where you work, you must have the right to take all of it with you if you leave that job.

No part of your IRA can be used to buy a life insurance policy, and the assets in your IRA cannot be combined with other property except in a common trust or investment fund.

If you have income that qualifies, you can start an IRA at any time up to the beginning of the year in which you reach age 70½, even though you may be receiving retirement income from Social Security or some other pension plan or IRA. Your IRA or IRAs do not affect your Social Security benefits or any other private pension benefits to which you are entitled. IRAs are intended to supplement all other pension benefits and cannot result in your losing any other retirement income.

The IRS doesn't care how often you contribute, or how large (up to the maximum) or small your contributions are. However, individual IRA sponsors may set their own minimum contribution requirements.

When Can You Set One Up?

You can set up an IRA any time between the beginning of one tax year and the due date for filing your federal income tax for that year, including extensions. For most people, this would be April 15 of the year following the tax year.

Consequently, you normally have a 15½-month period in which to set up and contribute to any IRA for any given tax year. *But if you make any contributions after the end of the tax year, be sure you clearly instruct the sponsor as to which year you want your contribution to apply. If you're making your final 1983 contribution in April 1984, for instance, make it clear that the contribution is for 1983, not for 1984.*

If you wish, you can set up an IRA with a sponsor before making any contributions. This would make sense if it involved a payroll or other regular deduction plan— automatic withdrawals from your checking or savings account, for instance—that would take effect soon after you authorized it, otherwise there isn't any advantage in doing it. You may decide later that another IRA is better suited for you—or your financial circumstances have changed and you can no longer afford the IRA. There's little point in setting up an IRA unless you're prepared to make contributions.

What Income Qualifies?

Any money you're paid for doing something is "compensation" and qualifies as income for the purpose of setting up an IRA. This includes all wages, salaries, tips, professional fees, bonuses, and commissions as well as royalties for books, songs, and inventions, and any other payments for your personal services.

It also includes your *net* income from self-employment, whether it be as a self-employed professional or as an owner and sole proprietor operating your own business. Net income is your *gross* income from self-employment less any expenses related to your self-employment or own business income. These expenses would be deducted on your tax return and must be subtracted from your gross income to arrive at your net income from that source for that year.

People who work full-time will easily earn more than $2,000, the minimum net income required to make the maximum $2,000 IRA contribution. Whether you can afford a $2,000 contribution is something else again.

Many people who earn less than $2,000 of qualifying income during the year may wish to contribute 100 percent of that amount. They include people who are supported by a spouse or have non-qualifying means of support, such as income from interest, dividends, and rents, and also have a small qualifying income. This could be from part-time work, self-employment, or a side business.

You *are* allowed to combine incomes from different sources to reach the total amount of qualifying income.

If you had a net income of $500 from freelance writing or a side business, and $1,600 from a part-time job, your total income for purposes of establishing an IRA would be $2,100, or $100 more than the $2,000 needed to contribute the maximum. And if one or more part-time businesses show a loss for the year, you are *not* required to deduct those losses from any salary or wage income.

If you are an active partner in a partnership and provide services to the partnership, your income from the partnership also qualifies as income for setting up an IRA. The key word is "active." If you are an inactive partner who simply invests in the business and doesn't provide services, your share of the partnership income does not qualify.

By the same token, earnings and profits from other investments for which you do no more than put up money do not qualify—this includes interest, dividends, rents, and short- and long-term capital gains. All amounts that you exclude from your taxable income, such as certain amounts earned by U.S. citizens working abroad, don't qualify either. And you are not allowed to use unemployment benefits as the basis for an IRA.

If your income is entirely from investments, interest, and dividends, you may be tempted to set up a corporation or otherwise structure your investments to pay yourself a fee or salary for managing them. You can then establish an IRA on the basis of the fee or salary.

But be forewarned: the IRS has thought of that and has classified paying yourself "unreasonable compensation" for managing your own investments as a *prohibited transaction*. If the IRS concludes that the fee or salary you pay yourself for managing your own investments is unreasonable, it will disqualify your IRA. All the money in it will be thrown into your income for that year, and you may be subject to additional tax penalties.

What Are Your Investment Options?

There are 3 kinds of Individual Retirement Arrangements: individual retirement accounts, individual retirement annuities, and individual retirement bonds.

If you have a pension, retirement, or profit-sharing plan at work and your employer is willing, you can also contribute up to $2,000 to that plan and deduct your contribution on your tax return rather than opening an IRA or IRAs of your own. The pros and cons of doing so are discussed in Chapter 8.

Individual retirement bonds were issued by the United States government but are no longer being sold.

Individual retirement annuities are issued by life insurance companies. They will build in value during the years you make contributions and, if you wish, can be used to provide guaranteed payments to you when you retire, with a number of payment options.

Any other Individual Retirement Arrangements you make are called individual retirement accounts. These include savings accounts at savings and loan associations, banks and credit unions, accounts at mutual funds and families of mutual funds, self-directed plans (meaning you make the investment decisions in which you can buy stocks, bonds, or anything else that attracts an IRA sponsor), and such lesser-known investments as real estate syndicates and deeds of trust.

One thing you can no longer do (as of the moment, anyhow) is set up a self-directed IRA to invest in "hard assets"—such things as coins, stamps, antiques, gold or silver bullion, gemstones, works of art, and collectibles. The 1981 Tax Act treats any "hard-asset" IRA established after December 31, 1981, as a premature distribution, in effect outlawing them.

Your investment options don't stop with one IRA, however. You can have as many as you wish provided you don't contribute more than the law allows each year. You could open a savings account for $2,000 this year, a mutual fund IRA next year, and an individual retirement annuity the following year, or spread your maximum allowable contributions among two or more different IRAs during the same year.

After you start, you're not required by the IRS to make additions to your IRA every year. If you need money for something else or your income falls, you can contribute less than the maximum—or even skip contributions. However, you are *not* allowed to carry forward unused contributions into following years.

If you decide to change IRAs, the IRS allows you to close one IRA and move those assets into another IRA. However, some IRA sponsors will penalize you for withdrawing before your investment matures or is held for a specified period of time. *And IRS rules must be followed in making the move. If the move isn't handled properly, the entire IRA could be thrown into your income for that year—and you may have to pay a 10 percent penalty besides.*

Generally speaking, you can switch assets from one IRA to another as often as you wish *provided* it is a transfer made from one IRA trustee or custodian to another and the assets are never directly under your control.

You are also allowed one rollover per IRA per year in which you may handle the assets directly yourself. You have up to 60 days in which to complete the rollover of these assets, giving you in effect an interest-free loan for that period. But these rollovers must be at least 12 calendar months apart.

If you are given a lump-sum distribution from your

employer's pension, retirement, or profit-sharing plan when you quit your job, are fired or retire, or when your employer terminates the plan, any part or all of this money can also be rolled into an IRA within 60 days and sheltered from taxation. If you don't mix these assets with other IRAs, you may later roll them back into another employer's plan if the new employer will allow it.

How Long Can You Contribute—and When Can You Take Money Out?

Rules covering withdrawals from IRAs and how long you may continue contributing to them are generally the same for all IRAs except for individual retirement bonds, which stop paying interest when you reach age 70½, whether you cash them in or not. These rules are:

• You cannot take money out of an IRA before age 59½ without paying substantial tax penalties unless you are disabled. Chapter 6 discusses these penalties, what the IRS means by "disabled," and other potential problems with the IRS.

• Between ages 59½ and 70½, you may withdraw as much or as little as you wish each year. At the same time, if you so desire, you may continue contributing to your IRA up to the limit allowed, assuming you are earning compensation that qualifies. Even if you are no longer working, compensation that qualifies includes royalties, commissions, fees, or other payments for work you did in the past.

• During the year you reach age 70½ you must decide whether to (1) cash in your IRA and pay taxes on it, (2) establish a payout plan based on your life expectancy or that of you and your spouse, (3) buy an annuity, or (4) begin a payout schedule that will pay the IRA out during your lifetime or the combined lifetimes of you and your spouse.

• After the beginning of the tax year in which you reach age 70½, you are no longer allowed to contribute to an IRA. (However, if you are one of the few people in what is called a Simplified Employer Pension [SEP], your employer may continue contributing to your IRA after you reach age 70½, even though you are no longer allowed to do so.)

• If you have more than one IRA, you are *not* required to establish the same withdrawal procedures for all of them. You could fully withdraw from as many as you wished at age 59½, withdraw all or part of others up to age 70½, and then fully withdraw from as many as you wished while establishing payout plans based on your life expectancy, or that of you and your spouse, for the remainder. After age 70½, however, the minimum amount you must withdraw is based upon the total of all your IRAs at the start of that year.

While these are IRS rules, some IRA sponsors may have more restrictive rules or penalties for withdrawing from specific investments.

Current government rules covering IRA plans at insured banks, savings and loan associations, and credit unions say that these institutions *may* waive premature withdrawal penalties for fixed-term savings instruments for people age 59½ and older. They are not, however, required to do so, and many don't.

If these institutions wish, they also have the right to refuse to allow any withdrawal from fixed-term savings instruments until these instruments mature. In practice, hardly any depository institution would do this, but it is possible. You also have to pay big penalties for pulling out of other IRA investments, especially some insurance company annuity plans, in the early years.

Paying Tax on Your IRA

Federal income tax on money contributed to your IRA over the years and on your IRA's earnings or gains is not eliminated, it is merely deferred.

Contrary to what some over-enthusiastic IRA marketers may suggest, an investment in an IRA is not "tax-free." In the end, there is no free lunch. Sooner or later, you must pay tax on the money accumulating in your IRA or IRAs. And if you do not live long enough to pay it yourself, your heirs or estate will pay.

Your moment of truth with the IRS arrives when you start withdrawing money from your IRA. The withdrawals are taxed as ordinary income for the years in which the withdrawals are made, and the usual income-averaging formula can be used if it is to your advantage.

In their promotional materials, IRA sponsors often state that taxes should be lower when you retire and begin withdrawing ''because you will probably be in a lower tax bracket.''

However, this isn't necessarily so—although that should be no reason for concern. The fact is that if you open your IRA at a young age and contribute regularly over the years, you may build such a large IRA that when you retire, you may not be in a lower bracket. If your IRA is big enough, your retirement income might even put you in a higher bracket.

Astoundingly, IRAs (and Keogh plans) have been criticized for this. But what's wrong with having so much retirement income that you don't fall into a lower tax bracket? And possibly even having more income than you enjoyed during your working years? If IRAs can do this for you, how more fortunate you are than people who find themselves with their incomes drastically reduced when they have to stop working.

The great thing about an IRA is how it helps you build a much larger retirement income than you could in any other way. You're much better off building a retirement fortune with an IRA during your working years and then paying taxes on it as you withdraw the money than you'd be paying little or no tax because you have little or no retirement income.

Your goal is not to be in a lower tax bracket when you retire, but to have a comfortable retirement income. Paying taxes on that income is a small price to pay for the security it will buy.

What You Must Do at Tax Time

When IRAs were first authorized, *all* taxpayers with IRAs were required to file a separate IRA reporting form along with their regular tax return. If you didn't file this form, you were subject to penalties. This caused a great deal of confusion. It also gave IRAs a bad name with the people who had to put up with this extra red tape.

But the IRS has simplified the rules. You're no longer required to file a separate IRA reporting form with your tax return unless you owe penalty taxes for that year.

If you have one or more IRAs but didn't contribute to any of them during the year and are not subject to penalties, you don't have to do anything at tax time. It's not even necessary to note anywhere on your return that you have an IRA or IRAs.

If all you've done during the tax year is contribute the allowable amount to one or more IRAs, your only obligation when you file your federal tax return is to enter the amount contributed—and then subtract it from your gross income, reducing your taxable income accordingly. It is not necessary to break this amount down into parts if you contributed to more than one IRA.

If you have withdrawn any money from an IRA or IRAs during the year, the amount must be listed on your Form 1040. This includes any taxable premature distributions from your IRAs as well as allowable distributions if you are age 59½ or older, or are disabled.

If you receive a rollover from any qualified employer plan into an IRA during the year, this must be reported according to instructions for filling out that year's Form 1040. These often change from year to year.

A separate IRS form, however, must be filled out and attached to your Form 1040 if you owe penalty taxes *for that year.* This is Form 5329, Return for Individual Retirement Arrangement Taxes. These penalty taxes include taxes for excess contributions, premature distributions, prohibited transactions, or excess accumulations.

If you owe penalty taxes but are not required to file a Form 1040 for that year, file the completed Form 5329 with the IRS at the time and place you would have originally filed your tax return, including a check or money order payable to the IRS for the tax you owe.

While IRA contributions can be deducted on your federal tax return, not all states recognize them as deductible. Now that Congress has greatly expanded IRA coverage, it's likely attempts will be made to make some of these state laws conform with the federal law.

If you itemize your deductions, the cost of professional advice about your IRAs is deductible. Lawyers frequently divide their bills into deductible and nondeductible items.

Any interest earned on IRA assets while they are in

your possession between rollovers is taxable as ordinary income during the year in which it is earned.

Supporting Tax Documents

All IRA sponsors are required to send you a full account of your IRA by June 30 following the end of your tax year. (It's not possible for sponsors to provide this information much sooner because so many people wait until April to make their final contributions.) It's up to you to keep track of your contributions and to report the correct total on your return.

These reports from IRA sponsors are for your information only and should not be forwarded to the IRS. Keep them in your files in case your return is audited.

If you receive a *total distribution* from any IRA during the year, the sponsor must send you a Form 1099R, Statement for Recipients of Total Distributions from Profit Sharing, Retirement Plans, and Individual Retirement Accounts. This form contains the amount distributed and indicates the types of distribution. These are a premature distribution; rollover; disability; death; prohibited transaction; other, normal distribution; excess contribution refunded, including earnings; or a transfer to an IRA for a spouse because of divorce.

The form 1099R is for your information only and need not be attached to your tax return.

If you receive periodic payments from your IRA, the sponsor must send you a Form W2P, Statement for Recipients of Periodic Annuities, Pensions, Retirement Pay, or IRA Payments. These include regular payments to people who have become disabled as well as people age 59½ or older who have started withdrawing from their IRA.

A copy of this form should be attached to your return.

IRAs Set Up by Employers and Labor Unions

An IRA trust account can be set up for you by your employer, union, or employee association. Employers that do this are usually small firms that do not want to be burdened with the red tape and other requirements of a regular employer pension or retirement plan.

With this kind of an IRA, the employer, union, or employee association makes all the arrangements. It decides where to invest the money and makes contributions to the IRA trustee on your behalf. You are allowed to deduct the contributions on your tax return, and your records are maintained separately from those of other participants in the plan. When you leave the company or union, you take the IRA with you.

If you have this kind of IRA, the maximum contribution to this IRA by your employer and by you to any IRAs you set up on your own is $2,000 (or $2,250 in the case of spousal IRAs). If your employer contributes the full $2,000, you may not contribute to any IRAs of your own. If the employer contributes less than $2,000, you may contribute the difference either to your own IRA or to the one set up for you by your employer, assuming your employer allows it. Usually it would be advisable to contribute the difference to an IRA of your own so it will be under your control. (Note: This is not the same as an SEP-IRA, discussed in Chapter 12, which has higher contribution limits and different rules.)

What Happens If You Die?

When you set up an IRA, you'll be asked to name a beneficiary or beneficiaries.

If you die before you withdraw all of your IRA, the balance must be paid to your beneficiary or beneficiaries. The entire amount the beneficiaries receive will be taxed as ordinary income.

Up to this point, that sounds simple. There are, however, several beneficiary options, and professional advice may be called for here.

When your IRA reaches a substantial size, you may want advice on whether or not to specify how your death benefits should be distributed and, if the answer is affirmative, what to specify. If your beneficiaries have options to exercise and don't fully understand the implications of those options, they should seek advice before doing anything.

Your beneficiaries may elect to receive the entire amount in a single sum, treat your IRA as their own, or apply the balance to purchase an annuity. Annuity payments must begin immediately and continue over the life of each beneficiary or over periods no greater than their life expectancy.

One important factor to be weighed in making these decisions is that if the death benefits are paid in installments over at least 36 months, or over the life of the beneficiary, they will not be includable in your estate for federal estate tax purposes. This won't matter if your estate isn't big enough to be subject to federal estate taxes, but could matter a lot if it is.

Another factor is that if your beneficiaries elect to treat their interests in your IRA as their own, they wouldn't have to start distributing the IRA to themselves until age 70½ and would be covered by all the other IRA payout rules.

The IRS will assume the beneficiaries will treat any assets remaining in your IRA as their own if they have not been distributed within 5 years of your death. This will also be the IRS's assumption if the beneficiaries make payments of their own into your IRA or roll your IRA into their own retirement account, annuity, or retirement bond. If your beneficiaries roll your IRA into IRAs of their own, the IRS will not consider it a distribution.

6

Pitfalls and Penalties: Avoiding Problems with the IRS

Your retirement fortune-building program can be slowed or even derailed if you get into trouble with the IRS.

Breaking IRS rules regarding IRAs usually results in tax penalties. In some cases your IRA will be disqualified no matter how large it has become, throwing all the assets into your ordinary income for that year. If this puts you in the 50 percent tax bracket, you'll have to give half of your IRA to the government, and you may have to pay a 10 percent penalty besides, leaving you with only 40 percent of your IRA to reinvest for taxable returns.

But for any IRS rule violation, the penalty applies only to the IRA involved. Any other IRAs you may have are not affected; another good reason for diversifying your IRA assets, especially if they are so large that they represent a substantial part of your net worth.

In general, people get into trouble with the IRS because they don't understand an IRA's limitations. When you open an IRA you're probably thinking more of the projections of your possible future wealth than of the fine print that spells out those limitations and your own obligations. Understandably, the sponsor is more concerned with emphasizing an IRA's benefits than with dwelling on pitfalls that may lie ahead. And in fact some people selling IRAs are themselves uninformed or misinformed about the rules and the trouble you can get into by breaking them, so understanding these rules is your responsibility.

Many rules that got people into trouble with the IRS in early years were eliminated by the universal IRA. You no longer need worry about whether you were an ''active participant'' in another pension or retirement plan at any time during the year, a provision which until 1982 disqualified large numbers of IRAs. Today everyone with income from services can have an IRA whether or not they are covered by a pension or retirement plan at work.

But other danger areas remain. In particular, try to avoid getting involved in what the IRS calls a *prohibited transaction,* which can trigger the most severe penalties. You also risk penalties that could be costly when you engage in IRA rollovers and transfers.

While it's easier to avoid now than it used to be, there are still circumstances that could find you making an *excess contribution,* which in some IRS literature is now called an *excess payment.* You may be able to correct the excess by withdrawing it, and the consequences for making one are usually less severe than for other rules' violations. But the rules themselves are complicated.

The other side of that coin comes if you are age 70½ and begin a regular withdrawal program from your IRA based on your life expectancy or the combined life expectancy of you and your spouse. If you don't withdraw enough money each year the IRS can penalize you for what it calls an *excess accumulation.*

Table 18 at the end of this chapter is a penalty box

which summarizes the major IRS rule violations regarding IRAs and the penalties that may be assessed.

Premature Distributions

One very common violation of IRS rules occurs when people find they need some or all of the money in their IRA before they reach 59½—and then proceed to withdraw it.

This often happens because they get carried away by the idea of opening an IRA. They fail to take a realistic look at their financial resources and their ability to do without the money until they are near retirement.

Some people simply don't bother to read and understand the rules even though they are clearly and prominently explained in the sponsor's literature. Others, despite the most realistic assessments and the best of intentions, find they need money for an emergency.

Nobody likes to pay a tax penalty to the IRS. But under some circumstances, the penalty for a premature distribution may not be all that serious.

When you make a premature distribution, the amount must be included in your gross income for the year in which it was withdrawn. Unless you're permanently disabled, you'll also have to pay a 10 percent tax penalty on the premature distribution.

Example: You've been building an IRA for many years and find you need $10,000 for a medical emergency. When you withdraw the $10,000, it is added to your gross income for that year. Unless you have lost at least $10,000 of ordinary income from some other source, this will probably push you into a higher tax bracket. If you're not permanently disabled you'll also have to pay the 10 percent penalty, which is $1,000.

The money that remains in your IRA, however, is not affected. This is an important point. All the premature withdrawal penalty affects is the amount withdrawn. (These are IRS penalties only. Depending on what kind of an IRA it is, the IRA sponsor may charge a penalty or withdrawal fee for withdrawing money before the end of an agreed-upon period.)

You are not allowed to "make up" the premature distribution by putting additional money back into your IRA or IRAs in future years. Consequently, another aspect of this penalty, insofar as the size of the retirement fund you can build, is the "hidden" loss of the tax-sheltered compounding power represented by the sum withdrawn. The earlier in the life of your IRA that the money is withdrawn, the greater this hidden loss.

You can use the B tables in Chapter 4 to estimate what this hidden loss would come to at various rates of return. Each $1,000 earning a constant 12 percent return, for instance, would grow to $3,105 in 10 years, $9,646 in 20 years, and $29,959 in 30 years (see Table 17). If you withdrew $10,000 that could have earned at this rate when you are at age 49½, you will have reduced the amount that would have been available penalty-free had you waited until age 59½ by more than $31,000. If you withdrew it at age 39½, you will have reduced it by nearly $100,000; and if you withdrew it at age 29½, you will have reduced it by about $310,000.

Table 17: "Hidden Loss" of IRA Compounding Power Due to Premature Distribution
(Assumes constant 12 percent annual return)

Amount Prematurely Withdrawn	What Tax-Sheltered Sum Would Have Grown To		
	10 Years	*20 Years*	*30 Years*
$ 1,000	$ 3,105	$ 9,646	$ 29,959
5,000	15,525	48,230	149,795
10,000	31,058	96,462	299,599

What the IRS Means by "Disabled"

The only way to avoid paying penalties for taking money out of an IRA before age 59½ is to be classified "disabled."

Obviously, there can be honest disagreements about exactly what disabled means. This is bound to start some people who suddenly need their IRA money thinking about becoming disabled just enough to meet the letter of the law—and to do so with disabilities that may be more imaginary than real.

Unfortunately for these people, the IRS has some fairly precise guidelines as to what disabled means. Unless you measure up to them, you'd better be prepared to pay the penalty if you take money out of an IRA before you reach age 59½.

According to the IRS, you are "disabled" only if you are "unable to engage in any substantial gainful activity." The disabling condition, which could be physical or mental, must have lasted or be expected to last for a long period or must be expected "to lead to death."

The IRS adds that a condition that can be corrected is *not* a disability. You will not be considered disabled if "with reasonable comfort and safety, the condition can be lessened so that the person can engage in substantial gainful activity."

To be certified "disabled," you must attach appropriate medical statements to your tax return. For the first year, this means a doctor's statement about the disability. You must also attach a statement explaining the effect of the mental or physical condition, why you're not able to engage in "substantial gainful activity," and the date the condition began.

From then on, each year's tax return must have an attached statement saying the condition has not lessened substantially and that it still affects "engaging in any substantial gainful activity."

Can a Sponsor Refuse to Pay You?

Most literature prepared by IRA sponsors does not stress the point, but if you insist on withdrawing money from your IRA before age 59½, in virtually all cases you can get it.

The exceptions would be if the sponsor's right to refuse was expressly stated in your agreement with the sponsor, as is the case with some depository institutions, and the sponsor actually exercised that right. To avoid public relations problems, most of those sponsors will allow you to take the money anyhow.

Sponsors Must Report All Distributions

Sponsors are required to report all distributions from an IRA to the IRS, just as they report your interest and dividends.

Consequently, one way of triggering an IRS audit would be to fail to report the premature distribution on your own tax return. The IRS computer capability for matching sponsor reports with individual returns has been greatly expanded and can be expected to continue to improve. And now that the IRA is universal, it can be expected that the IRS will watch this area of possible abuse closely.

Does It Ever Pay to Take a Premature Distribution?

While we strongly advise against breaking IRS rules, the fact is that as the rules are now written there are circumstances where it could pay you to withdraw money from an IRA before age 59½.

This step should probably not be undertaken without consulting an attorney, accountant, or tax adviser, especially if it involves a substantial sum or there is a large sum in your IRA. The closer you get to age 59½, the more cautious you should be about jeopardizing the entire IRA by making a technical misstep or being unaware of a change in IRS rules and regulations or in the tax law itself.

Circumstances could arise, however—the loss of a job or other relied-upon income, catastrophic medical bills, or a need for more cash to keep your business from going bankrupt—that would make the need for immediate cash more important than the penalties for withdrawing the money.

Under those circumstances, the longer you've maintained your IRA and the more it has grown, the more likely that after paying the penalty you'd come out ahead.

A $2,000 investment each year for 20 years at a 12 percent return would build an IRA worth about $160,000, toward which you had invested only $40,000. If your income was entirely cut off because you lost your job, you could make gradual withdrawals from the IRA to cover your living expenses until you found another job. These withdrawals could be at the same rate, or less, at which you were earning income, so you would not be thrown into a higher tax bracket.

If it took you a whole year to find another job and your living expenses and other financial obligations required withdrawing $40,000 from the IRA, your total tax penalty would be the 10 percent premature distribution tax, or $4,000. Meanwhile your IRA would continue earning at the tax-sheltered 12 percent rate and would be worth more than $135,000 at the end of that year.

You would have suffered a slowdown in your retirement fortune-building program. But the penalty you paid for covering all living expenses and other financial obligations for you and your family during that year would make it a bargain,

In fact, even if the money withdrawn did push you into a higher tax bracket, in time your IRA would grow to the point where you could take the withdrawal into your income and come out ahead of investments with comparable safety on which you had to pay taxes all along.

Inevitably, some people will devise investment strategies around this. Even before the universal IRA became effective, *Business Week* reported that tax experts at Peat, Marwick, Mitchell & Co. developed a computer model showing how an investor with a retirement nest egg already assured from other sources could use an IRA as "a pure investment play." They found that depending on tax-rate and interest-rate variables, an investor who wanted to accumulate funds to be used 10 or 15 years down the road could close out an IRA investment, pay the taxes and the stiff penalties, and still come out ahead of any "reasonably conservative" investment program.

Keep in mind, though, there is always a possibility that if investment strategies built around deliberately violating IRS rules on premature withdrawals become widespread, Congress will stiffen the penalties—and people who set up IRAs for this purpose will find their strategies will no longer work.

Some Prohibited Transactions Disqualify Your Entire IRA

The penalty for engaging in what the IRS calls a *prohibited transaction* can be far more serious than that for taking a premature distribution. For some prohibited transactions, the entire IRA will be disqualified as of the first of that year.

A prohibited transaction is defined as "any improper use" of your IRA account or annuity. Three specific transactions that can trigger the disqualification of your entire IRA are:

• Borrowing money from it.
• Selling property to it.
• Receiving "unreasonable compensation" for managing it.

Having your entire IRA disqualified for one of these prohibited transactions would be serious enough at any time. But if it happened after you had built your IRA to six figures or larger, or had rolled over a sum of comparable size from an employer pension plan, the consequences could be financially disastrous.

If you had a $300,000 IRA and engaged in one of

these transactions, however small, you'd have to take the entire $300,000 into your income for that year, knocking you into the highest tax bracket. If that was the 50 percent bracket, it would cost you $150,000—half the value of the entire IRA—right off the top. If you were under age 59½ and were not disabled, you'd also have to pay the 10 percent premature distribution penalty, adding another $30,000 to your tax bill. When it was all over, instead of a $300,000 IRA, you'd have only $120,000 left to invest at taxable rates of return.

Actually these 3 prohibited transactions are simple and reasonable restrictions aimed at preventing self-dealing. If you're strapped for cash you'd be better advised simply to take a premature distribution from an IRA for what you need, especially if you don't need much, rather than trying to borrow from your IRA. Borrowing from almost any other source would be a better alternative.

Selling property to your own IRA would also put you in an obvious self-dealing situation, as would paying yourself unreasonable compensation for managing it.

If you engage in any of these prohibited transactions your IRA will stop being tax-sheltered as of the first day of the year in which the transaction occurs, and the fair market value of all assets in the IRA must be included in that year's gross income. "Fair market value," according to the IRS, means "the price at which the IRA could change hands between a willing buyer and a willing seller when neither has any need to buy or sell, and both have reasonable knowledge of the relevant facts."

Prohibited Transactions by an Employer

If you're in an IRA set up by your employer, labor union, or employee association and the prohibited transaction is engaged in by the employer, union, or employee association, you do *not* have to pay any penalties. Your account will not lose its IRA status, and you won't be subject to the premature distribution tax.

But if you knowingly participate in the prohibited transaction with your employer, union, or employee association, you will have to suffer the consequences. Your account or annuity will no longer be treated as an IRA, and if you are under age 59½ and not disabled you'll have to pay the 10 percent premature distribution penalty.

Other Prohibited Transactions

There are 2 other prohibited transactions for which the penalties are not as severe. These are:
- Using your IRA as security for a loan.
- Investing in collectibles (after December 31, 1981).

If you use any part of your IRA to secure a loan, that part is treated as a distribution. You must include it in your gross income for that year. If you're under 59½ and are not disabled, you'll also have to pay the 10 percent tax on premature distributions.

Pledging part of your IRA for a loan, however, does *not* disqualify the entire IRA. The part of the IRA not pledged to secure the loan retains its IRA status. (However, if you have an IRA annuity contract and borrow against it, you must include the entire contract's fair market value as of the first day of the tax year in your gross income. If you are under age 59½ and are not disabled, you'll also have to pay the 10 percent premature distribution tax.)

The ban on IRA investments in collectibles took effect in 1982. Collectible IRA investments made before that year may be retained and need not be liquidated.

The IRS defines collectibles as including "art work, rugs, antiques, metals, gems, stamps, coins, alcoholic beverages, and certain other tangible property." After 1981, any IRA investment in collectibles will be considered distributed and included in your income for the year in which you made the investment. If you're under 59½ and not disabled, you'll also have to pay the 10 percent premature distribution tax.

This provision of the tax law is controversial. Collectible dealers are trying to persuade Congress to make collectibles permissible as IRA investments again.

Can You Borrow to Buy an IRA?

In a word, yes.

There is some confusion on this point. While you may borrow money to buy tax-exempt investments— municipal bonds, for instance—the IRS will not allow you to deduct the interest on those loans.

IRAs, however, are not tax-exempt. Sooner or later, someone pays income tax on the contributions and on the earnings of those contributions. And so if you borrow money and use it to buy an IRA, you *can* deduct the interest under current IRS regulations.

Excess Contributions

The danger of making an excess contribution has been reduced substantially by the law that made IRAs universal.

Before 1982, your IRA contribution was limited to $1,500 or 15 percent of qualifying income, whichever was less. You had to make this calculation in addition to determining what your income for purposes of contributing to an IRA would be. These requirements led to many complications. Sometimes they resulted in people making excess contributions even though they did all they could to follow the letter of the law.

To make an excess contribution based on your annual income now, you'd have to contribute more than 100 percent of your income that qualifies for purposes of an IRA. Your income would have to be less than $2,000 if it's your IRA alone, or no more than $2,250 if a spousal IRA is involved. Most people can easily see if they are violating those rules.

Nevertheless, there are still many ways in which you could make an excess contribution. Usually the penalties for doing so aren't that serious—but under some circumstances they can be very serious and costly. In any event, the complicated rules governing excess contributions illustrate why there is nothing "simple" about IRA tax laws.

The most serious tax consequences for making an excess contribution stem from rollovers and transfers involving large sums. If a technical error is made in making these moves, part or all of the assets being moved may not qualify as tax-free and could become excess contributions, costing you thousands of dollars.

The tax consequences for simply contributing more to your IRA than you thought you could are less serious, but are annoying and involve you in additional red tape at tax time.

One problem arises if you plan to contribute the limit allowed, but aren't sure what your limit is. You may have financial support or income from other sources, with additional part-time qualifying IRA income from part-time work, self-employment, or a part-time business.

Only *net* income counts toward an IRA. Business expenses deducted on your tax return must be subtracted first. Misunderstandings or calculating errors could result in an excess contribution.

You could also make an excess contribution if you misunderstood the rules about "compensation" and included income from investments or other non-qualifying sources, such as a business in which you are not an active investor or partner.

You'd also wind up making an excess payment if you contributed a substantial sum early in January, but something happened to cut off your income for the remainder of the year—a serious illness, accident, or loss of a job. It's true that the sooner you make your IRA contributions each year, the faster they'll grow. But it would be prudent not to make a substantial contribution in early January if you're not reasonably sure of earnings sufficient to cover it—in severance pay if you lost your job, if nothing else.

Excess contributions could also result if you are in a plan where the employer makes contributions for you—to an SEP-IRA, to an IRA set up by an employer or labor union, or to the lesser-known 401(k) plans—and the employer contributes too much. In some cases it will be up to you to withdraw the excess contribution, even though the employer made the payment.

Finally, you could make an excess contribution simply through carelessness. You might forget that you contributed a few hundred dollars to an IRA back in January. Or you could fail to give proper instructions to an IRA sponsor as to which year you wish a payment to apply. This could happen for any contribution made between January 1 and April 15 of any year. Your IRA payments between those dates could apply either to the current year or to the previous one.

It's also possible that despite your instructions, a sponsor will credit your payment to the wrong year.

Penalties and Options for Excess Contributions

The penalty for an excess contribution is a 6 percent excise tax for each year it remains in your IRA. If you're under age 59½ and not disabled, you'll also be subject to the 10 percent premature distribution tax on the excess contribution's earnings.

More importantly, if your total contribution for the tax year in which the excess contribution takes place is more than $2,250—apparently indicating a clear intent to contribute more than is allowed—you also risk having the entire excess contribution included in your gross income whether you have deducted it on your tax return or not. This could result in your paying double the tax on the excess.

This picture isn't as bad as it appears at first glance, although it would still be best to avoid making an excess contribution. But if your total contributions come to no more than $2,250, you can avoid most of these penalties by withdrawing the excess payment and its earnings before the date on which your tax return is due. (And of course you must *not* deduct the excess payment on your tax return.)

This will excuse you from the 6 percent excise tax and from having the excess contribution included in your gross income. However, if you are under age 59½, you'll have to pay the 10 percent premature distribution tax on the earnings or other income of the excess contribution.

You also have the option of allowing the excess contribution to remain in your IRA and carrying it over to the following year (or years). To qualify for this, your total contributions for the tax year (including the excess contributions) must be no more than $2,250. (You are *not* allowed to carry *back* an excess contribution, applying it to an earlier year in which you may have contributed less than allowed.)

If you take the carry-forward option, you'd pay the 6 percent excise tax on the excess contribution for the year in which you made it and carry the excess forward into the following year.

Example: You contributed $2,200 to an IRA in 1983 when you were only allowed to contribute $2,000. You carry the excess $200 forward into 1984 and can contribute only up to $1,800 in that year. For 1983 you would pay an excise tax of $12 ($200 × .06 = $12), plus a 10 percent penalty tax on the earnings of the $200. These earnings would also be taxable.

But if your total contribution for the tax year, including excess contributions, is more than $2,250, you are not allowed to carry the excess forward. If the excess is still in your IRA after the date you file your tax return, you'll have to include it in your gross income even though you didn't originally deduct it.

In effect, this could force you to pay tax on the excess twice. If the excess is $750 and you're in the 30 percent bracket, you must pay an additional tax of $225 ($750 × .3 = $225) even though you didn't deduct the $750 on your return. If you're under age 59½ and are not disabled you'll also have to pay a 10 percent premature distribution tax of $75, increasing your total tax bill by $300.

Simple? Of course not. IRAs are indeed great investments—but nobody except an IRA sponsor ever said IRAs were simple.

How Long Should You Keep IRA Records?

It would be prudent to keep all records concerning your IRAs for at least as long as you maintain them.

You'll need those records in case of an IRS examination or audit. But while it's not likely the IRS will examine your return after 3 years have passed from the date of filing, there are many other situations where these records might be useful—or even essential.

These records may be needed to establish your rights to the assets in the IRA. They may also be needed by your heirs or estate to establish their rights to the assets if you die, or by whoever handles your affairs if you become permanently disabled in such a way that you are unable to handle your affairs yourself.

They may become essential if an IRA sponsor becomes insolvent or the sponsor's records are lost or destroyed. Conceivably, records could be lost in a fire, earthquake, or other disaster. Questions about your IRA could also arise if records are lost or misplaced in a takeover of one financial institution by another.

The larger your IRA and the more it represents in terms of your total financial assets, the more important keeping all these records in a safe place becomes. It would be a good idea to put them in a safe-deposit box and/or make copies of them to be held by others, such as your attorney or your beneficiaries.

Table 18: Penalty Box

Action	What IRS Calls It	Penalty
Taking money out before age 59½ (if you are not disabled)	Premature distribution	• Take amount into income for that year. • Pay 10 percent penalty on amount.

Contributing more than the limit	Excess payment or excess contribution	• If total contributed is less than $2,250, pay 6 percent excise tax each year on excess amounts remaining in your IRA. • If excess is withdrawn before due date of tax return, no excise tax due. However if under age 59½ and not disabled, pay 10 percent premature distribution tax on earnings of the excess contribution. • If total contributed is more than $2,250, include excess in gross income even if it was never deducted.
Borrowing money from your IRA	Prohibited transaction	• Account no longer treated as IRA as of first of the year. • All assets considered distributed and included in your income for that year. • If under age 59½ and not disabled, also pay 10 percent premature distribution tax.
Selling property to your IRA	Prohibited transaction	Same as above.
Receiving "excess compensation" for managing your IRA	Prohibited transaction	Same as above.
Using IRA as security for a loan	Prohibited transaction	• Part used as security considered distributed and included in your income for that year.

Table 18: Penalty Box (*Cont.*)

Action	What IRS Calls It	Penalty
		• If under age 59½ and not disabled, also pay 10 percent premature distribution tax.
Borrowing on IRA annuity contract	Prohibited transaction	• Value of entire annuity considered distributed and included in income for that year. • If under age 59½ and not disabled, also pay 10 percent premature distribution tax.
Investing in collectibles after 1981	Prohibited transaction	• Amount invested considered distributed and included in your income for that year. • If under age 59½ and not disabled, also pay 10 percent premature distribution tax.
Beginning in year in which you reach age 70½, fail to withdraw minimum amount.	Excess accumulation	• Pay 50 percent excise tax on the excess accumulation. (Can be excused if you demonstrate "good reason" for having the excess.)

7

Women, Husbands and Wives, and Widows

If an IRA can do wonders for one person's retirement income, it can do even more for a married couple's. If both spouses work and can afford the contributions, it can double their IRA retirement income and make retirement fortune-building that much easier.

Even if only one spouse works and has an IRA, the added benefits can be substantial. In this case, the law allows what's called a "spousal" IRA to be created for the non-working spouse. While the total contribution limit for this couple is only $250 more than for a single IRA, this can still increase retirement income by a respectable sum.

More importantly, the spousal IRA offers an opportunity—perhaps the only one non-working spouses, usually wives, will ever enjoy—to have an independent retirement fund under their control. And because up to $2,000 of the total $2,250 limit can be contributed each year into the IRA of the non-working spouse if desired, for a non-working spouse the spousal IRA has all the fortune-building potential, at least, of a regular IRA.

As with any IRA, couples should undertake commitments only if they're in a position to afford them. In many marriages, both partners must work because they need the money for living expenses. Little or nothing would be left over for an IRA.

Other couples could afford an IRA only by dipping into their savings—assuming they had savings. And if they might need those savings before reaching age 59½, this would not be prudent.

Still other couples could afford an IRA or IRAs—perhaps easily—by cutting expenses here and there, but for one reason or another may prefer not doing so. It might require their giving up things they value more than they value an IRA at that point in their lives.

These are personal decisions. What means most to you? A vacation? A new car or wardrobe? Eating out several times a week? Having a child? Financing an older child's college education? An investment opportunity? A hobby? A coveted work of art? Starting a business, or keeping one going? Supporting an aged parent? Or earmarking more money for retirement?

Alternative uses for the money you and your spouse could contribute to an IRA are endless and involve all aspects of your lives. As with all important domestic decisions, if a couple disagrees on goals and priorities, it may lead to spirited—and sometimes bitter—arguments. In short, if you're married, IRA decisions could affect both you and your spouse profoundly—and both of you should be involved in making them.

How IRAs Can Help Wives

The IRS words its IRA rules and regulations carefully to make it clear that they apply evenly irrespective of the sex of one spouse or another. In reality, when the IRS refers to a "non-working spouse," it is usually a woman.

Whether a wife works or not, IRAs offer retirement income opportunities that were not available to her before. One day this extra source of retirement income could prove more important to her than she dreams.

The facts are that the average age of widowhood is 56, and one-third of all widows are far below the official poverty line. Yet according to the Older Women's League Educational Fund of Oakland, California, less than 10 percent of all widows receive survivor benefits, and two-thirds of all widows live alone.

Three-fifths of all women over 65 are unmarried, while three-fourths of men over 65 live with their spouses. At age 75, there are twice as many women as men—and women outnumber men in nursing homes by more than 2 to one.

When a husband dies, the wife often loses her rights to part or all of her husband's pensions. Other than Social Security, all she may have left is what income she can get from an IRA or other pension plan of her own.

Many also lose part or all of the husband's pension rights if there is a divorce. In researching the plight of divorced or widowed homemakers and pension benefits, a committee of the Illinois Commission on the Status of Women found that only 20 percent of older women received *any* pension based on their own or their ex-husband's employment records. When there is a divorce, the husband may keep all of his pension benefits—and when he dies, there may be some doubt as to what happens to it.

At least to some extent, an IRA can help a woman offset these potential financial disasters. Even if the IRA is her husband's, it does not end when the husband dies. The money is still there. If he has named her as beneficiary, she can take all of it within 5 years, buy an annuity, or make the IRA her own.

A wife's right to receive benefits may end after a

divorce. A woman may be married to a man for his entire working life, bearing and rearing his children while he pursues a business career. But if there is a divorce, he may direct that someone else receive benefits after he dies—and she may be cut off without a cent of his retirement money.

A spousal IRA can give a non-working wife the advantage of having a retirement nest-egg in her own name, one she can do with as she pleases just as if it were built with her own earnings. (And in fact it *can* be built with her own money if the contributions are from her savings or from interest, dividends, rents, or other investment income she receives, even though this income does not qualify for an IRA based on her own earnings.)

If the non-working wife later goes to work, she can change the spousal IRA into a regular IRA by simply taking her contributions as deductions on her tax return or on a joint return filed with her husband.

IRAs are also advantageous for working wives. In many cases, wives must follow work patterns during their lifetimes that make it difficult to establish retirement income of their own in any other way. Many leave the work force during child-bearing and child-rearing years, or must change jobs frequently if their husband is transferred from one location to another. These interrupted work patterns may make it difficult or impossible to build retirement credits at work, but working wives can now build a retirement fund of their own with an IRA.

Even a wife who works full-time throughout her marriage can benefit from an IRA by building her own independent source of retirement income. It will protect her against the loss of retirement income if her husband should die or there is a divorce. If her IRA is large enough, it could assure her financial independence in old age after her husband's death. It will also help offset the inequity that finds a working wife's contributions unrecognized in calculating Social Security benefits if her husband's earnings have been higher.

IRAs and Single Women

These are things single women should also be thinking about. If you never marry, an IRA gives you the same opportunity all workers have of sheltering some income from taxation each year and using the money to build your own source of retirement income. But if you marry and leave the work force, at least you'll have one source of retirement income of your own, rather than having to depend for retirement finances on decisions your husband-to-be might make or on other forces beyond your control.

Even if you stop making contributions after you're married, the tax-sheltered earnings alone will increase the IRA's value substantially over the years. If a woman marries at age 25, has a $1,000 IRA earning at a conservative 10 percent rate of return, and makes no more contributions to it, it would be worth more than $45,000 when she reaches age 65. A $2,500 IRA at age 25 would be worth $113,000 and a $5,000 IRA would be worth $226,00.

IRA Rules for Working Couples

If both spouses work, each can have his or her own IRA or IRAs, and the rules governing IRAs in general apply to each. Their maximum combined total contribution is $2,000 each, or $4,000.

A working couple's IRAs must be established and maintained separately. Funds cannot be commingled in a jointly owned IRA. Because they are separate, these IRAs need not be with the same IRA sponsors, or even in the same type of investment. One spouse may have IRA contributions deducted from paychecks by an employer, while the other splits them among savings accounts, mutual funds, and insurance annuities.

Each spouse has control over what is done with his or her IRA. This includes naming beneficiaries and transferring or rolling over the IRA from one investment to another.

In practice, most couples will consult with one another before making investment and other decisions involving their IRA or IRAs—but they're not required to do so. Of course, they *are* required by the IRS to report on contributions, withdrawals, and any violations of IRS rules and regulations and penalties due on their tax return.

However, it's not necessary for working couples with their own IRAs to file a joint return, as they'd have to do with a spousal IRA. If both spouses work, and they wish to do so, they may file separate returns—although in most cases, the joint return would be more advantageous.

If the working couple can afford to contribute the maximum to their IRAs, their fortune-building potential will double. If each contributes $2,000 a year that earns at a constant 12 percent return, after 30 years they'd have IRAs totaling substantially more than a million dollars.

As with any other IRAs, contributions need not come directly from wages or other sources that qualify as income for the purposes of having an IRA. You can make your IRA payments from savings or other non-qualifying sources, including interest, dividends, capital gains, rents, and gifts. To make the maximum $2,000 annual contribution, all either spouse need do is earn at least $2,000 of compensation that does qualify during that tax year.

But a couple that is unable to contribute the limit and may even have to skip years when there is no money to spare for IRAs can still build a much larger retirement savings pool than a single worker in similar circumstances.

Irrespective of the age of the other spouse, each may continue contributing to the IRA (assuming there is qualifying compensation) until the year in which he or she becomes age 70½, when withdrawals must begin.

When Only One Spouse Works: The Spousal IRA

When one spouse works and the other doesn't, the IRS allows a "spousal" IRA to be established. This involves setting up an IRA for the spouse who doesn't earn any compensation.

To qualify for a spousal IRA, the working spouse must have an IRA too—and the couple must file a joint tax return. The maximum total annual contribution to both IRAs is $2,250 or 100 percent of income, whichever is less.

The spousal IRA gives couples with a non-working spouse the opportunity to contribute $250 a year more toward an IRA than a single person with a $2,000 limit can contribute. The couple must be married at the end of the tax year and meet all other IRA requirements.

The opportunity to contribute an extra $250 each

year won't make a great difference in the beginning. But the difference becomes significant as time goes on.

After contributing $2,250 each year for 5 years at a constant 12 percent return, the spousal IRA would have a total of $16,009 compared with $14,230 for the maximum single IRA contribution, a difference of $1,779. After 10 years, the spousal IRA total would be $44,222, compared with $39,308 for the single IRA, a $4,914 difference. After 20 years, the spousal total would be $181,571 compared with $161,396 for the single IRA, a $20,175 difference. And after 30 years, it would be $608,157 compared with $540,584 for the single IRA, a $67,573 difference (see Table 19).

Table 19: Sample Spousal IRA Gains
(Assumes constant 12 percent return with investments made at the start of each year)

Plan Years Completed	(Single IRA Maximum) $2,000	(Spousal IRA Maximum) $2,250	Difference
5	$ 14,230	$ 16,009	$ 1,779
10	39,308	44,222	4,914
15	83,506	93,944	10,438
20	161,396	181,571	20,175
25	298,666	335,999	37,333
30	540,584	608,157	67,573
35	966,926	1,087,792	120,866
40	1,718,284	1,933,070	214,786

Note: To see spousal IRA growth rates in detail, see tables in Chapter 4.

How Will You Divide Your Spousal IRA?

The other aspect of a spousal IRA is that it gives the non-working spouse—usually the wife—an opportunity to have an independent source of retirement income. But how much of each year's combined contributions should go to the IRA of the non-working spouse?

Until 1982 the IRS required that contributions to spousal IRAs be divided equally between the two spouses. If one had a $500 contribution during the year, the other had to have a $500 contribution, too.

The Economic Recovery Tax Act of 1981 changed that. Beginning in 1982, a spousal IRA can be divided in almost any way. The only limitations are that at least $250 must be contributed to the IRA of the non-working spouse—and the higher account may receive no more than $2,000 in one year.

In practical terms, this means up to $2,000 can be contributed to the IRA of the non-working spouse each year. But it also means $2,000 can be contributed to the IRA of the working spouse, leaving only $250 to the IRA of the non-working spouse.

This requires couples with a spousal IRA to make what could be a difficult decision on how to allocate their contributions. Many factors may have to be weighed. They include any assured retirement income from other sources, the assets owned jointly or separately by the couple, and the income-producing potential of both spouses. Also, which spouse has the better financial judgment? Will the offspring make demands on their retirement funds, a situation not unusual today? And if one spouse has a company retirement plan, shouldn't the other get the bulk of the spousal IRA?

The way spousal IRA contributions are divided can

vary from year to year to adapt to changing conditions. Up to $2,000 could go into the working spouse's IRA in tax year 1982, for instance, with only $250 going to the IRA of the non-working spouse. But in 1983, this could be reversed, with the IRA of the non-working spouse getting $2,000 and only $250 going to the IRA of the working spouse.

The 1981 Tax Act did *not* change the status of earlier contributions. These cannot be switched from one spouse's IRA to the other's. The liberalized rules on splitting contributions apply only to contributions made for tax years 1982 and later.

Just as with a working spouse, the non-working spouse has control over his or her IRA, including the right to name the beneficiary and to transfer or roll the IRA over into another investment. The spousal IRA is set up just as any other IRA. If the working spouse already has an IRA, all that need be done is establish one for the non-working spouse.

How Long May Spousal Contributions Continue?

If you are the working spouse, when you reach age 70½ you must stop contributing to your own IRA. However, rules have been proposed that would allow you to continue contributing to your spouse's IRA until he or she reaches age 70½. For the latest on this, consult a tax adviser.

At age 70½, you must begin taking distributions from your own IRA. However, your spouse doesn't have to start receiving distributions until the tax year in which he or she reaches age 70½.

If the non-working spouse is older, the working spouse must stop contributing to his or her spouse's IRA in the tax year in which the non-working spouse reaches age 70½—and the spouse must then begin receiving distributions.

You may still continue contributing to your own IRA as long as you have earnings that qualify. However, after your spouse has reached age 70½, your annual contributions to your own IRA will be limited to the ceiling for an individual—currently $2,000 or 100 percent of your income, whichever is less.

Working Just a Little Could Pay Off Big

While a spousal IRA allows an additional $250 to be sheltered from taxation each year, that's a far cry from being able to shelter up to an additional $2,000. A couple whose everyday living expenses are being comfortably met by the working spouse would come out much further ahead if the non-working spouse worked just enough to make a bigger contribution to his or her IRA.

In view of the likelihood that she will outlive her working husband, this would be a prudent step for a non-working wife to take—assuming she's in good health and has no objection to working. If she worked just long enough each year to earn the $2,000 or so needed to qualify for the maximum contribution, she'd soon have a substantial retirement fund that would be hers no matter what happened to her marriage in the future. It would provide some independence and protection in case her husband died and she was cut off from part or all of his retirement benefits, or they later divorced and she lost all rights to his benefits.

Even assuming the best of all eventualities—that the couple remained together and in good health well into old age—the additional retirement income she creates could make a difference between a comfortable retirement and one with financial worries.

Assume that a couple is age 55 with the husband earning enough to meet all of their needs and the children are grown and gone. If the wife worked just enough to earn $2,000 for the next 10 years and contributed the limit to an IRA each year, at a constant 12 percent return, she'd have nearly $40,000 ($39,308) when the husband retired at age 65—and it would be in her name, to do with as she pleased.

If she went to work at age 50 and contributed $2,000 for each of the next 15 years, the couple would have an additional $83,506. And if she started at age 45, in 20 years they'd have $161,396 in her IRA or IRAs.

Of course, this advice is easier given than followed. Where you live, there may not be many opportunities for finding a source of income paying up to $2,000 or so each year, but possibilities exist. Stores may be happy to hire a responsible adult willing to work part-time, especially at busy seasons like Christmas or Easter. Many offices would welcome part-time help too. If you have office skills, you could register with an "office temporary" firm and work just enough to earn as much as you pleased.

Babysitting or cottage industry income—from the sale of arts and crafts, for instance—also qualifies. If you earn less than $2,000 after paying expenses, you could contribute and deduct the entire sum. You'd owe no added taxes on those earnings until you began withdrawing from your IRA or IRAs. (But you would have to pay Social Security tax.)

Should You Put Your Spouse to Work for $2,000?

If you own or control a corporation, are the sole proprietor of a business, or have a business partnership, it may occur to you to hire your non-working spouse just long enough for him or her to earn the $2,000 maximum IRA contribution—assuming the spouse is agreeable. This is perfectly legal if:

• The spouse actually performs useful duties. If he or she merely shows up at the office and spends the day working crossword puzzles or making social telephone calls, it won't suffice. Work must be performed, and the work must relate to your business.

• In the case of a corporation, you withhold Social Security taxes. You can't have it both ways; if your spouse is going to take a deduction for an IRA, he or she must also pay the taxes other employees pay. (When one spouse is a partner in the business, you do not withhold Social Security taxes for wages paid to the other spouse by the partnership or unincorporated business.)

• The rate of pay is reasonable for the duties. If your spouse's principal duty is answering the phone and greeting visitors to your office, the IRS will not allow you to compensate him or her at the same rate you compensate your attorney.

If you are unable to demonstrate actual services performed and it appears that in putting your spouse to work you are merely shifting income, the deduction for the spouse will be disqualified and penalties will be assessed. But if service was rendered and the compensation is reasonable, the wages will qualify for an IRA.

IRAs Affect Marriage Penalty Tax Deduction

If a couple filing a joint return has one or more IRAs, it may affect the marriage penalty tax deduction—but not to a great extent.

Beginning in 1982, a two-earner married couple filing a joint return is allowed to deduct from gross income up to 5 percent of the first $30,000 of income earned by the lower-earning spouse. This deduction increases to 10 percent in tax year 1983 and thereafter.

But if the lower-earning spouse also has an IRA, the IRA deduction must be taken first. This will reduce that spouse's earned income for purposes of the marriage penalty tax deduction.

For instance, if the lower-earning spouse earned $20,000 in tax year 1983, the deduction without an IRA would be 10 percent of that, or $2,000. But money contributed to an IRA would have to be subtracted from the $20,000 before calculating the penalty deduction.

If the lower-earning spouse had contributed $2,000 to an IRA in 1983, this would reduce the sum on which the penalty tax deduction is calculated to $18,000. Ten percent of that would be $1,800, or a $200 smaller deduction than if the lower-earning spouse did not have an IRA.

You'll always come out ahead with the IRA. All you're giving up is 10 percent of your marriage penalty tax deduction (or 5 percent, if it's for tax year 1982). In return, you're getting 100 percent of the IRA deduction —and the tax-sheltered money in the IRA may grow manyfold.

What If There's a Divorce?

If there's a divorce, an IRA can be transferred from one spouse to the other by the divorce decree or other written document related to the divorce.

This transfer is *not* considered a distribution by the IRS and is tax-free. Beginning on the date of the transfer, the IRA is treated as the property of the spouse who receives it.

There's one important difference between an IRA transferred as a result of a divorce decree and other IRAs. In this instance, because the IRA was not originally set up for the benefit of the receiving spouse, he or she is allowed to make withdrawals before age 59½ without paying the 10 percent premature withdrawal penalty.

This being the case, it would be wise not to make any further additions to this IRA but to set up a different IRA instead.

Special rules apply to spousal IRAs. Until 1982, no contributions for the IRA of the non-working spouse were allowed for the tax year in which the divorce or legal separation took place. Beginning in tax year 1982, contributions *are* allowed after the divorce into the IRA of a non-working spouse—*but only under certain conditions and with limitations so strict that most divorced spouses will be unable to take advantage of this tax break.*

Contributions to the IRA of the non-working spouse may be continued if the spousal IRA was established by the individual's former spouse at least 5 years before the divorce. Also, the former spouse must have contributed to the spousal IRA for at least 3 of the 5 years preceding the divorce.

If these conditions are met, each year income can be

contributed to the divorced spouse's IRA up to the lesser of $1,125 or the sum of the divorced spouse's compensation, alimony, or separate maintenance payments. (If the divorced spouse has income of more than $1,125, the most that can be paid or deducted is your total compensation, or $2,000, whichever is less.)

But if these conditions are not met and there is a divorce or legal separation, there can be no contributions to the IRA of the non-working spouse during that tax year or later unless the spouse earns compensation that qualifies.

It makes no difference what time of year the divorce or separation occurs or when contributions are made. If you made the spousal contribution in January and the divorce or legal separation didn't occur until December, you still can't deduct it. All contributions to the non-working spouse's IRA during the year will be treated as excess contributions subject to the 6 percent excise tax unless withdrawn before the tax return for that year is filed.

The divorced non-working spouse, however, may continue maintaining the IRA on an inactive basis. All earnings will be tax-sheltered until the spouse begins withdrawing from the IRA. Unlike the case with an IRA transferred as a result of a divorce decree, if money is withdrawn from this IRA before the age 59½, it is subject to the 10 percent premature distribution penalty and must go into ordinary income for that year.

If the divorced spouse starts earning compensation, the IRA can be reactivated by making more contributions to it, or he or she can start another IRA or IRAs. The divorced spouse also has the right to transfer or roll the IRA over into another investment at any time.

8

IRAs and Your Retirement Plan at Work

If you're not participating in an employer pension, profit-sharing, or thrift plan at work, skip this chapter. But if you are participating in one—or will find yourself participating in one in the future—this chapter is must reading for you.

One of the most important provisions of the law authorizing the universal IRA is that if your employer allows it, you can now make voluntary contributions to your employer's retirement or pension plan and deduct those contributions instead of contributing to an IRA.

Many—in fact most—employers will not allow you to make these voluntary, tax-deductible contributions to their plans. But if your employer does allow it, you may contribute up to $2,000 to your employer's plan instead of to your own IRA. Or if you wish, you may split your contributions between your employer plan and one or more IRAs of your own.

This means that if you are in a company plan that allows you to make voluntary deductible contributions, you must decide whether your voluntary contributions will be deductible or non-deductible. If your financial resources are limited, you may also have to decide whether you'll come out ahead by setting up your own IRA or contributing to an employer plan—or by making voluntary non-deductible contributions to a company thrift or savings plan which are matched by contributions from your employer.

What Are Your Investment Options?

Before 1982, no voluntary contributions to an employer plan could be deducted from your income. They had to be made with after-tax dollars. The benefit was that your contribution's earnings would compound tax-sheltered in the plan. And if you later took a lump-sum distribution from the plan, you enjoyed very favorable tax treatment.

If your employer plan still allows non-deductible voluntary contributions, you may still continue making non-deductible contributions.

And you are not allowed to deduct any voluntary contributions to a company thrift or savings plan that are matched by your employer. These do not affect the amount you may contribute to an IRA.

The total of your deductible employer-plan contributions and the amount you contribute to your IRA or IRAs can be no more than $2,000 annually, but you may split the $2,000 any way you wish. You could make a $1,200 deductible contribution to your employer's plan and contribute another $800 to an IRA—and make non-deductible contributions to your employer plan too.

If you participate in more than one employer plan during the year you may make deductible contributions to all of them and to an IRA or IRAs as well—provided the total contributed is not more than $2,000.

If you deduct your employer-plan contribution, the

amount you deduct is not subject to withholding by your employer.

Characteristics of Employer Plans

A "qualified employer plan" means any IRS-qualified pension, profit-sharing, bonus, or annuity plan for employees. This includes profit-sharing, stock bonus, and bond purchase plans as well as the Simplified Employee Pension (SEP).

It also includes government, military, and teacher pension and retirement plans and annuities at all levels of government—federal, state, and local—as well as plans under which tax-exempt educational, political, and other organizations buy annuities for their employees.

One big advantage of an employer plan is that it is built with the employer's money. Contributions are made on your behalf, but are not considered part of your income for tax purposes. This money continues to compound earnings that are sheltered from taxation each year.

Another big advantage is that you may enjoy favorable tax treatment on distributions when you retire. You can use 10-year averaging for a lump-sum distribution, which reduces the tax bite considerably. You may also enjoy favorable capital gains treatment for unrealized gains on employer stock, and when you die your beneficiary can take advantage of a $5,000 death benefit exclusion.

Ten-Year Averaging

Basically, 10-year averaging allows you to pay tax on a lump-sum distribution just as though you had received it in equal amounts over a 10-year period rather than in a single year. Even when the lump sum goes over $100,000, the total tax due will be less than the top 20 percent capital gains rate.

Smaller distributions fare even better because of a minimum-distribution allowance. Half of the distribution or $10,000, whichever is less, is not subject to federal taxes. This means that for distributions up to $20,000, you pay tax on only half. This tax computation is independent of your computation on your other income.

Another potential tax advantage of an employer's lump-sum distribution is that employer contributions made before 1974 can be treated as long-term capital gains if you wish, rather than using 10-year averaging for that portion of the distribution. You or your tax adviser would have to figure the tax both ways to see which is best.

Employer Plan Pros and Cons

As you can see, an employer retirement plan is a good thing to have.

The bulk and sometimes all of the benefits stem from the employer's contributions, but you don't pay tax on those contributions as part of your income. And just as with an IRA, you don't pay tax on the earnings of those contributions as they continue to compound over the years. You may also enjoy substantial tax advantages for lump-sum distributions when compared with IRAs, which cannot use 10-year averaging.

On the other hand, the employer dictates the plan's terms and makes the investment decisions. You may have to work for the employer for a specified period of time before you're entitled to retirement benefits or have vested rights, which means being able to take your share of the plan with you when you leave the company.

If you're in a profit-sharing plan, you're not assured of any contributions from the company unless the company operates profitably and there are profits to share.

And you have no control over your contributions to the plan. You have no say as to how your contributions will be invested. And if you are dissatisfied with the progress of those investments, you cannot take the money out and invest it somewhere else.

If your employer allows it—and so far the majority of employers do not allow it, although there are some major exceptions—should you make a non-deductible contribution to an employer plan? Or should you make a deductible contribution to your employer's plan or to an IRA or IRAs of your own?

Under some circumstances, the favorable tax treatment you may enjoy upon receiving a lump-sum distribution when you retire may be the determining factor. You would of course have to be reasonably sure that you would be offered a lump-sum distribution. Not all companies offer one, and those that do often limit the option to executives and higher-paid employees.

The tax treatment is not an easy projection to make, and it depends on your life expectancy after taking the lump-sum distribution and on your other financial resources. However, the longer you would be expected to live and the longer you could keep the IRA's tax-sheltered compounding power working for you, the more likely you'd come out ahead making your voluntary contributions to an IRA rather than to an employer plan.

Contributing to your employer's plan is convenient, especially if your contributions are simply deducted from your paycheck. So, if you're one of those people who finds it difficult to save in any way other than through "forced savings" plans, this may be best for you.

If you want to put $2,000 into your company pension plan (or into an IRA through a company payroll deduction program) for next year, the company could deduct $38.46 from your paycheck every week beginning the first week of January. Of course this means that you won't be able to maximize the fortune-building power of your contributions by bunching them near the start of the year. But you will be able to reach your goal in a relatively painless way.

Also, weigh the probable return from the employer's plan against what you may be able to receive elsewhere. Some employer plans have done much better than others. If the employer's literature shows that the plan is earning substantially less than what an IRA could earn with reasonable safety, consider setting up your own IRA or IRAs instead.

One of an IRA's major advantages is that it is much more flexible than the employer plan. You always own 100 percent of it and can decide what to do with it. If you move to another part of the country, change jobs, or become aware of a better investment opportunity, you can move the IRA accordingly.

But what happens to your voluntary deductible contributions if you change jobs? Can you take them with you? Or must you leave them with the company plan until you are age 59½? Get the answers to these questions before making your decision.

With your own IRA, you're not tied to the fortunes of your employer's plan. As with any other investments, just because your pension plan has done well in the past does not mean it will continue to do well. A change in the management of the plan—or in the company itself— could result in a change in the plan's investment policies.

How well is your company doing? If it's a leader in its field or is clearly holding its own, you should have no hesitation about making voluntary contributions to its pension or retirement plan, assuming the plan's return is as good as what you could earn on your own.

But if your company is in trouble, it may be prudent to put your discretionary retirement dollars into an IRA rather than in that company's retirement plan. Certainly if the company is reporting losses every quarter, must depend on consortiums of bankers to keep afloat financially, and is closing some income-producing properties and selling others just to meet expenses, you'd be well advised to avoid further voluntary contributions. At this writing, IRA voluntary contributions are not covered by the Pension Benefit Guarantee Corporation, the federal agency that insures the assets of employer pension plans. (They would, however, be a preferred claim against the assets of the plan.) In any event, if there is any question about the solvency of your company plan, stop contributing to it and contribute the maximum to an IRA instead.

Another factor is the time you expect to continue working for the company. If you don't plan to remain long enough to earn vested rights in the plan, contributions made by your employer may be forfeited. In this case you'd also be better off setting up your own IRA. This is especially true if you change jobs often, either because of the nature of your work or because you don't like staying at one place too long.

If you can afford it, one strategy would be to contribute $2,000 to your own IRA each year—and then contribute as much as you can to your employer's plan on a non-deductible basis. This would give you the full $2,000 deduction while earnings continue to pile up tax-sheltered in your employer plan too, with the possibility of substantial tax advantages if you later take a lump-sum retirement distribution.

Employer Thrift and Savings Plans

Another set of factors comes into play with employer thrift and savings plans to which your employer makes matching contributions.

You are not allowed to deduct any of your own contributions that are matched by your employer. As a rule, these plans allow you to invest from 2 percent to 6 percent of your pay. The employer then matches some or all of your contributions.

Typically, an employer might match your contribution by 50 percent. If you contributed $2,000 to the plan, the company would contribute another $1,000, giving you an immediate 50 percent return on your investment.

That's a pretty tough deal to beat. No IRA will give you an immediate return remotely comparable to that. If the plan is earning any kind of reasonable return, your investment results will better those of most IRAs. If you can't afford to invest in both and must decide between investing in an IRA and making non-deductible contributions to a plan where the employer makes a substantial matching contribution, usually your best bet will be the company thrift plan, where you may also be allowed to make withdrawals before you reach age 59½ without penalty.

Many thrift plans, however, have one big drawback if you don't remain with the company long enough: you must be vested before you can keep the employer's contribution. If you quit or are fired before you are vested, you lose your rights to the employer's contribution.

Also, there's a point at which the matching contributions aren't big enough to overcome the tax advantage of deducting each year's contribution to an IRA. *Money* magazine reports that a study by the employee-benefits consulting firm of Towers, Perrin, Forster & Crosby, Inc., in New York City showed that for the employee to come out ahead, the employer should match at least 25 percent of your contributions.

Similarities Between Deductible Employer Contributions and IRAs

In general, the rules covering deductible employer-plan contributions and IRAs are similar. For instance:

• If you receive a distribution of deductible contributions from a qualified employer or government plan, you must pay a 10 percent penalty tax for the tax year in which you receive it if you are under age 59½. There is no penalty, however, if you are 59½ or older, or in the case of death or permanent disability.

• You are not allowed to make voluntary contributions to the employer plan and deduct them after the year in which you reach age 70½. (One difference, however, is that unlike an IRA, you are *not* required to begin withdrawals from an employer plan at age 70½ if the plan itself does not require it.)

• Contributions can be made after the end of the tax year until April 15 of the following year. This gives you flexibility in allocating contributions between employer plans and IRAs.

Warning: If you are in an employer plan that allows deductible contributions, it is your responsibility to notify the plan administrator if you intend your contributions to be non-deductible instead. Unless the administrator has designated some other date, this notification must be made by April 15 of the year following the tax year.

If you fail to notify the administrator, it will be assumed that your contributions to the plan will be deductible.

Whether you want them to or not, they'll count toward your $2,000 IRA contribution limit for that year. If you contribute $2,000 to an IRA and then contribute $500 to an employer plan that allows deductible contributions but fail to tell the administrator that it is to be a nondeductible contribution, you'll have made a $500 excess contribution to your IRA.

Distributions Are Taxed Just as IRAs Are Taxed

One thing you do *not* gain by making deductible contributions to an employer's plan rather than to an IRA is the favorable tax treatment on the portion of the plan represented by your deductible contributions. The portion of the plan represented by your employer's contributions continues to enjoy it, but the portion resulting from your voluntary contributions is taxed as an IRA distribution would be taxed.

If you're given a lump-sum distribution from an employer plan, the portion represented by your deductible contributions (and their earnings in the plan) must be included in your gross income for that year. Five-year averaging is available, however. You may also defer taxes by rolling this money into an IRA and later into another employer plan, assuming the other plan also permits holding the distribution as accumulated deductible employee contributions.

If taken other than in a lump sum, the distribution of your deductible voluntary contributions and their earnings must be under the annuity rule. This means regular payments must be made over your anticipated life span or the money must be used to buy an insurance annuity.

In that case, the tax treatment of the distributions gets tricky. The IRS assumes that your deductible contributions to the plan (and their earnings or gains) will be distributed after the non-deductible ones. The exception would be if the employer's plan states otherwise. In any event, this complicates figuring the tax on the distributions. Once again, you'll probably need professional help.

Many Employers Offer IRA Payroll Deductions Instead

For a number of reasons, the majority of employers, at this time at least, will not allow you to make voluntary deductible contributions to their retirement or pension plans. Doing so would require amending their present plans or undertaking a lot of paperwork and costly changes to set up new programs.

As an alternative, many employers have established payroll deduction programs for investments in regular IRAs. There is great variety in how these programs are organized. Sometimes the employer gives the employees the option of having the money deducted from their paychecks and sent to the IRA of their choice. Other employers offer specific IRA packages. Often these have been set up by investment management firms, insurance companies, mutual funds, or other IRA sponsors. These packages usually give employees a wide choice of investments. (Employers prefer that you have a choice because they don't want to be held responsible if you select an investment that doesn't do well. If they offered just one IRA and you lost money investing in it or didn't even do as well as the average investment, it would create problems in morale as well as other areas.)

Typically, these packages include several mutual funds—a money market fund and perhaps a stock, bond, or government securities fund. IRA packages are also provided by banks and thrift institutions with a variety of insured savings plans. In short, although your contributions are deducted from your paycheck at work, you still face the problem of sifting through all the sponsor literature and deciding which IRA is best for you.

On the other hand, sponsors of these packages often allow investors to participate in investments at lower commissions than would be charged if you bought these investments on your own. You also have the option of switching from one investment vehicle to another without worrying about breaking IRS rules and subjecting yourself to a big penalty, which is a major advantage.

Convenience is also a major advantage in contributing to these IRAs through payroll deductions—and the "forced savings" aspect of this approach may be essential for some people.

The payroll plan, however, may limit you to IRAs you don't like or that you don't believe are appropriate for your circumstances. You may also wish to set up your IRAs elsewhere if you don't think you'll be with that company for very long.

Some employers have decided not to get involved with IRAs at all, except perhaps to distribute some explanatory literature. As an executive of one major firm put it to *Business Week:* "There is just so much you can deduct from a person's paycheck."

Payroll Deduction Pros and Cons

A payroll deduction is certainly the easiest way to start an IRA, and it has a "forced savings" element that will help millions of people enjoy a bigger retirement income than they could ever have achieved otherwise.

But it also has major drawbacks.

One is that your choice of the investment vehicles is limited to those selected by your employer. You must invest either in the employer's own qualified pension or retirement plan and/or in investment options selected by your employer. Before signing up for any payroll deduction plan, compare the track records of those investments with investments you could make elsewhere. And by all means be sure you understand the nature of these investments.

If you don't know what a mutual fund or a money market fund is, don't commit your retirement dollars to them until you do know. Any investment that you understand and feel comfortable with is appropriate for an IRA, but don't sign up for any payroll deduction option that is unfamiliar to you.

Take your time. Study the options in your payroll deduction plan. One advantage of payroll deduction plans is that you can move money around from one investment to another without worrying about running into trouble with the IRS.

Technical Payroll Problems

There are some technical problems involved with any IRA program that depends on a payroll deduction plan.

One is that, in most cases, the deduction plan must

of necessity be built around the convenience of the payroll computer system. It may be prohibitively expensive or inconvenient for the computer to bunch contributions early in the year—or to extend them into the following year.

Another is that when an employer deducts your IRA contributions from your paycheck, the IRS authorizes adjusting your income tax withholding to reflect the new exemption in your gross income. However, not all companies will do this. If this change is not made, you could wind up over-withholding.

What's more, the government does not pay you any interest during the time it holds your money. By all means, before signing up for a payroll deduction IRA, learn if your employer is going to adjust your withholding accordingly.

The other side of this coin involves what could happen if you start a payroll deduction IRA plan for which your employer adjusts your withholding accordingly, but you later drop out of the plan. If your company's payroll department fails to readjust your withholding schedule, you could find yourself owing the government extra money at income tax time.

9

IRA-to-IRA Rollovers and Transfers

Sales literature prepared by IRA sponsors usually gives the impression that once your money is in their IRA it will remain there forever—or at least until you are happily retired and begin making withdrawals.

Actually you have a lot of flexibility in moving money (and other assets) around from one IRA to another. If you decide you don't like the performance of an IRA or think you see a better investment opportunity in some other IRA, you can move funds without paying any tax penalties provided you follow the IRS rules.

This flexibility is a great retirement fortune-building tool. It allows you to restructure your IRA investments to maximize profits (or cut your losses) by adapting to changing conditions or perceptions.

If you conclude that the stock market will be down for the next few years, you can get out of it. If you think stocks will take off and register gains far greater than what savings certificates or money market funds are paying, you can get in it. Or if you made an investment that isn't doing well, you can dump it.

You may also wish to move IRA funds for personal reasons. If you change jobs, move from one city to another or even from one part of town to another, you may wish to move your IRA to a sponsor with an office more convenient to your new job or home. If you opened an IRA simply because you had a business or personal relationship with that sponsor and that relationship ends, you may want to switch to a different sponsor. Or you may decide to move an IRA simply because people you deal with in a sponsor's office are rude or make mistakes processing your accounts.

Rollovers can also be made into an IRA or IRAs from a qualified employer pension plan under some circumstances—and can be rolled back into another employer plan if the second employer will permit it. These rollovers, which are covered by special rules, are discussed in the next chapter.

But after those employer plan assets are rolled into an IRA, you can move them from one IRA to another. So long as they remain in an IRA, they are governed by the same IRA-to-IRA rollover and transfer rules as any other IRA.

Two Ways in Which Tax-Free Movements Can Be Made

There are 2 ways in which tax-free movements of assets in and out of IRAs can be made: rollovers and transfers.

Both are allowable contributions, but obviously you cannot deduct them from income on your tax return. Your IRA deductions are limited to your regular contributions, if any, for that tax year.

Rollovers and transfers give you great flexibility in moving assets, but each move must be made with care. Before undertaking a move, be sure you understand the rules covering that particular move and the penalties for violating those rules, knowingly or unknowingly.

There are no IRS dollar limits on amounts that can be rolled over or transferred. This means that the IRS penalties for making a mistake when rolling over a large sum could be a major setback in your retirement fortune-building program—or even spell the end of it.

Some people tend to overuse the rollover and transfer devices. Some IRA investments require time and patience to work out. Before making a move, give yourself a cooling-off period to review all aspects of it. Is the new investment really all that better? Or are you getting caught up in an investment fad that could fade as fast as it arose? And up to this point, what has been your track record in moving other IRAs? Have the new investments usually worked out better than the old ones? Or would you have been better off sticking with the old ones?

Penalties Apply Only to That IRA

If a mistake *is* made in rolling over or transferring an IRA, any IRS penalties apply only to that IRA and do not affect any other IRAs you own.

This is another good argument for not putting all of your IRA dollars in the same investment basket once your IRA begins to reach what to you is a substantial size. Even if you wish to concentrate on one type of IRA investment, split your contributions among several sponsors. That way if you make a technical error in a rollover or transfer, your entire IRA portfolio won't be penalized.

IRA-to-IRA Rollovers: The One-Year Rule

A rollover is a tax-free movement of part or all of the cash or other assets from one retirement program to another. It is a movement where either the actual physical transfer is made by you or, at some time in the process, the assets are under your direct control.

Rollovers usually involve people moving money between IRAs—receiving a check from one IRA sponsor, for instance, and then using it to set up an IRA with another sponsor.

IRA-to-IRA rollovers must be at least one full year apart to qualify as tax-free. It isn't enough for an IRA to have one rollover in 1983 and another in 1984. At least one full year must elapse. If you make an IRA-to-IRA rollover on October 1, 1983, that IRA wouldn't qualify for another rollover until October 1, 1984. (You could roll other IRAs over, however. The one-year rule is *one year per IRA*.)

If you made a rollover of that IRA before the full year elapsed, it would be considered an excess contribution. If you withdrew the money before the date on which you filed your tax return, you would have to take it into your ordinary income for that year. If you are not disabled and are not under age 59½, you would also have to pay the 10 percent premature distribution tax.

If you didn't withdraw the money before filing your tax return and the attempted rollover was for more than $2,250, you'd still be required to withdraw the entire sum, take it into ordinary income, and pay the 10 percent penalty, if applicable. But if the rollover was less than $2,250, you could keep it in the IRA and the penalty would be a 6 percent excise tax for that year. You would also have to reduce your IRA maximum payment for the following year accordingly.

Example: In examining your return, the IRS finds that you made a $12,000 IRA-to-IRA rollover that did not meet the once-a-year requirement. Because the rollover was for more than $2,250, you have to take the

$12,000 out of the IRA and into your income as a premature distribution and pay tax on it. If you are in a 40 percent bracket, your tax bite for the disallowed rollover would be $4,800. In addition, if you are under age 59½ and are not disabled, you'll have to pay the 10 percent penalty; in this case $1,200, for a total of $6,000 in penalties.

Example: You make a $1,500 IRA-to-IRA rollover that does not meet the once-a-year rule. Because the rollover is for less than $2,250, instead of withdrawing it and paying tax on it as ordinary income (and paying the 10 percent penalty if you are under 59½ and not disabled), you pay the 6 percent excise tax on the rollover as an excess contribution for that year, which is $90 ($1,500 × .06 = $90). The $1,500 would then become a deductible IRA contribution for the following year, and you could contribute up to another $500 to a regular IRA or $750 to a spousal IRA.

The Same Property Must Be Rolled Over

In IRA-to-IRA rollovers, you must roll over to the new IRA exactly the same amount or property you received from the old IRA. If you receive stock from the first IRA, you must contribute the same stock to the second IRA. You cannot sell the stock and roll over the proceeds, or sell it, buy back an equivalent amount of stock, and roll the new stock over.

If you receive money in a rollover and the money earns interest or dividends between the time you take it from the first IRA and roll it over into the second one, the interest or other earnings cannot be included in the rollover. You must take it into your ordinary income for that year. Similarly, interest and dividends paid to you during this period on stocks or bonds being rolled over must be taken into your ordinary income. (You do *not,* however, have to take into your income *accrued* interest that may accumulate during this period but is not paid until after the rollover is completed.)

In considering an IRA-to-IRA rollover, don't forget to weigh penalties or fees that could be levied by IRA sponsors. These include early withdrawal penalties at banks, thrift institutions, and credit unions that under some circumstances could cut into your principal. They may also include substantial "back load" fees charged by many insurance companies for pulling out of their plans before a specified period of time. Self-directed IRAs and mutual funds may also have withdrawal fees.

Use these other fees or penalties as a factor in your decision to be sure the rollover you're contemplating is really all that good a move. You may find that by delaying your rollover a few weeks or months and waiting for an investment to mature, you could avoid an expensive sponsor penalty.

You Have 60 Days to Complete IRA-to-IRA Rollovers

You have 60 days in which to complete rollovers from one IRA to another.

This creates an interesting situation. As we've seen, in a rollover you may take physical control of the money or other assets. When the first sponsor gives you a check for funds to be rolled over, you needn't take it directly to the second sponsor. You could put it in your own checking or savings account or do virtually anything else you please with it for the next 60 days.

For all practical purposes you could give yourself an

interest-free loan to meet a big college tuition bill for one of your children, buy a car, make a down-payment on a house, pay off a gambling debt, take a world tour or whatever, provided you rolled over a like sum into the second IRA within 60 days.

Some tax advisers won't even tell their clients about this 60-day option unless asked. They know that people who start playing games with IRA money are running great risks, particularly if the rollover involves a large sum. If you are making a six-figure rollover, the consequence of not completing it within the 60-day period could be financial disaster.

If the rollover is not completed within 60 days, the IRS will require that you include the entire amount withdrawn from the first IRA as income for that year and pay tax on it. If the attempted rollover was for $200,000 and you are in the 50 percent tax bracket, you'd have to give the government $100,000 for failing to complete the rollover on time. If you are below age 59½ and not disabled, you'd also owe another $20,000 as the 10 percent premature distribution penalty.

If any payment is made to the second IRA, it is viewed by the IRS as a regular payment. You may deduct only the portion that qualifies for an IRA. If you had made no other IRA contributions that year, the maximum would be $2,000. But if you had attempted to roll over $200,000 as in the previous example, you would have to withdraw all of it before you file your tax return because the excess is above the $2,250 limit.

In short, if something goes wrong with a rollover involving big money during this 60-day period, you can find yourself in a lot of trouble.

Let Someone Know What You're Doing

The longer you hold IRA assets during the 60-day roll-over period, the greater the chance something could go wrong.

For one reason or another—illness, an incapacitating accident, simple forgetfulness, or death—the assets received from the first IRA may never get to the second one within 60 days. If this happens, the person who is penalized—or that person's beneficiaries, if the person dies and the beneficiaries are unaware that the rollover was in progress—would blame the tax adviser for providing information on the procedure.

Nevertheless, the option is there, and under some circumstances is useful. Ordinarily if you know what you're going to do with money or other assets received in a rollover it would be best to complete the rollover as soon as possible.

But this option does give you the ability to pull money out of an IRA quickly if you see you've made a serious investment error, have concerns about the sponsor's financial condition, or want to get out of that investment for any other reason. It could also be useful if you're moving from one part of the country to another and want time to investigate IRA sponsors where your new home will be located. Finally it would be a convenience if you knew you'd have no trouble finding money to complete the rollover and wanted to take advantage of an immediate investment opportunity or great bargain by giving yourself a temporary loan.

If you decide to make a rollover of a large sum for any reason, let someone close to you or someone who handles your financial affairs know about it. This could be your spouse, a family member, business associate, attorney, or financial adviser. If you are in the process of rolling over a large sum and suddenly are unable to communicate with anyone because of an accident, stroke, or other incapacitating illness, this person may be able to arrange to complete the rollover in time for it to remain tax-free. Doing so may require that someone have your power of attorney, which should be arranged in advance of the rollover.

Transfers from One IRA to Another

While IRA-to-IRA rollovers must be made at least one year apart, transfers from one IRA to another can be made at any time.

The difference between a rollover and a transfer is that with a transfer, the assets are never under your direct control. Rather than moving assets from one IRA to another yourself, the transfer is made directly between the IRA trustees, custodians, or contract issuers.

To make a transfer you instruct the trustee, custodian, or contract issuer of the first IRA to transfer the funds or other assets to the trustee, custodian, or contract issuer of the second IRA. This must be done in writing.

The trustee, custodian, or contract issuer of the second IRA should be informed that the transfer is to take place. And often, in fact, the sponsor of the second IRA will help prepare the paperwork and arrange the transfer for you. This transfer can also be handled by tax advisers, insurance brokers, and financial planners.

However, it is best to do the actual signing of all these documents yourself and be directly involved in the process until you receive confirmation that the transfer has been completed from both sides of the transfer. Keep track of the transfer—and if the paying trustee or custodian is slow to act, nudge them a little.

When a transfer is made, at no time may the assets be in your possession even if just long enough for you to carry a check across the street from one office to another —or even down the hall. If this happens, the transfer becomes an ordinary IRA-to-IRA rollover and is governed by those rules.

If it's been more than a year since your last rollover of that IRA, all you've lost is the chance to roll it over again for a year. But if you have broken the one-a-year rollover rule, the entire sum is now an excess contribution and could trigger all the IRS penalties. It could result in the entire amount becoming taxable income for that year, and subject you to the 10 percent premature distribution penalty besides.

Transfers Are Usually Preferable to Rollovers

The main drawback to a transfer is that it usually takes more time to arrange. It may take a couple of weeks (or more) to complete a transfer, while under some circumstances you could complete a rollover in a single day.

In making transfers, some IRA sponsors may be in no hurry to transfer your money or other assets to their competitors—or they may simply have inefficient office procedures for handling a transfer. For obvious reasons, they may be more interested in concentrating on procedures for getting IRA money into their financial institution than in letting it out.

If a sponsor doesn't complete your transfer within a reasonable time—two weeks would seem more than ample time under most circumstances—start phoning and writing the first sponsor to demand that the transfer be carried out. If this doesn't produce results, take your case to whatever government agency or agencies regulate that sponsor (assuming the sponsor is under government regulation).

All things being equal, if there's no need for speed you'll be much better off arranging a transfer than making a rollover. There's no limit to the number of transfers you can make. So making a transfer would preserve the right to move that IRA again in less than a year with a rollover if you believed it had to be moved very quickly —if you saw the investment turning sour, for instance. With a rollover you could cut your losses by getting your money out in one day, rather than seeing them deepen as you waited for the trustees or custodians to complete transfer arrangements.

With a transfer you also avoid the risk of something happening to prevent the rollover from being completed within 60 days after you take possession of the assets.

10

Rollovers Between IRAs and Employer and Other Pension Plans

From the beginning, people have used IRAs as a tax shelter for lump-sum distributions from employer pension and retirement plans. Now that IRAs have become universal and more people are beginning to understand them, this use for an IRA will increase.

You may not have other pension or retirement plans now because you're sure you'll remain covered by your company plan until you retire, at which time you expect to take monthly benefit checks rather than a lump-sum distribution. But during your working lifetime, circumstances could change greatly. Some of the most important decisions affecting your retirement finances (or those of your beneficiaries) may involve rolling assets from other pension plans into an IRA—and later, possibly rolling them back into another employer plan.

Some differences between IRAs and qualified employer plans—which include government and teacher plans as well as those offered by private employers—are discussed in Chapter 8. Insofar as they relate to potential rollovers of lump-sum employer-plan distributions in and out of IRAs, the major difference is that in general the tax treatment of a lump-sum distribution from an employer plan is more favorable than for an IRA. A portion of the lump-sum distribution may be taxable as long-term capital gains, and all of it may be subject to a favorable 10-year averaging rule. Money rolled into an IRA from an employer plan will continue to pile up tax-sheltered earnings and, in time, more than offset the less favorable tax treatment given IRA distributions when you begin withdrawing money.

Complicating your choices, if you are given a lump-sum distribution that you would be permitted to roll over into an IRA during your working years, is the fact that you may wish to use the IRA as a "conduit" and roll it back to a new employer plan at some later date—if the new employer will allow it.

Consequently, when you are given a lump-sum distribution from a qualified pension, profit-sharing, or stock bonus plan, there are many important implications. You may have only 60 days in which to make decisions that could profoundly affect your financial situation for decades.

The rules covering employer-plan rollovers are also among the most complex related to IRAs. Again, this is a situation where professional advice may be needed.

When Can Employer Rollovers Be Made?

Circumstances under which the IRS will allow a tax-free lump-sum rollover from an employer pension, profit-sharing, or stock bonus plan into an IRA (assuming your employer permits it) include:

• You leave your job for any reason, whether voluntarily or because your services have been terminated.

• You are age 59½ or older.

• Your employer ends a pension plan or permanently stops making payments to a profit-sharing or stock bonus plan and gives you your complete share.

• You die—in which case your beneficiary or beneficiaries may roll your death benefits from the plan into an IRA if they wish.

Although your complete share in the employer plan need not be paid to you in a single installment, to qualify as a tax-free rollover into an IRA it must be received within a single tax year. If you were paid part of the distribution in 1983 and part in 1984, you could not roll over either portion because this would not meet the one-year test.

You Cannot "Quit" Self-Employment

One exception to these rules involves the self-employed. The IRS will not allow you to "quit" self-employment and give yourself a lump-sum distribution from your IRA before you are age 59½. Obviously, if you were able to do this, you could get your hands on the money while avoiding the 10 percent premature distribution tax.

If you stop being self-employed, you must still keep the money in an IRA until age 59½—or pay the tax penalty if you take it out before then.

However, if you are self-employed and become permanently disabled, you *are* allowed to take a lump-sum distribution of everything in your IRA without a tax penalty. Of course, you'd have to report the distribution as income for that year and pay tax on it.

Employer Plan Rollovers Must Also Be Made Within 60 Days

As with IRA-to-IRA rollovers, rollovers from an employer plan must be completed within 60 days of the date the assets are distributed to you.

While the assets are under your control, any earnings paid to you must be taken into your income for that year. If you rolled $50,000 into a money market mutual fund, the earnings from the $50,000 would remain in the fund. You could contribute no more than $50,000 to the IRA when you complete the rollover.

These Rollovers Can Be Made More Than Once a Year

One important difference between employer plan rollovers and IRA-to-IRA rollovers is that rollovers out of or into employer plans are not subject to the once-a-year rule. They can be made at any time.

If you lose your job and roll an employer-plan distribution into an IRA, you could roll that money right back into another employer plan if you got a new job and the employer allowed the rollover.

When the assets are in your IRA, however, movements to any other IRA would be covered by the IRA-to-IRA rules. If you moved them to another IRA with a rollover, the move would be covered by the once-a-year rule. But if you transferred them from one IRA trustee or custodian to another, you could move them as often as you like.

To Keep the "Rollback" Option, Don't Mix IRA Assets

After you roll assets from an employer plan into an IRA, the law allows you to roll them back (along with any tax-sheltered earnings while they were in the IRA) to another employer plan at a later date.

For most people, retaining this option would be a good idea. Even if you have no intention of rolling these assets back to an employer plan now, you could change your mind later.

But if you wish to roll these assets and their IRA earnings back into another employer plan at any time in the future, you must never mix these assets with any other IRA assets.

Do not roll money or any other assets from an employer plan into any other IRA if you wish to retain this option. Even if the IRA you roll the assets into has only a few dollars in it, you'd lose the right to make a tax-free rollback later.

Rollover from Employer Plan

Set up a separate IRA for the assets being rolled over from the qualified employer plan. And, as long as you wish to retain the rollback option, do not make any more contributions to this IRA.

If you mix assets and then attempt to roll this IRA into another employer plan, the entire amount will be considered distributed to you and taxable for that year. If you are under age 59½ and are not disabled, you'll also have to pay the 10 percent premature distribution penalty. Again, if you made this technical mistake and this was a six-figure IRA, it would prove to be a financial disaster.

You Needn't Roll All the Assets Over

When you receive a distribution from a qualified employer plan under conditions that permit rolling it into an IRA, you are *not* required to roll *all* of it over. If you wish, you may roll over part of the assets tax-free and keep the remainder.

There is, however, an important trade-off if you split the distribution and that is you will *not* be allowed to use the favorable 10-year averaging treatment for the amount that you keep. You will be eligible for the regular 5-year averaging treatment if you qualify, but the special tax treatment for other qualified employer-plan distributions is not available.

You may also split the rollover assets into more than one IRA. The same rules about later rolling those assets back into another employer plan apply. To retain the rollback option, these IRA assets must never be mingled with other assets. However, if you commingle only some of the assets with those from some other source, only that commingled IRA is disqualified from rolling back into an employer plan tax-free.

These rules give you a lot of flexibility, particularly with a large employer-plan distribution. If you receive a $100,000 distribution from an employer plan, you could keep $20,000 as part of your ordinary income for that year and split the remainder by setting up 8 separate IRAs for $10,000 each—or as many IRAs as you wish, for that matter—in a wide variety of investments. If you were willing to give up the option to roll this money back into another employer plan later, you could also roll these assets into one or more existing IRAs.

Non-Deductible Voluntary Contributions Can't Be Rolled Over

For years, some employer plans allowed employees to make voluntary contributions that you were not allowed to deduct from your income. Although the employer's plan sheltered the earnings of those contributions from taxation, the contributions were made with after-tax dollars. Before 1982, all voluntary employer-plan contributions were of this type.

If you roll your share of an employer plan into an IRA, you are not allowed to roll over the portion that consists of these voluntary, non-deductible contributions. Before completing the rollover, take those contributions out and keep the money. (Your employer will give you a statement totalling your voluntary contributions.)

That money doesn't have to be added to your income, however. It has already been taxed or will be included by the employer in your current year's earnings statement, if the contributions were made in the current year.

Example: You're given a $100,000 lump-sum distribution from an employer plan, but $5,000 of that represents your own non-deductible contributions. You subtract the $5,000 and may roll over up to the remaining $95,000 into an IRA—tax-free. If you roll over any portion of your non-deductible contributions, that portion will be viewed as an excess contribution even though you have already paid tax on this money.

Deductible Voluntary Contributions Can Be Rolled Over

Beginning in 1982, if an employer allows it, you are permitted to make voluntary contributions to your employer's plan and deduct them instead of making contributions to an IRA.

If the employer later gives you a lump-sum distribution, these contributions *can* be rolled over into an IRA or another employer pension plan. Your employer will give you a statement telling you what they are.

If you decide to keep these voluntary deductible contributions rather than rolling them over into an IRA, they will be considered distributions from the plan. You'll have to take them into income for that year and pay tax on them. If you are under age 59½ and are not disabled, you'll have to pay the 10 percent premature distribution penalty.

The rollover rules covering voluntary contributions are complicated, to say the least. It shouldn't be surprising if some IRA sponsors don't fully understand them. And so if you can show that your rollover resulted in an excess payment because the sponsor gave you incorrect information, the IRS says in its Publication 590, which discusses Individual Retirement Arrangements, that it will allow you to withdraw the excess without having to include it in your gross income.

Rollover or Sale of Property Received in a Distribution

A distribution from an employer plan may also include property—most typically stock in the employer company.

Unlike an IRA-to-IRA rollover where the exact property received must be rolled over, you *are* allowed to sell property received from an employer plan and then to roll it (or a portion of it) into an IRA—tax-free. In fact, many financial institutions are unwilling to accept the responsibility for being caretaker to your stock in an IRA. Their IRA agreement with you may specify that if you turn over stock, the institutions will convert it into cash.

The ability to roll over proceeds from sale of property greatly widens your options. However, it could also complicate the preparation of your tax return—so much so that at this level, you should definitely be receiving professional guidance.

Things are still relatively simple if you roll all of the property, or all the money you receive from the property's sale, into another IRA. In that case, there would be no gain or loss to report on your return for that year.

If your employer gave you a distribution of $100,000 in stock in the company and you sold it within the 60-day period for $120,000 and rolled the entire amount into an IRA, you do not have to report the $20,000 as a gain. (Similarly, however, if you sold the stock for $80,000, you couldn't take the loss.)

Procedures become more complicated if you decide to sell property but do not roll over the entire proceeds. In this event, you'll be taxed on the part you do not roll over. Part of that will be a capital gain or loss on the sale, and part will be on ordinary income. And as with an all-cash distribution, any portion you keep and do not roll over does not qualify for the favorable 10-year tax treatment.

The fair market value of the property (after subtracting any non-deductible contributions you may have made) on the date it was distributed to you will be taxed as ordinary income. The difference between the fair market value on the date you received the property and what you obtained when you sold it will be a capital gain or loss.

You must designate on your tax return how much of the ordinary income and capital gain portion was retained by you and how much of each was contributed to the IRA.

Annuity-to-IRA Rollover

You may also roll a lump-sum distribution from a tax-sheltered annuity into an IRA. However, you can roll over only the part of the annuity that would normally be taxed, which is the part that does not represent your non-deductible contributions.

As with rollovers from employer plans, these rollovers must be completed within 60 days.

The assets can later be rolled into another tax-sheltered annuity, but only if they have not been combined with IRA assets from any other source. And you are not allowed to roll these assets into an employer plan—only into another annuity.

Keogh-to-IRA Rollover

Under some circumstances, a lump-sum distribution may be rolled over from a Keogh plan into an IRA, although there are few self-employed people who would want to do so. If you're not disabled and are under age 59½, you must completely terminate the Keogh plan when making the rollover.

If you're age 59½ or older, the Keogh plan can be maintained. But to qualify as a lump-sum distribution, the assets you roll out of the plan must have been in it for at least 5 years. If you wish to roll over assets that have been in your Keogh plan for less than 5 years, you must terminate the entire plan and roll all the assets over.

Some pros and cons of Keogh plans and IRAs are discussed in Chapter 12.

If you are an employee covered by a Keogh plan and leave the job, you may roll your portion of the Keogh plan over into an IRA within 60 days—tax-free. You may not, however, roll this money into an employer plan.

Rollover by a Surviving Spouse

A surviving spouse is allowed to roll over an employer's lump-sum distribution into an IRA of her or his own. This could happen either upon the employee's death or because of the termination of the employer's plan after the employee's death.

Under some circumstances, the surviving spouse may be allowed to exclude up to $5,000 of this lump-sum distribution from income during the year of the distribution. This is called the death benefit exclusion, and no part of it can be rolled into an IRA.

The surviving spouse may keep these IRA assets separate from any other IRAs, mingle them with other IRAs, or make additional contributions to them. *Under no circumstances, however, can any assets received from an employer plan by a surviving spouse be rolled into any other qualified plan.*

Employer Rollover Pros and Cons
If You're Still Working

Many circumstances could find you contemplating or receiving a lump-sum distribution of your entire share of an employer's qualified plan while you're still in your working years. The choices you may have to make include:

• *If you have the option, should you leave the money in the company plan and allow it to grow there tax-free?* This will depend largely on how you feel about the company, how well the company plan is doing (and might be expected to do in the future), and whether you have an immediate and pressing need for the money.

It might also depend on whether you can roll over the assets to a plan with a new employer immediately, or whether you'll have to put them in an IRA "conduit" instead, possibly not knowing if you'll ever find another employer willing to accept them.

If the employer has terminated your services abruptly or you are leaving because you are dissatisfied, you'll probably want to take the distribution in any event. However, if you're the kind of person who knows that once you get your hands on the money you'll spend it, consider leaving it in the employer plan anyhow. Having some additional retirement income from that employer's plan will be better than frittering the money away.

• *Should you roll the entire employer-plan distribution into an IRA?* If you still have many working years ahead and there is no immediate need for this money, you'd be well advised to roll all of it into an IRA even though you may risk losing the favorable tax treatment given to employer plans if you take a lump-sum IRA distribution later. The tax-sheltered earnings in your IRA could more than offset the difference.

If invested at a constant 12 percent rate of return, money would double in the seventh year, triple in the tenth year, quadruple in the thirteenth year, and quintuple in the fifteenth year. If you kept it in the IRA for 20 years, it would multiply nearly tenfold.

At this rate, $100,000 rolled over into an IRA when you are age 45 would have grown to approximately $176,000 in 5 years, $310,000 in 10 years, $550,000 in 15 years, and $965,000—nearly a million dollars—in 20 years at age 65, when you may be ready to retire.

Of course, if you have a pressing need for the money, take it. If you've lost a job and have no other financial resources, you may need the distribution to live on. Or you may conclude that its best use would be to assure a child's college education, buy a home, take advantage of an investment opportunity, start your own business, or attain some other personal goal.

You may also have so much assured retirement income from other sources that you may prefer taking the IRA now. You'll receive the favorable employer-plan tax treatment and can do what you wish with the money, including investing in collectibles or other investments barred to IRAs.

• *Should you take part of the money and pay tax on it, and roll the remainder into an IRA?* For most people this would be a poor choice. By taking only part of the distribution, you would lose the employer plan's favorable 10-year averaging tax treatment.

But there are circumstances where being taxed at the higher rate wouldn't make much difference. If you had little or no income from other sources that year—perhaps because you lost your job with the employer who gave you the distribution—the tax difference might not be significant either.

• *If you roll all or any portion of the employer-plan distribution into an IRA, should you preserve the option to roll it back to some other employer plan by always keeping these assets separate from your other IRA assets?* Definitely. Even if you have no intention of putting money into another employer plan now, circumstances could change. One day you might find yourself going to work for an employer who has an excellent plan—and is willing to accept a rollover for your IRA or IRAs.

In setting up this IRA or these IRAs, however, avoid making long-term commitments, at least at the start. If you think you may be rolling these assets back into a new employer plan soon, a money market mutual fund or passbook IRA at a depository institution, where there would be no sponsor penalties if you wanted to move the money, would be your best bet. Avoid buying insurance annuities with big penalties for pulling out in the early years, or long-term savings certificates with early withdrawal penalties that could cut into your principal. You can always move assets to a longer-term IRA later if it becomes apparent you won't be rolling them into another employer plan soon.

Employer Rollover Pros and Cons When You Retire

A different set of factors comes into play if you're given the opportunity of receiving a lump-sum distribution from an employer plan when near or at retirement.

Many people will never have a chance to make this choice. In the past when people retired, they almost always received retirement benefits in the form of fixed monthly payments for the rest of their lives, with some additional death benefits for their beneficiaries. But this pattern is changing, and especially for middle- and upper-level employees and executives. *Dun's Review* notes that the demand for lump-sum payments is becoming so insistent—particularly from executives—that nearly every pension plan may have to offer them sooner or later.

The demand for taking pensions in a lump sum stemmed from the creation of IRAs in the Employment Retirement Income Security Act of 1974 (ERISA), which also allowed lump-sum rollovers into IRAs from employer plans. The rationale for this was to allow people to protect themselves against inflation by investing the money themselves. Inflation was eroding the value of fixed payments to retirees. It was reasoned that if you didn't need the lump sum immediately, you could keep compounding it at a relatively high tax-sheltered rate, allowing you to buy a retirement income far higher than would be the case otherwise.

Not all financial advisers think this is a good idea— and not all companies allow employees to take a lump-sum distribution. In fact, the majority of employers still don't offer them, although the list of those that do is growing. The opportunity is given most often to executives, and some firms grant them only to employees who demonstrate that they have retirement income from other sources.

If you're given this option when you retire, you may have to make these decisions:

• *Should you take the lump-sum distribution or regular monthly benefits for the rest of your life?* Again, many factors must be weighed. Are you the sort of person who spends everything you get? If so, don't accept the lump-sum payment unless you are assured of a generous retirement income from other sources.

Beyond this, are you capable of investing a large sum yourself? Even if you are, would you worry a lot if you had to do so? And how long can you reasonably be expected to live? Or to continue earning income, if you're still earning or plan to continue in a different line of work? What are your other retirement income sources? Is there a spouse or other beneficiary or beneficiaries relying on your retirement income? If so, what death benefits would your beneficiaries receive under the employer plan if you died?

• *If you decide to take the distribution, should you roll all of it into an IRA or keep it all?* The same factors are involved along with some others, including taxes. If you keep it all, you can use the favorable employer-plan treatment with 10-year averaging. If you roll everything into the IRA, you'd lose the favorable treatment—but if the money remains in the IRA long enough and is earning at a good rate, you'd come out ahead anyhow. To help you make your estimates, the fixed-investment growth tables in Chapter 4 show how any sum would grow at various interest rates.

Taxes aside, for many people this choice comes down to what you *want* to do rather than what a financial adviser might think "best." It's not uncommon for people receiving a large employer distribution at or near retirement—usually more than they've ever owned in a lifetime—to pay the tax and use the remainder for luxuries they could never afford before. The pleasure that money buys them more than offsets the loss of additional retirement income in their minds—and if they die soon after taking the money and spending it, they'll have won the game.

On the other hand, if your goal is to build as big a retirement fund as you can, roll everything into an IRA and don't touch it until you have to. Allow the IRA's tax-sheltered leverage to work for you as long as possible. If necessary, exhaust any lower-yielding retirement assets before you begin using your tax-sheltered IRA.

• *Should you take part of the distribution and roll part over?* Because a distribution at or near retirement would probably involve a relatively large sum, for most people this would be an even more unwise choice than if made when given a distribution earlier in your working life. By rolling any part of the distribution into an IRA, you lose the favorable 10-year averaging treatment for what you keep.

All things being equal, it would be better to either keep the entire distribution and pay taxes at the more favorable 10-year rate or roll everything into an IRA and continue sheltering the earnings from taxation.

11

Age 59½ and After: Taking Money Out of Your IRA

Between age 59½ and the year in which you reach 70½, you have a great deal of flexibility in paying distributions to yourself from your IRA or IRAs.

Each year you may pay yourself as much or as little as you wish. Assuming you're still earning the compensation to qualify, you may also continue making contributions to your IRA—and if you can afford them, you should.

If you're in the 30 percent tax bracket, for each dollar you earn in a non-sheltered investment, you must give the government 30 cents—but each dollar you contribute to an IRA will continue compounding with no additional tax due in the year contributed. For many people, the period after age 59½ includes some of their peak earning years when it is easiest to afford maximum contributions. With no federal tax penalty for withdrawing from an IRA after age 59½, the only penalties you may have to worry about are those that might be levied by IRA sponsors for withdrawing before specific investments mature. With a little planning, those are easy to avoid.

IRAs as an Income-Leveling Device

Between ages 59½ and 70½, IRAs can be used as an income-leveling device. All distributions from your IRA are taxable as ordinary income in the year received, but proper timing can minimize the overall tax cost. Try to plan your distributions so your tax bracket doesn't change substantially from one year to another.

If a source of income is unexpectedly cut off or reduced, you could make up the difference by paying yourself a distribution from an IRA. Under these circumstances, you may wind up in no higher a tax bracket than if your income remained stable and you never touched your IRA. On the other hand, you may not wish to take any distributions during years when your income is high.

During this period, you may also be in a position to use your IRAs for any major expenditures you may not be able to handle out of regular income—a medical emergency, down-payment on another home, gift to a child, or what-have-you.

If maximizing your retirement income is your goal and you are still earning income (all things being equal), try to avoid distributing assets from your IRA to yourself until such non-sheltered investments as savings accounts and E-bonds have been exhausted. Normally the tax-sheltered IRA's earnings will be much higher than after-tax earnings you can get elsewhere with equal safety.

The one asset you may wish to hold even though it could be liquidated for a relatively large sum is your home, if you own one. The many personal and emotional factors involved with a home often far outweigh dollars-and-cents considerations in making this decision.

If you make withdrawals from your IRAs between

age 59½ and 70½, you are *not* required to file any additional documents with your federal income tax return. However, you are required to list the distributions as part of your income for that year.

Pros and Cons of Taking It All

At any time between ages 59½ and 70½, you may also elect to distribute everything in your IRA or IRAs to yourself. (Should you do so, you are still allowed to open another IRA before age 70½ if you have income that qualifies.)

In deciding whether to take it all, you must weigh many of the same factors that must be weighed by an employee given an opportunity to receive a lump-sum distribution from a qualified employer plan.

First, consider the tax consequences. If it's a big IRA and you take it all, you'll have to pay a big tax bill. If the distribution puts you in the top tax bracket—currently 50 percent—you'll have to give half of the money to the government by April 15 of the following year. Unless you have a desperate need for the money, try to avoid doing this.

While the lump-sum IRA distribution doesn't qualify for the special tax advantages available for an employer-plan distribution, it does qualify for 5-year averaging (as would any other ordinary income you receive). If you decide you must take a lump-sum distribution, try to do it after several years in which you had relatively little income so 5-year averaging may be of some help.

Next, look at yourself. If you're the type of person who is unable to manage or hold onto money, take as little from your IRA as possible. If you need money, arrange for a periodic withdrawal system, either from your IRAs or by using your IRAs to buy an annuity from an insurance company.

What are your other income sources? If your needs are comfortably being taken care of by them, you may wish to delay drawing from your IRA as long as possible while further compounding the tax-sheltered earnings.

How long can you reasonably be expected to live? If you are in poor health and know that your life span is very limited, you may wish to take much or all of your IRA now and pay the tax—unless you have a beneficiary or beneficiaries you wish to inherit your IRA after your death. If you are in good health and come from a family whose members often live to a very old age, you may wish to make your retirement income from your IRAs last as long as possible.

Just as with someone taking a distribution from an employer plan, much depends on what *you* want rather than what might shape up on paper as "best." If you have adequate retirement income from other sources and would like to use the money in your IRA for travel or other luxuries you've denied yourself throughout your working life, go ahead and enjoy your IRA retirement fortune. That may have been your goal all along.

After You Reach Age 70½

The whole idea behind an IRA is to provide money for retirement. Consequently, after you reach the year in which you become age 70½, you can no longer contribute to an IRA—and you *must* start a withdrawal program.

Your choices at this point are (1) take everything out and pay tax on the entire distribution, (2) use your IRAs to buy an insurance annuity, (3) begin a payout schedule that will pay the IRA out during your lifetime or the combined lifetimes of you and your spouse, or (4) start making regular withdrawals based on your life expectancy and that of your spouse. If you fail to take enough out of your IRA to meet IRS minimum requirements each year after you reach age 70½, you will have to pay a penalty of one-half of the excess amount not distributed.

• *Taking everything out.* The major pros and cons were discussed earlier. If you haven't built a very large IRA by age 70½ or you've withdrawn so much that only a small sum is left, you may not have much to lose by taking it all immediately instead of buying a small income far into the future. But if it's a relatively large sum, you'll be much better off stretching the payout (and the tax bite) rather than taking it all at once.

• *Buying an insurance annuity.* The IRS gives you the option of ordering the trustee or custodian of your IRA to use the money to buy an annuity contract for you (and in fact you can do so at any time after age 59½). You won't be taxed when you receive the contract, but will be taxed when you begin receiving payments.

This may be your best course if you don't trust yourself to handle your own affairs. It can also assure that you won't outlive your savings. On the other hand, if you know you can manage money, you'd probably be better off investing it conservatively and paying yourself out of your IRA rather than buying an annuity. Obviously when you buy one, some of the money must go for a fee or commission.

Annuity-type payments are also vulnerable to a loss of buying power due to inflation. And you want to be sure to select the type of annuity best suited for your circumstances. With some annuity plans—a so-called life annuity, for instance—benefits will be paid for as long as you live. But after you die, no payments are made to your beneficiaries. Other plans will pay your beneficiary for only a relatively short period of time.

• *Paying the IRA out over your lifetime, or the lifetimes of you and your spouse.* In effect, pay yourself as much or as little as you like, just so you don't pay less than the minimum described in the next section. And you have a lot of leeway, because the IRS allows you to take credits for payments over the minimum in earlier years.

• *Starting a withdrawal program based on your life expectancy.* The IRS has devised a formula for estimating your life expectancy (or the combined life expectancy of you and your spouse) for the purpose of calculating the minimum you must withdraw from your IRAs by the end of each year after you reach age 70½.

Actually, you may not have to make these calculations yourself. Your IRA sponsor will probably have tables from which someone can quickly tell you the minimum amount you must withdraw from your IRA each year to avoid the "excess accumulation" penalty.

However, it would be advisable to know how this formula works so you can confirm the sponsor's estimate with your own calculations. Sponsors and their employees can make mistakes—and so can you, especially if someone gives you numbers over the telephone.

Currently, the IRS formula assumes that after reaching age 70½, men will live another 12.1 years and women will live 15.0 years.

Consequently, by the *end of the year* in which a man reaches age 70½, he must have made withdrawals equal to *his entire IRA balance at the beginning of the year divided by 12.1*. In the following year, this multiple is reduced by one to 11.1; in the third year, to 10.1, and so on.

For women, the amount withdrawn by the end of the

year in which age 70½ is reached must equal the entire balance at the start of that year divided by 15.0, with the multiple reduced by one in each subsequent year.

Examples: A man has $100,000 in an IRA at the start of the year in which he reaches age 70½. To avoid the IRS penalty, by the end of that year, he must withdraw at least $100,000 divided by 12.1, or $8,624.46. If the IRA balance at the start of the second year is still $100,000 (because of growth during the first year), he must then withdraw at least $100,000 divided by 11.1, or $9,009.01, and so on.

A woman with a $100,000 IRA at the start of the year in which she reaches age 70½ would have to withdraw at least $100,000 divided by 15, or $6,666.67. If the balance at the beginning of the second year was still $100,000, she must withdraw $100,000 divided by 14, or $7,142.86, and so on.

The IRS has also constructed tables for what it calls the "expected return" multiples for married couples with an IRA. Tables 20 and 21 are the IRS life expectancy tables as of early 1982.

The IRS Two Lives table works the same as the multiples for single men and women. If the husband owns the IRA and his wife is age 68 in the year he becomes 70½, the multiple for determining their minimum withdrawal by the end of that year would be 19.2. If the IRA was worth $100,000 at the start of the year, they would have to withdraw at least $100,000 divided by 19.2 by the end of the year, or $5,208.33. The multiple would be reduced to 18.2 in the following year, and so on.

If the spouse who does not own the IRA dies, the owner's multiple reverts to that for a single person. If in the previous example the wife died in the third year after the husband reached age 70½, the multiple would be 10.1 for that year instead of the 17.2 it would have been had

Table 20: One Life—Expected Return Multiples

Owner of Individual Retirement Arrangement	Multiple
Female	15.0
Male	12.1

Table 21: Two Lives—Joint Life and Last Survivor—
Expected Return Multiples

Owner of Individual Retirement Arrangement	Age of Spouse (in year you became age 70½)						
	61	*62*	*63*	*64*	*65*	*66*	*67*
Female-Multiple	21.6	21.1	20.7	20.3	19.9	19.6	19.2
Male-Multiple	23.0	22.4	21.8	21.2	20.7	20.2	19.7
	68	*69*	*70*	*71*	*72*	*73*	
Female-Multiple	18.9	18.6	18.3	18.0	17.8	17.5	
Male-Multiple	19.2	18.7	18.3	17.9	17.5	17.1	
	74	*75*	*76*	*77*	*78*	*79*	
Female-Multiple	17.3	17.1	16.9	16.7	16.6	16.4	
Male-Multiple	16.7	16.4	16.1	15.8	15.5	15.2	
	80	*81*	*82*	*83*	*84*	*85*	
Female-Multiple	16.3	16.2	16.0	15.9	15.8	15.8	
Male-Multiple	14.9	14.7	14.5	14.3	14.1	13.9	

she lived. (If the spouse who owns the IRA dies, the IRA's disposition will then be determined by the beneficiary or beneficiaries.)

You are *not* required to make only the minimum withdrawal as determined by these IRS formulas. You may make larger withdrawals (or have larger insurance annuity payments) if you wish. Your only obligation after the year in which you become age 70½ is to take out at least the minimum—and you can take credits for over-withdrawing in earlier years.

While these are the latest IRS life expectancy multiples as of the publication date of this book, they could change at any time to reflect the fact that Americans are living longer. If you are age 70½ or older and have an IRA, check with the IRS and your IRA sponsor periodically to be sure your calculations are based on the most recent multiples.

The IRS life expectancy tables and a worksheet for determining if you owe tax for an excess accumulation are part of the IRS Instructions for Form 5329: Return for Individual Retirement Arrangement Taxes.

You do *not* have to file a Form 5329 with your tax return unless you actually owe the IRS a tax penalty of one kind or another. You may, however, wish to obtain a copy of the Form 5329 instructions from any IRS office so you will have the latest IRS life expectancy tables in your files.

In using the IRS tables, the total for all of your IRAs (if you have more than one) and withdrawals from them are what count. If you have $100,000 in one IRA at the start of the year, $25,000 in another, and $10,000 in another, you must base your calculations on the total $135,000 at the start of the year. You cannot treat each IRA individually. You may allocate withdrawals from the IRA in any manner you please, but to avoid penalties, the total withdrawn must at least equal the amount calculated using your multiple if you are to avoid IRS penalties.

Penalties for Excess Accumulations After Age 70½

If in any year after you reach age 70½ you withdraw less than the minimum amount calculated under the IRS life expectancy tables, the difference between what you withdrew and the minimum is viewed by the IRS as an *excess accumulation.*

The IRS penalty for an excess accumulation is substantial—50 percent of the excess. If you were supposed to withdraw at least $10,000 in any given year according to the tables but you withdraw only $6,000, the difference would be $4,000. Your penalty tax would be half of that, or $2,000.

If you withdraw less than the minimum and are subject to the penalty, you must file a Form 5329 with your federal income tax return, listing the tax due. However, the government recognizes that it is easy to be misinformed about the minimum contribution by plan sponsors or financial advisers—and how difficult it is for many people to make the right calculations. If you have a good reason for an excess accumulation in an IRA, the government provides an out. You may not have to pay the penalty tax if you can demonstrate that whoever sold you the IRA or advised you on it gave you the wrong advice—or that you made an honest mistake in using the IRS tables or did not understand them.

If you can demonstrate that your excess accumulation was due to a reasonable error and that you are making additional distributions to correct the situation, the

IRS may waive the penalty. The IRS has indicated that it will accept erroneous advice or your own good efforts to understand the instructions as acceptable reasons.

Detail your case in writing. Attach your letter to the Form 5329 when you file your tax return, and pay the penalty tax at that time. If the IRS decides to waive your penalty, it will refund the money.

Stretching Out Payments for Maximum Return

Not everyone electing to make IRA payouts based on the IRS life expectancy payment tables will be in a position to withdraw only the minimum each year, especially if you must rely on an IRA as your main source of retirement income.

But the fact that the remainder of your IRA continues to compound tax-sheltered after you start making withdrawals means that although you can no longer make contributions, your IRA may continue to grow for many years.

If you are in a position to stretch this payout to its maximum, just reverse the approach taken when building the IRA during your working years. The calculation that determines the IRS minimum annual withdrawal is based on your account balance as of the beginning of the year. However, you don't have to take the money out then. Instead, you can maximize its earning power by leaving it in the account and not withdrawing it until the very end of the year.

The following example shows what could happen to a $100,000 IRA when distributed for a maximum stretch-out by a couple where the wife is age 65 would begin at

20.7—which is to say, the IRS is assigning them a combined life expectancy of about 21 years.

The example assumes that this couple's IRA is earning at a constant 12 percent rate and that they don't make any withdrawals until year-end.

Payments would begin at $4,831 in the first year and increase at a growing rate thereafter. Nevertheless, the balance in the account would continue to increase until the thirteenth year, when it will have peaked at $181,192 (see Table 22). It will still remain over $100,000 until the nineteenth year, when it would drop to $95,514.

Withdrawals would reach $7,784 at the end of the fifth year, $14,268 at the end of the tenth year, $26,777 at the end of the fifteenth year, and $56,886 in the twenty-first and final year.

The total payout for this $100,000 IRA at the end of the 21 years would be $459,228. And actually, even now, many people reaching age 70½ have IRAs much larger than this because of rollovers from employer pension plans. A $250,000 IRA in this example would grow to $1,148,640, and a $500,000 IRA would grow to $2,297,280.

Obviously, in the real world, few people will have the discipline or resources to carry out this kind of program to an extreme. But these examples illustrate that to the extent you can stick to minimum withdrawals and bunch them toward the end of the year rather than making them at the beginning of the year, you will maximize your IRA's retirement fortune-building power.

Table 22: Stretching Minimum Payout on $100,000 IRA
(Assumes 12 percent constant return, with wife age 65 during year husband reaches age 70½. All withdrawals made at end of year.)

Year	IRA at Start of Year	IRS Multiple	Amount Withdrawn	IRA Earnings
1	$100,000	20.7	$ 4,831	$12,000
2	107,179	19.7	5,441	12,861
3	114,599	18.7	6,128	13,752
4	122,223	17.7	6,905	14,667
5	129,985	16.7	7,784	15,598
6	137,999	15.7	8,777	16,536
7	145,558	14.7	9,902	17,467
8	153,122	13.7	11,177	18,375
9	160,320	12.7	12,624	19,238
10	166,934	11.7	14,268	20,032
11	172,698	10.7	16,140	20,724
12	177,282	9.7	18,276	21,274
13	180,280	8.7	20,722	21,634
14	181,192	7.7	23,531	21,743
15	179,404	6.7	26,777	21,528
16	174,155	5.7	30,554	20,899
17	164,500	4.7	35,000	19,740
18	149,240	3.7	40,355	17,909
19	126,794	2.7	46,965	15,215
20	95,514	1.7	56,185	11,462
21	50,791	0.7	56,886	6,095
22	-0-			

TOTAL WITHDRAWN: $459,228

12

Other "Do-It-Yourself" Retirement Plans: SEP-IRAs, Keogh Plans, and 401(k)s

In addition to the universal IRA, the government has three other "do-it-yourself" retirement programs: Simplified Employee Pension (SEP) plans, Keogh plans (which are only for the self-employed), and a plan called the 401(k), which some analysts see as the "super IRAs" of tomorrow.

These plans differ in many respects but have one thing in common. Under most circumstances, if you're participating in one you are also allowed to establish a separate IRA or IRAs and contribute up to the universal IRA limits.

Simplified Employee Pension IRAs

If your employer has a Simplified Employee Pension plan, you actually set up an IRA or IRAs on your own, but your employer makes the contributions.

The employer includes these contributions as income

on your W-2 Form for that year. You then shelter this income from taxation by deducting the contributions on your tax return.

SEPs were created in the Revenue Act of 1978. The idea was to help smaller businesses provide retirement benefits for employees without so much of the red tape and administrative burden associated with regular employer pension plans. But as so often happens, what the government calls "simplified" is in many respects not simple at all. In fact, as the prospectus for one major family of mutual funds (Stein Roe) puts it, "Although the Internal Revenue Service has published some regulations with respect to SEPs, there are still many unresolved issues and consequently, there are a number of questions about SEPs for which no definite answers can presently be given." These unresolved questions are probably one reason SEPs are as yet not widely used.

In general, an IRA or IRAs you set up under an employer's SEP are governed by the rules covering all other IRAs. You must be given a free choice as to IRA sponsors and the type of IRA you wish to set up.

Once the employer makes the contribution, the employer surrenders all control over the money to the plan's trustee or custodian, or to the insurance company, if it's an individual retirement annuity. This gives you the same control you'd have over a regular IRA—and subjects you to the same rules and penalties for rule violations.

One advantage of an SEP is that the employer's contribution limits are much higher than those for a regular IRA. They are the same as for Keogh plans—$15,000 or 15 percent of income, whichever is less.

The employer, however, is not required to contribute the limit—or even to make any contributions at all in any given year—just so long as everyone is treated alike.

Contributions may vary from year to year provided each person covered by the plan receives the same percentage of income as a contribution. There must be a written allocation formula. If the employer gives a $100,000-a-year employee a $10,000 contribution, which is 10 percent of income, a $20,000 employee must be given a $2,000 contribution, and so on.

Whatever the employer does, you are also allowed to contribute up to $2,000 a year (or 100 percent of income) to that IRA or to any other IRA or IRAs. And if the employer contributes less than the $2,000 (or 100 percent of income) to the SEP-IRA, you may make up the difference as part of your universal IRA $2,000 contribution for that year.

For instance, if your employer contributes $5,000 to your SEP-IRA, you are permitted to contribute another $2,000 to that IRA or to any other IRA. But if your employer contributes only $1,000, your own contribution is still limited to $2,000 to that or any other IRAs.

One other difference between SEP-IRAs and other IRAs is that if you are still working after you reach age 70½, you are allowed to continue deducting your employer's contributions. However, you are no longer allowed to make your own contributions.

One disadvantage of an SEP is that if an employer offers one, it must be accepted by all employees who have reached age 25 and have been employed by the firm for 3 of the immediately preceding 5 calendar years. Apparently, this includes part-time and seasonal employees. If even one employee who meets these qualifications elects not to participate, the plan is disqualified. (However, employees who are part of a collective bargaining unit or who are nonresident aliens earning no U.S.–source income from the employer may be excluded from consideration.)

You may select any qualified individual retirement account or individual retirement annuity for your SEP plan.

If you are an employer, you may include yourself in the SEP—but must always pay your employees the same proportion of income that you pay yourself. The favorable 10-year-averaging procedure that can be used with a Keogh plan lump-sum distribution is not available for an SEP, which would make a Keogh plan a better choice if you are self-employed.

If your employer pays too much into your SEP-IRA, you must withdraw the excess amount before you file your tax return. If you fail to withdraw it, *you* will be liable for the 6 percent excise tax. If the employer's contribution was $15,000 or less, however, you won't have to pay the 10 percent premature distribution tax.

Setting up an SEP-IRA usually involves you and your employer both signing Form 5305-SEP, Simplified Employee Pension-Individual Retirement Accounts Contribution Agreement. You keep one copy, and your employer keeps the other. This form is not filed with the IRS.

The form includes a question and answer section on SEP-IRAs. An employer setting up an SEP-IRA plan is required to give you a disclosure statement that includes a description of the SEP, requirements concerning employer payments, information on deducting the employer's contribution, and questions and answers about the SEP.

The IRS adds that if your employer "selects, recommends, or substantially influences" your choice of IRAs, you must be given a "clearly written explanation" of the terms of those IRAs. And if they prohibit withdrawals, the Department of Labor may require that you be given still more information. The choice as to where to set up an SEP-IRA must always be yours, no matter what your employer may want you to do.

Employer contributions to an SEP for any given tax year may be made as late as 3½ months (by April 15) after the end of the calendar year. If you leave an employer who has an SEP, or your employer terminates the plan, you may continue making your own contributions to the former SEP-IRA or IRAs.

Keogh Plans for the Self-Employed

A Keogh plan may be opened by anyone who has income from self-employment, whether full- or part-time.

Typically, Keogh plans are maintained by professional people, including doctors, dentists, attorneys, and other professionals with their own practice. They may also be opened by owners of sole proprietorships, business partners, and farmers, as well as anyone else working for themselves—independent contractors, writers, artists, composers, freelance photographers, and so on.

But moonlighting or part-time self-employment income also qualifies. If you make extra money as a freelance writer or have a small side business, the net profits from these ventures can be used as the basis for Keogh plan contributions even though you may have an employer pension plan and a full-time job.

And, of course, under the universal IRA, anyone with a Keogh plan may also contribute up to $2,000 or 100 percent of earned income, whichever is less, to an IRA as well.

In many ways, Keogh plans and IRAs are similar— but there are some significant differences. If you are self-employed but are unable to contribute the limit to both types of plans in any given year and must decide whether to select one or the other, these differences may sway your decision.

As with an IRA, your Keogh contributions are deducted from your taxable income return. Earnings are sheltered from taxation until you begin withdrawing from the Keogh plan, which can begin any time after age 59½ but must begin by the year in which you reach 70½. Prohibited transactions for both types of plans are also similar, and you have the same range of investment options—everything from insured savings accounts and certificates to mutual funds, families of mutual funds, insurance annuities, and self-directed plans.

IRA-Keogh Pros and Cons

For a self-employed person, the main advantages of a Keogh plan over an IRA are:

• Contribution limits are much higher—currently $15,000 or 15 percent of income, whichever is less. In other words, you could earn up to $100,000 after deducting business expenses and contribute up to $15,000 to your Keogh plan or plans.

Obviously you can build a much larger retirement fortune with a Keogh plan than with an IRA. If you're fortunate enough to be able to earn $100,000 from self-employment after deducting expenses on your Schedule C, contributing $15,000 to a Keogh plan each year at a constant 12 percent return would give you about $107,000 in 5 years, $295,000 in 10 years, $625,000 in 15 years, $1,200,000 in 20 years, and $2,240,000 in 25 years —and if you wished, you could have been contributing another $2,000 to an IRA each year too.

• Tax treatment of money withdrawn from Keogh plans may be more favorable than for IRAs. IRA lump-sum distributions are taxed as ordinary income, but

Keogh lump-sum distributions are given the same favorable 10-year averaging treatment as qualified employer plans. (However, you are not allowed to take 10-year averaging for *both* a Keogh plan and a qualified employer plan. If you have both types, you can only use 10-year averaging with one of them.)

The Keogh distribution may be taxed partly as ordinary income and partly as capital gains if that formula is more favorable than 10-year averaging. When the owner of a Keogh plan dies, the beneficiary may also take advantage of a $5,000 death benefit exclusion.

The main disadvantages of a Keogh plan as opposed to an IRA are:

• If you have full-time employees who have been with you for 3 years or more, you must include them in a Keogh plan, but you do not have to include them in an IRA. If you have a Keogh plan with employees, you must also meet additional reporting requirements with the IRS.

• In general, penalties for breaking the rules are stiffer for a Keogh plan than for an IRA and are more likely to result in disqualification of the entire plan. In addition, you may be barred from personally contributing to another Keogh plan for 5 years. (Although you can open one for your employees if you wish.)

While these are the main differences between IRAs and Keogh plans, there are a number of others. In general, all things being equal, a self-employed person with no employees is better off with a Keogh plan than an IRA, but if you can afford it, to contribute the limit to both.

As a starting point for research on this question, consult IRS Publication 560, "Tax Information on Self-Employed Retirement Plans." Compare this information with that in this book and in IRS Publication 590, "Tax Information on Individual Retirement Arrangements."

If you have self-employment income and are thinking of opening a Keogh plan, discuss it with a tax adviser to be sure you understand the privileges and obligations, particularly if one or more employees will be included.

If Your Employer Has a Keogh Plan

If your employer has a Keogh plan and you are in it, you may also contribute up to the $2,000 maximum each year to your own IRA or IRAs.

Some employers with Keogh plans allow employees to make additional voluntary contributions of up to 10 percent of their income. These voluntary contributions do not affect your IRA contributions because your voluntary Keogh contributions are not deductible. Your advantage in making these voluntary contributions is that all earnings are sheltered from taxation in the plan.

If you're given the option of taking a lump-sum distribution from the Keogh plan, you will also benefit from the favorable 10-year averaging treatment. For employees, another advantage of a Keogh plan over some employer plans is that once the employer makes a contribution for you, you are never forced to forfeit benefits. In addition, employer funds committed to your Keogh plan can never be used for anything but pension benefits. If you leave the employer, you can roll the distribution over tax-free into an IRA.

If You're Covered by a 401(k)

A very few employees are covered by what is called a 401(k), a little-used tax shelter written into the Internal Revenue Act of 1978. If you are one of these people, consider yourself fortunate.

Some analysts believe that if these plans continue to be structured as they are now, the 401(k) plans could become the "super-IRAs" of the future.

If your employer decides to offer one, it will reduce your compensation from the top and treat the reduction for tax purposes as a company contribution to a qualified savings program. If your compensation is $40,000 and the company's contribution is $3,000, you'll be taxed as though your income for that year is $37,000. The other $3,000 will be viewed as an employer contribution to an employer plan.

This is a particularly good deal if you are earning above the maximum Social Security income level. The "reduction" in your income under this plan affects neither your Social Security contributions nor your eventual Social Security benefits. And as the IRS proposed the rules, your employer would continue calculating your pension, insurance, and health benefits on the basis of your full salary, no matter what the supposed salary "reduction."

These rules also allow you to deduct your own contributions. In the case of profit-sharing plans, they give you the option of taking some or all of the money in the form of an immediate cash payment—in effect, a taxable addition to your salary. The deferred compensation under this plan qualifies for the favorable 10-year averaging tax treatment. Finally, you'll also be able to contribute up to $2,000 for an IRA, assuming you can afford all of those contributions.

For a variety of reasons, not all employers will want to offer the 401(k). There are some very complicated rules regarding nondiscrimination in offering these plans to employees. All lower-paid employees must get the same proportionate benefits as higher-paid employees. And unlike IRAs, these plans allow early withdrawal without any tax penalty before age 59½ in the case of "hardship," which is up to the employer to define. Nevertheless, check with your employer to see if a 401(k) plan may be offered in the future.

If All You've Ever Had Is an IRA

It's ironic, but if all you've ever had in the way of a retirement plan is an IRA, the universal IRA law has done the least for you.

IRAs were created for you in the first place. They were designed for people who didn't have pension or profit-sharing plans at work. For the most part, this meant people of modest means working for small businesses and Mom-and-Pop operations that couldn't afford pension plans. Being allowed to set up an IRA gave you your first opportunity to build your own retirement fund. Or in some cases, instead of offering you a qualified retirement plan, your employer or union set up an IRA for employees instead.

Your only gain under the universal IRA law is the opportunity, since the start of 1982, to make bigger IRA contributions—up to $2,000 for individuals compared with $1,500 before, and $2,250 for spousal IRAs compared with $1,750.

Meanwhile, everyone already covered by an employer plan at work can now make IRA contributions as big as yours—and self-employed people can contribute the full IRA limits even after contributing up to $15,000 in a Keogh plan.

So in a sense, the people for whom IRAs were created have been sent back to square one. Everyone else now enjoys the full benefit of an IRA—but you enjoy little more than you had before.

Perhaps Congress will do something to correct this situation one day, but don't count on it. The biggest red-tape problem with the original IRA law was defining people who were "active participants" in other plans, and hence ineligible for IRAs. This created a red-tape nightmare, and Congress is not likely to bring it back.

If all you had in the way of retirement benefits before Congress approved the universal IRA was an IRA, the only way you can protect yourself is by contributing all you can afford to an IRA. It's still the greatest retirement tax break around for ordinary people.

And let your representatives in Congress know you're aware of how the universal IRA has sent you back to square one. If you yell loudly enough, Congress may devise a simpler formula for giving you a better retirement tax break.

PART III

Which IRAs Are Best for You?

Setting up an IRA may involve little more than signing your name to a standard trust agreement and designating a beneficiary or beneficiaries. But the decision as to where and what kind of an IRA you set up is important.

It's true you can transfer or roll over assets from one IRA to another if you don't like the first IRA. But when you open an IRA, you should hope to be satisfied with its performance and never have to move it. There are hazards in making rollovers and transfers. If a technical error is made, you could wind up suffering an inconvenience at the least or paying costly penalties at the most. The less often you roll over or transfer assets from one IRA to another, the better.

But there's also the inertia factor. Many people, once they've established an IRA, leave it with that sponsor for years no matter how poorly it does simply because moving it would take time and trouble. In short, it pays to ask the right questions before you set up any IRA.

Setting up and maintaining one or more IRAs requires your obtaining as much information as you can on that general type of investment and on the specific IRA or IRAs you are considering. IRS rules and regulations change constantly, and you should try to find out about these changes. The time may also come when you'll need professional advice on how to handle your IRA or IRAs.

Chapter 13 discusses some general considerations in setting up and maintaining an IRA, including some things anyone with an IRA should know about the IRS. Chapter 14 discusses sources of more advice and information.

Finally, you must decide on the specific IRA that best meets your needs. This may be your most difficult decision. The law that allows everyone who works to have an IRA has triggered a marketing battle of epic proportions. Banks, thrift institutions, mutual funds, insurance companies, and brokerage houses are all scrambling for a piece of this pie. The effective date of the universal IRA at the start of 1982 was signaled by a massive advertising and promotional blitz.

Trying to weigh the merits of the thousands of IRAs already in the marketplace would be difficult enough, but new schemes are being launched almost daily. And if your employer allows you to make contributions to your company or profit-sharing plan at work, you have still another decision to make.

A discussion of the marketing battle for your IRA investments and the major IRA investment options open to you is in Chapter 15.

13

Setting Up and Maintaining an IRA

It's all too easy to put off the decision to set up your first IRA until a few weeks or even days before the deadline —for most of us, April 15 of the following year. *But try not to wait until the last minute.*

You may have intended to open an IRA for months, but never got around to it. Or you may not even have considered setting one up until your tax preparer suggested it. But with only a few weeks or days in which to set up your first IRA, you could make a big mistake.

You could rush out seeking advice—perhaps from your neighbor the stockbroker, your cousin the insurance agent, or the friendly banker you chat with on the commuter train—and get advice not really in your best interest.

Naturally your neighbor, the customer's representative at a stock brokerage firm, will suggest buying shares in a front-end load mutual fund on which he or she will earn a commission, or perhaps opening a self-directed plan for buying and selling stocks, which raises the happy prospect of many more commissions in the future.

Your cousin the insurance agent will advise buying an insurance annuity, which may cost you a substantial commission. And the banker will sell you on the virtues of his institution's federally insured IRA plans.

These people are all giving you the best advice as they know it. But if you had taken time to investigate mutual funds, you may have found a good-performing no-load fund where you wouldn't have had to pay an 8.5 percent commission at the start. Or if your heart were really set on an insurance annuity, comparison shopping might have uncovered a much better deal.

And you can make a big mistake by opening an IRA at just any bank, savings and loan association, or credit union. The time when all savings plans at these institutions were virtually the same is long gone. These institutions now offer a vast and bewildering variety of IRA plans. With time to research the market, you may find a significantly higher return or a plan much better suited to your circumstances.

Before setting up your IRA, try to give yourself time to weigh the options. These may include contributing to your employer's retirement plan (if it's allowed) or having IRA payroll deductions where you work. Visit, phone, or write local financial institutions, mutual funds, insurance companies, or other IRA sponsors and study their sales literature.

If you must set up an IRA at the last minute, don't tie up your money for a long time. Put your money in a passbook savings account or a money market fund. Later, it can be moved to some other investment without penalty after you've had time to do some research.

Given a Choice,
Set Up Your IRA Close to Home

Whatever investment you select, you'll have to make a choice among sponsors offering that type of investment.

All things being equal, try to set up your IRA or IRAs

with sponsors whose offices are convenient to where you live or work.

However, this should not be your overriding consideration, particularly if the sponsors located near your home or place of business do not offer the type of investments you conclude are best suited for you. If you decide that a mutual fund or family of funds is best for you and there are no nearby offices, don't let that stop you. Investors have been dealing successfully with distantly located mutual funds and other investment sponsors for years by mail, telephone, or wire transfer.

But if you are fortunate enough to have the choice, there are 2 reasons why it would be better to select a nearby IRA sponsor. First, if it's easy for you to go to the sponsor's office yourself, it will be easier to settle misunderstandings that may arise—or to effect a rollover out of that IRA at some later date.

Second, if you're one of those people who waits until the last minute to make your final IRA contribution (or to make your entire contribution for the tax year, as so many people do), it will be easier—and safer—to meet the April 15 deadline by carrying your contribution to the office yourself if necessary.

If it's the last minute and you're dealing with sponsors hundreds or thousands of miles away, there could be problems. The closer you get to April 15, the more the mails get clogged. And while telephonic and wire transfer instructions are usually reliable, mistakes can happen—especially if the volume of those instructions is unusually heavy.

When you carry a contribution to a sponsor's office, always ask for a dated receipt, especially if it's near the deadline. The receipt will prove you made the contribution in the proper tax year even if someone in the sponsor's office makes an error posting your contribution.

Some Questions to Ask

Whatever the type of IRA investment, ask these questions:

• *What are the fees to get in?* An IRA's great fortune-building advantage is that you can compound the earnings tax-deferred until you start withdrawing. To the extent that fees and commissions are charged, you're losing compounded earning power.

IRA investments with high fees in the early years are especially inappropriate if you plan to retire soon or run a high risk of job turnover. You may have to retire and start benefits before you've had time to make up those hefty early-year fees. Or if you lose a job and exhaust your other financial resources, you may have to draw money from your IRA. The hefty sponsor fee would come on top of the 10 percent premature distribution penalty if you are under age 59½ and are not disabled.

• *How much must you contribute to get in and stay in?* Are the minimum investments required higher than you can handle comfortably? Try to be realistic. Don't commit yourself to an IRA that requires contributions so large that you'd have trouble getting the money together. IRAs are a great investment, but don't punish yourself to start one.

• *What does it cost to maintain the IRA?* Normally maintenance fees are minimal. But check the fine print (and the sponsor's disclosure statement) to see if there are additional fees beyond the regular fees.

• *What will it cost to get your money out, perhaps rolling it over into another IRA?* Many IRAs charge only minimal termination fees if you switch to a different IRA, but others may charge stiff termination fees. Don't put your money in an IRA with a high termination fee if you can find a similar investment that doesn't charge one.

• *How long must you tie up your money?* Does the contract require that you keep money in this IRA for a specified period? Does it penalize you for taking money out after you reach age 59½?

This won't be an overriding consideration for everyone. All savings certificates at banks, savings associations, and credit unions are required to penalize early withdrawals if you're below age 59½ and the investment has not matured.

If you're investing for the long-term in these institutions, there's no need to be concerned about tying up your money for any reasonable period. The early withdrawal penalties shouldn't discourage you from making these investments if you believe they best suit your needs. But if you're nearing (or above) age 59½, learn if you can withdraw early without penalty after age 59½. Select the institution that allows you to do so.

On general principle, avoid tying up money for very long. A lot can happen—including changes in your circumstances and in financial markets. And given the inventiveness of IRA marketers and the planned deregulation of savings rates, new and better IRA investments may be available in the near future.

• *If it's a fixed-rate investment, how much will you have at the end of a given period of time?* This is the key question for any fixed-rate investment. Compounding methods for fixed-rate investments may vary greatly. Be sure you understand how the actual return after a fixed period for any one investment will compare with another.

• *Will this IRA meet your retirement investment goals and needs?* To the extent possible, use the sponsor's IRA disclosure statement to estimate whether that plan

SETTING UP & MAINTAINING AN IRA   **231**

will give you the additional retirement money you'll need at the time you think you'll need it.

The Disclosure Statement

When you set up an IRA, the plan's sponsor is supposed to give you a disclosure statement about your program. This statement covers all the key points about the IRA. *Read it carefully.* Seek out the sections on fees so you understand what buying and maintaining the IRA will cost.

You must be given this statement 7 days before the IRA is set up or purchased. As an alternative, the sponsor may give you the statement when you set up the plan. You then have a 7-day cooling-off period in which to cancel.

With some IRA programs, written or oral cancellation or both may be required. Oral notification may be by phone during regular business hours. If your notification is by mail, the regular postmark is used. Certified or registered mail uses the date of certification or registration.

If you cancel, you're entitled to a full refund of everything you paid. There should be no charge or commissions, expenses, or changes in market value.

The disclosure statement is supposed to discuss the tax requirements, eligibility, and penalties regarding IRAs in general. It is also supposed to provide details about that particular IRA investment. These include:

• If possible to do so, growth projections of the program's value.

• Whether and for what period the growth projections are guaranteed—and if not guaranteed, a statement of the earnings rate and terms on which the projection is based.

• Any sales commissions to be charged each year.

• If applicable, the part of each annual contribution used to buy life insurance, which is not deductible, for each year.

Sponsors making growth projections must give illustrations of dollar amounts available at retirement and at specified points during the life of the investment.

Establish a Record-Keeping System

Right at the start, set up a record-keeping system for keeping track of your IRA investments.

This may not seem important at first, but the longer you maintain your IRA or IRAs, the more important it will become, particularly if you establish a number of IRAs or move them around often.

These records should be in addition to your file of IRA statements and other materials received from sponsors, which you should keep indefinitely.

There are at least 2 good reasons for starting and maintaining complete, easy-to-follow records for your IRAs:

• To keep track of how they're doing—how much you have invested in each IRA and how far you are ahead (or behind). Periodically, compare returns to your IRA investments with those on comparable investments.

• To assure that if something happens to you—death, or an incapacitating accident or illness—someone can look at the record and reconstruct the history of your IRAs. This would be especially important if the IRS later raised questions about some aspect of your IRA investments.

Any record-keeping system you feel comfortable with will do. If you were investing in a mutual fund or self-directed IRA, you would, of course, also want to list the number of shares purchased and the price and the names of the companies involved, if applicable. You could also do this with some of the standard investment-record materials available at stationery stores.

Naming Your Beneficiaries

When you set up an IRA, you'll be asked to name a beneficiary or beneficiaries to inherit it if you die.

This decision may be made in the few moments spent looking at the question on the application form and then be forgotten. But it's worth more time and thought, especially since over a period of time, an IRA could grow to a large sum.

Many people mistakenly believe they must name a wife, child, or other close relative as their beneficiary. But you may name anyone you wish—or may name a charity or an institution. You may also submit a list of beneficiaries in an order of preference—or you may name your estate.

If the sponsor's form contains only one line for naming a beneficiary, you are not bound by that limitation. You may insist on writing in as many beneficiaries as you wish, or writing them in an order of preference—on an attached list, if necessary.

Whatever your circumstances, it's usually a good idea to have at least a second beneficiary designated to inherit the IRA if the first beneficiary dies. If you have only one living relative and name that person as your beneficiary, if that person dies before you and you don't name another beneficiary, mostly likely the state in which you live will wind up with your IRA's assets.

This could also happen if you have no will and your only living relative, perhaps your spouse, dies simultaneously with you in an accident or disaster, such as a plane crash. How ironic that you build a retirement fortune with an IRA during your working lifetime only to have your efforts merely enrich the treasury of the state in which you lived simply because you failed to name an alternate beneficiary.

In addition to naming one or more beneficiaries, you may also specify the method of distribution. Some IRA sponsors request this information. Generally speaking, the payment options are a lump-sum payment, installment payments, the purchase of an insurance annuity contract with the full value of the death benefits, or the assumption of your IRA by your beneficiaries.

Keep Your Beneficiaries Up to Date

You may change your IRA beneficiaries as often as you wish.

Just as you keep track of your IRA investments, remember to change beneficiaries in accordance with changes in your circumstances—and theirs. If a spouse or someone else you have named as a beneficiary dies or becomes incapable of handling his or her affairs, make the change right away—especially if you didn't name a secondary beneficiary and there is a risk the IRA will be claimed by the state if you die.

You can also change beneficiaries for any other reason. As time goes on, your point of view about family members or others you have named as beneficiaries may change—even toward those you once believed would always be closest to you. For one reason or another, some people may decide they no longer want their children as beneficiaries. There could also be good reasons for not naming your own spouse, such as the spouse becoming so incapacitated that he or she could no longer make responsible financial decisions.

As your IRA increases in size, it would be advisable to seek professional advice to be sure that your IRA assets are really disposed of as you wish after you die, perhaps correlated as part of a general estate plan. If it is a large IRA, you may be able to reduce the tax consequences by naming a number of beneficiaries rather than leaving everything to one or 2.

Can You Give Away or Transfer an IRA?

Technically you can give away an IRA at any time. However, the entire gift would be included in your taxable income for that year. Consequently, such a move should be avoided. If the gift was made before you reached age 59½, you'd also have to pay the 10 percent early distribution penalty.

A transfer of interest in your IRA or any part of it— to satisfy a creditor, for instance—would have the same consequences as a gift.

Don't even consider giving an IRA away or transferring any part of one to someone else without getting professional advice. Even then, do so only if confronted with very unusual financial problems.

How Old Shall You Say You Are?

Needless to say, we strongly urge that you give the sponsor your correct age when you set up an IRA.

But as many accountants, attorneys, and other financial and legal advisers have learned, there are some people who consistently lie about their age, concealing their true age from friends, employers, and members of their family. Unfortunately, as these people approach the critical "income tax ages," they are inviting embarrassment and perhaps a delay in receiving Social Security benefits—and may even be violating income tax regulations.

For instance, your family and friends may "know" you to be age 60. But, when your real age reaches 65 you'll want to collect Social Security benefits. At this point, proof of age will be required—and all will be revealed.

The vanity involved in these deceptions is so great that some people have delayed claiming Social Security benefits for years for fear of exposing their correct age— particularly to a spouse who may believe them much younger.

These deceptions are practiced by both men and women. In fact, the practice has increased recently because so many people are entering into second or third marriages today and joining new "families." Unlike relatives who knew you when you were a child and can't be fooled, members of these new families will accept any reasonable age you claim to be.

Some people begin concealing their true age when they reach their forties. It may be to make a more favorable impression on members of the opposite sex—or to deceive employers or business associates who might otherwise view them as "over the hill."

The universal IRA will compound problems for people seeking to conceal their true age and induce other people to consider lying about their age for the first time.

Some people will be tempted to lie because the Form

1040 on which you file your federal tax return does not require that you give your age or date of birth.

What's more, when you set up an IRA the trustee or custodian does not ordinarily demand proof of age. All you will be asked to provide is a birth date. It is inevitable that some people will be tempted to give a birth date that will say they are 59½ or older earlier than their real date of birth simply so they can later withdraw money from the IRA without paying the penalty tax. However, if they keep the assets in that IRA, they will have to start withdrawing from it when the sponsor's records show they have reached age 70½, even though they may be much younger.

On the other hand, people who have been understating their age to their family for years and then open an IRA face other problems. If they understate their age to the IRA sponsor, they will delay their ability to receive distributions from the IRA without paying the tax penalty. They also risk creating a situation where they would be violating IRS regulations if they didn't start a withdrawal program by the year in which they reached the true age of 70½.

It's likely the universal IRA will see more people misstating their age than ever. But because there will be so many more opportunities for them to be found out, they will be exposing themselves to consequences that may range from embarrassment to chagrin, anger, disappointment, and even social dislocation—not to mention the risk of stiff IRS penalties, disqualification of the entire IRA, and even criminal prosecution if the IRS believes the offense warrants it.

If you decide to conceal your true age from an IRA sponsor, you may get away with it—for a while, at least. On the whole, the IRS has little control over that situation unless a deception is called to their attention by an accidental disclosure. *But taxpayers who deliberately falsify their age to receive tax benefits are violating one or more IRS Code sections, some with very serious consequences.*

The IRS and Your IRA

There will be tens of millions of IRAs before long—and IRA deductions will be as commonplace as those for home mortgage interest and real estate taxes.

Under the universal IRA law, there is little reason for the IRS to challenge your deductions if you contribute to qualified programs and do not over-contribute. Normally, your IRA deduction should be automatic.

Under the old IRA law, the focus of IRS monitoring was on whether you qualified to have an IRA. Many IRAs were disallowed because people were covered by a pension or retirement plan at work at some time during the tax year.

Now that IRAs are universal and everyone who earns income qualifies, the IRS monitoring emphasis has changed. One area of concentration involves proper and adequate reporting of withdrawals from an IRA. All IRA custodians are required to send the IRS information forms on every payment from an IRA. This allows cross-referencing to your tax return by IRS computers, just as the IRS can now cross-reference payments to you of interest and dividends by financial institutions and by companies in which you own stock.

The IRS can also be expected to have an important monitoring program for reporting correct ages when people receive a payout. If this area becomes a problem, it is likely efforts will be made to include a line for your year and/or date of birth on the Form 1040.

Currently, it is not easy for the IRS to trace rollovers from qualified employer plans into an IRA, and later back to another qualified plan, but its reporting system is getting more efficient and more sophisticated all the time. Although false reporting may go undetected for long periods, the chances of detection are increasing constantly—and ultimate detection may trigger serious consequences.

Our tax system is one of voluntary compliance. Every responsible tax preparer is pledged to support that system, and no responsible preparer will countenance tax cheating if he or she has knowledge of it. Preparers also face severe penalties if they conspire with a client to defraud the government. What many people fail to realize until too late is that when the IRS invokes special penalties, the dollar amounts involved in the offense may not be the main criterion. Rather, the IRS may be more concerned with the flagrancy of the offense and the obviousness of intent to defraud, whether the amount be large or small.

While many millions of items of information on IRAs will be reported to the IRS by IRA sponsors and taxpayers in future years, monitoring this voluminous body of information will become increasingly accurate and routine. New computer techniques and equipment will make the problem rather simple. The IRS already does a fairly thorough job of monitoring the voluminous information filed with it every year in such areas as savings accounts, dividends paid, and accounts with stock brokers.

If you decide to rely on the massive nature of the IRS reporting system to conceal irregularities in your IRA, you are courting big trouble. Despite the stories about false and inaccurate tax reporting, the use of Social Security numbers as tax identification numbers has made the total system far more encompassing—and will lead to increased detection of false reporting in the future. If you build a retirement fortune with an IRA, you'd be foolish to risk losing it through disqualification because you broke the rules.

Keeping Up with Changes in IRA Rules

There is nothing permanent about tax rules and regulations. When you open an IRA, do so with the understanding that the tax rules governing it are in a constant state of change. As best you can, try to keep up with the changes to avoid making costly mistakes.

The basic statutes referred to as the "tax laws" are in the Internal Revenue Code. Only Congress can change the tax law itself. If nobody has a reason for making changes, a section in the Tax Code may remain unchanged for years.

However, because of the broad coverage of the universal IRA and the many financial institutions and other IRA sponsors involved, you can expect at least some new legislation affecting IRAs to come out of almost every Congress.

In part, these changes will be in response to desires for change from the general population as expressed through their representatives in Congress. If any areas of IRA abuse stem from the 1981 law, Congress will probably correct them, just as it acted in 1978 to correct abuses in the sale of certain insurance annuities.

Pressure for change will also come from banks, thrift institutions, mutual funds, brokerage firms, and insurance companies seeking to expand their IRA authority or to correct what they perceive as cumbersome or unreasonable requirements. The banks and thrift institutions will always be seeking higher federal insurance coverage for IRA deposits. And as soon as the 1981 law was passed, representatives of coin dealers, antique dealers, and other dealers in collectibles announced they would try to get Congress to change its mind and make collectibles legal for IRAs again.

Changes in the basic tax law are just the beginning. After Congress passes a law, the IRS studies it and issues its regulations. These are clarifications of and elaborations on its application of the Tax Code.

Once the regulations are issued, interested parties are constantly making special requests of the IRS for interpretations of special sets of facts that may not be covered completely in the Code or the regulations. These special requests are called requests for "rulings."

For the most part, the rulings are "private letter rulings" valid only for the parties who requested them. Private letter rulings are published in technical journals and generally read only by professionals with a special interest in tax matters.

But occasionally the facts have a much broader application than just for the requesting parties and may have an impact on many taxpayers or, in the case of IRAs, IRA custodians. The IRS may then write and release an "Official Revenue Ruling," which is its interpretation of how it will view those circumstances for tax purposes. Although official revenue rulings are not absolutely incontestible, they are taken seriously by all professionals and are not challenged without good cause.

Change may also emanate from the courts. Many taxpayers take exception to IRS findings in a tax audit. If a taxpayer feels strongly enough about the issue involved and is willing to pay the cost, the case can be presented to one of several courts for adjudication—and may even be heard by the Supreme Court.

These court decisions become precedents for tax

professionals in applying the law in subsequent (and even prior) situations. Meanwhile, at its option, the IRS may announce either that it acquiesces in the decision or that it is nonacquiescing—which means it won't be guided by the court's findings in future cases. If this happens, you are on notice that you may have to go to court yourself if you wish to be supported on a similar set of facts.

In any event, you can see that the so-called tax laws are really a complex combination of statutes, Treasury Department regulations, IRS private and general rulings, and court decisions. All this adds up to a constant series of changes, some important and sweeping in nature and others of relatively minor concern to the public at large.

If there's a major change affecting most or all IRA owners or potential owners, it will be reported in the news media and money management magazines. Many C.P.A. firms mail newsletters to clients discussing changes of this nature. If the changes benefit thrift institutions, banks, insurance companies, brokerage firms, or other IRA sponsors by liberalizing their services, they will advertise that fact in their promotional campaigns.

Some changes are technical and will require that your IRA custodian amend your plan. In this case, you'll be sent the amendment for safekeeping with your copy of the plan. You may also be asked to sign a new document if the change requires you to make some kind of decision.

Regular readers of the *Wall Street Journal, Barron's, Business Week, Fortune,* or business periodicals will sometimes find references to less far-reaching changes; otherwise, you could be unaware of many of them. While these changes may be of less significance to most people, it is always possible one or more may apply to your special circumstances or to some move you are thinking of making.

If you see a tax preparer each year, ask if any changes during the past year apply to you. Get a new IRS Publication 590 each year to compare how it differs from previous years. And don't overlook the better annual tax guides published for general readers, which are generally accurate and well-written.

14

Advice and Information: Who Needs It and Where to Get It

When you walk into a bank, savings and loan association, credit union, brokerage house office, or insurance agency seeking advice on financial matters, you might assume that the people you're talking to are IRA experts.

Many are knowledgeable and do a good job of answering basic IRA questions. But if asked questions that go beyond the basics, they may supply you with misinformation. They're not trying to deceive you—it's just that most of these people don't know all the facts about IRAs and shouldn't be expected to know them.

Most IRA sponsors have training programs for people who sell IRA investments to the public, and some of these programs are thorough. However, IRA rules and regulations are so complex that even professional tax experts admit they don't know all the answers.

Most people rely on IRA marketers for information on what they can or cannot do. But, however comprehensive their training program, few employees of IRA marketers can be expected to have more than a peripheral education on the tax ramifications stemming from IRAs. It would be unreasonable to expect insurance agents, investment counselors at banks and thrift institutions, and customers' representatives at brokerage houses to know all the ins and outs of IRA rules when even the tax professionals don't know them, especially since most of these people have many other responsibilities in addition to talking to people who want information about IRAs.

By all means, ask questions. Many of these people have excellent back-up research materials in their office. Some can get answers on especially difficult questions over the phone from IRA experts on special "hot lines." (And the best of these people will admit when they are in over their heads on some questions and will suggest you seek professional advice.)

But however sound their sources of information and no matter how hard they try to help, in the last analysis you must seek answers to the most difficult questions on your own. Don't rely entirely on IRA sponsors for advice if a large sum is involved. Even the IRS won't guarantee that its advice is correct. And if that's so, it would be foolish to rely on advice from IRA sponsors if the penalties for making a technical mistake are severe.

By the same token, don't accept all the information you see in IRA promotional materials and advertisements as gospel. Although these materials are usually checked by tax experts, these people can make mistakes too. One major institution continues printing incorrect IRA information in its brochures even though the error was pointed out several years ago. The "especially trained retirement counselors" who advise the public on behalf of this institution still give out this misinformation every business day, and sincerely believe it to be true.

Promotional materials may also be rendered obsolete

by changes in IRA rules, new IRS and Tax Court interpretations, or changes in the law. The longer these materials remain in your file, the more likely that at least
some of them are out-of-date.

Need for Professional Advice Increases with Time

Almost anyone should be able to open an IRA without
seeking professional advice. Even so, if you have a tax
adviser, by all means discuss your IRA with him or her.
Ask questions on what you don't understand and get the
benefit of the adviser's thinking on investments (but
don't feel obliged to follow it!).

If you're truly confused about how IRAs work or by
your IRA investment options, seek independent professional advice right at the start. By "independent professional advice" we mean the kind you pay for, not the
kind offered by someone with a vested interest in selling
you something. People who want to sell you something
are professionals too—and many give excellent advice.
But your own best interests demand that you put the
greatest reliance on advice from someone who has nothing to gain if you take it.

As time passes, the need for professional advice will
increase. The larger the sum involved or the greater the
proportion of your total assets the IRA represents, the
better it would be to obtain expert opinion before proceeding with any important move or change involving
your IRA or any part of it.

Also, seek professional advice the closer you get to
retirement. If you make a serious mistake in handling an
IRA early in your working life and some or all of your

IRA is disqualified (or you make a bad investment), you still have time to build other IRAs. But if you make an error with only a few years to go—or are already retired—you won't have time to start over again.

Certainly anyone about to receive a large lump-sum distribution from an employer plan or contemplating any IRA move in which a large sum is involved should get advice from an independent professional *before doing anything*. Similarly, widows or other beneficiaries who have the option of receiving a large distribution from an employer plan or an IRA, or taking annuity-type payments instead, should seek advice before making a decision.

The experience of independent tax professionals is that the most serious mistakes in handling IRAs are made when people act first and seek advice afterwards. In all too many cases, by then the damage has been done.

Free Information from the IRS

Before paying for advice, obtain what is available for free. This will also make any sessions with an independent professional adviser more productive. The more you already know, the less time your adviser will have to spend explaining IRAs to you—and the smaller your bill will be for the adviser's services.

One free IRS publication everyone with an IRA should have is IRS Publication 590: "Tax Information on Individual Retirement Arrangements." It is updated every year.

This publication covers all IRS rules and regulations pertaining to IRAs in detail. While not so authoritative as the actual IRA regulations, it answers most questions anyone would want to ask. As is the case with many government documents, it is sometimes hard to follow and by trying to cover everything may fail to adequately distinguish between what is most important and what really doesn't matter much.

Nevertheless, it is comprehensive and covers all major aspects of current IRA rules and regulations. You should obtain a new copy each year and compare it with the old one to see what major revisions have been made.

Other free IRS publications that relate to IRAs in one way or another include:

No. 448: "Estate and Gift Tax"
No. 506: "Income Averaging"
No. 560: "Tax Information on Self-Employed Retirement Plans" (Discusses retirement plans for self-employed persons and certain partners in partnerships who are eligible for Keogh plans.)
No. 575: "Pension and Annuity Income" (Explains how to report pension and annuity income on your federal tax return as well as special tax treatment for lump-sum distributions from pensions, stock bonus, or profit-sharing plans.)

The most recent editions of these publications can be obtained by visiting any IRS field office or writing the IRS "Documents Distribution Center" for your state. If there is more than one center for your state, send your order to the one nearest you. The addresses of these field offices are:

Alabama—Caller No. 848, Atlanta, GA 30370
Alaska—P.O. Box 12626, Fresno, CA 93778
Arizona—P.O. Box 12626, Fresno, CA 93778
Arkansas—P.O. Box 2924, Austin, TX 78769

California—P.O. Box 12626, Fresno, CA 93778

Colorado—P.O. Box 2924, Austin, TX 78769

Connecticut—P.O. Box 1040, Wilmington, MA 01887

Delaware—P.O. Box 25866, Richmond, VA 23260

District of Columbia—P.O. Box 25866, Richmond, VA 23260

Florida—Caller No. 848, Atlanta, GA 30370

Georgia—Caller No. 848, Atlanta, GA 30370

Hawaii—P.O. Box 12626, Fresno, CA 93778

Idaho—P.O. Box 12626, Fresno, CA 93778

Illinois—6000 Manchester Trafficway Terrace, Kansas City, MO 64130

Indiana—P.O. Box 636, Florence, KY 41042

Iowa—6000 Manchester Trafficway Terrace, Kansas City, MO 64130

Kansas—P.O. Box 2924, Austin, TX 78769

Kentucky—P.O. Box 636, Florence, KY 41042

Louisiana—P.O. Box 2924, Austin, TX 78769

Maine—P.O. Box 1040, Wilmington, MA 01887

Maryland—P.O. Box 25866, Richmond, VA 23260

Massachusetts—P.O. Box 1040, Wilmington, MA 01887

Michigan—P.O. Box 636, Florence, KY 41042

Minnesota—6000 Manchester Trafficway Terrace, Kansas City, MO 64130

Mississippi—Caller No. 848, Atlanta, GA 30370

Missouri—6000 Manchester Trafficway Terrace, Kansas City, MO 64130

Montana—P.O. Box 12626, Fresno, CA 93778

Nebraska—6000 Manchester Trafficway Terrace, Kansas City, MO 64130

Nevada—P.O. Box 12626, Fresno, CA 93778

New Hampshire—P.O. Box 1040, Wilmington, MA 01887

New Jersey—P.O. Box 25866, Richmond, VA 23260

New Mexico—P.O. Box 2924, Austin, TX 78769

New York—
  Albany: P.O. Box 1040, Wilmington, MA 01887
  Buffalo: P.O. Box 240, Buffalo, NY 14201
  New York City: P.O. Box 1040, Brooklyn, NY 11232
*North Carolina—*Caller No. 848, Atlanta, GA 30370
*North Dakota—*6000 Manchester Trafficway Terrace,
  Kansas City, MO 64130
*Ohio—*P.O. Box 636, Florence, KY 41042
*Oklahoma—*P.O. Box 2924, Austin, TX 78769
*Oregon—*P.O. Box 12626, Fresno, CA 93778
*Pennsylvania—*P.O. Box 25866, Richmond, VA 23260
*Rhode Island—*P.O. Box 1040, Wilmington, MA 01887
*South Carolina—*Caller No. 848, Atlanta, GA 30370
*South Dakota—*6000 Manchester Trafficway Terrace,
  Kansas City, MO 64130
*Tennessee—*Caller No. 848, Atlanta, GA 30370
*Texas—*P.O. Box 2924, Austin, TX 78769
*Utah—*P.O. Box 12626, Fresno, CA 93778
*Vermont—*P.O. Box 1040, Wilmington, MA 01887
*Virginia—*P.O. Box 25866, Richmond, VA 23260
*Washington—*P.O. Box 12626, Fresno, CA 93778
*West Virginia—*P.O. Box 636, Florence, KY 41042
*Wisconsin—*6000 Manchester Trafficway Terrace, Kan-
  sas City, MO 64130
*Wyoming—*P.O. Box 2924, Austin, TX 78769
*Foreign Addresses—*Taxpayers with mailing addresses
  in foreign countries should send requests for publi-
  cations to: Director, Office of International Opera-
  tions, Internal Revenue Service, Washington, DC
  20225.
*Puerto Rico—*Director's Representative, U.S. Internal
  Revenue Service, Federal Office Building, Chardon
  Street, Hato Rey, PR 00918
*Virgin Islands—*Department of Finance, Tax Division,
  Charlotte Amalie, St. Thomas, VI 00801

You can also get free advice from IRS personnel. However, these people have heavy workloads, particularly in the months and weeks just before April 15, so it's often difficult or impossible to get through on the phone, and they may not be able to devote much time to you.

While IRS information is free, it is *not* guaranteed. If someone working for the IRS gives you information that turns out to be incorrect, the IRS is not responsible if you act on that information and make a costly mistake. Consequently, if a lot of money is involved in what you're thinking of doing, you're still better advised to pay for an independent professional opinion.

Free Advice from IRA Sponsors

Most IRA sponsors will be glad to send you free literature on their plans. Obviously, advice from an IRA sponsor must be weighed with the understanding that the sponsor wants you to buy its product. The sponsor's literature will describe the benefits of that product and ignore or play down those of competing products.

Much general and technical material in sponsor literature can be helpful, and some of it may go into greater detail on some topics than this book does. Some sponsors have taken considerable time and expense to do a thorough job of explaining how IRAs work. Sponsor material may also give valuable information on the past performance of that particular IRA investment, which you can then compare with the performance of other IRA investments.

But while this technical material may have been researched with great care, don't rely on it as the final word if you're considering an important move with your IRA or if a large sum is involved. IRA sponsors can make mistakes too, and it's always possible that some material is out-of-date.

Free Advice from Trade Associations

You can also get free advice on IRAs from trade associations of IRA sponsors. The leading ones are:

The American Bankers Association, 1120 Connecticut Avenue N.W., Washington, D.C. 20036. Information about IRAs offered by commercial banks.

Credit Union National Association, P.O. Box 431, Madison, WI 53701. Information about IRAs offered by credit unions.

Investment Company Institute, 1775 K Street N.W., Washington, D.C. 20006. The Institute provides information on all types of mutual funds. It has a free booklet and free membership list. In addition to including the names, addresses, and phone numbers of members, the list categorizes them by types of funds. These include aggressive growth funds, balanced funds, bond funds, growth funds, growth and income funds, income funds, money market funds, and options funds.

If you're interested in a particular type of mutual fund, the Institute will provide specialized lists, such as those that invest only in common stocks or in such specialized areas as gold and precious metals.

No-Load Mutual Fund Association, Inc., Valley Forge, PA 19481. For $1 the Association will send you its latest directory. This booklet lists more than 200 no-load funds. The funds are grouped by investment objective. The booklet details investment requirements, services, addresses, and toll-free telephone numbers for the funds.

United States League of Savings Associations, 111

E. Wacker, Chicago, IL 60601. For people sending a self-addressed, stamped envelope, the League will provide a comprehensive question and answer brochure covering IRAs as well as other retirement savings changes that took effect in 1982.

Advice from the News Media

IRA advice in newspapers, magazines, and on television and radio news and information programs is obviously more objective than that from IRA sponsors and trade associations. But in technical respects, it may be less reliable. This is particularly true if the story or article must compress a lot of information into a short time period or space, necessitating that important details or qualifications be omitted.

Materials from most IRA sponsors and all major trade associations have been checked out by attorneys and other professionals who work closely with IRS rules and regulations. But articles and commentaries in the news media usually reflect the research of the writers. Many must work under tight deadlines and rely on outside sources of information.

The most reliable information is from writers, commentators, and publications specializing in business, finance, or money management. Publications such as *Money, Changing Times, U.S. News and World Report, Business Week,* and *The Wall Street Journal* have knowledgeable staff writers and researchers preparing this material. On the whole, material in magazines is probably a little more reliable than that in newspapers simply because magazines may have more time in which to check facts. The least reliable stories are those in newspapers or on television or radio reporting a major new development the moment it has been announced, before there has been time to doublecheck the details and analyze the announcement's implications.

As a rule, IRA advice on television and radio is most reliable when given by network business news or money management specialists, or by experienced business reporters with local stations. The least reliable information is from general news reporters for local stations, who on short notice often must present complex material they haven't had time to learn much about.

While news stories, articles, and commentaries on IRAs can broaden your understanding of them and keep you abreast of major changes in the law, they're no substitute for professional advice related to your unique circumstances.

When You May Need Independent Professional Advice

When your IRA or IRAs begin representing a substantial portion of your assets or when you are nearing retirement, it might pay to have an independent professional adviser review your retirement program every few years.

The situation can be likened to a checkup with your physician or dentist. Often a professional can anticipate a problem before it comes to a head—and in the long run, save you a lot of money and grief.

Beyond this, consider seeking independent professional advice about your IRA or IRAs when:

• You're not sure if you qualify for an IRA or for a spousal IRA.

• You're uncertain about how to start an IRA or what IRA investment is best for you at this point.

• You can't decide whether you'll be better off making deductible contributions to your company retirement or profit-sharing plan or setting up your own IRA.

• You're uncertain as to what long-term investment goals are most appropriate for your temperament or circumstances.

• You're trying to relate your IRA to a total financial planning and retirement program.

• You're considering a rollover or transfer of a large sum.

• You're about to begin a program of withdrawals from an IRA or IRAs. (Will they be qualified withdrawals? Are they financially sound? Is the timing right? Most people should seek advice at this crucial period.)

• You're planning a will or trust agreement involving an IRA.

• Your logical heir has a physical or mental disability and you want to be sure the funds are managed prudently if you die.

• You're getting married or divorced.

• Your economic circumstances have changed significantly—for better or for worse.

• The IRA plan you are in is amended in a way you don't understand.

• Congress makes changes in the IRA law.

• You are uncertain of the consequences of any action you are thinking of taking with an IRA.

Who Provides Independent Professional Advice?

Independent professional advice on IRAs is provided by Certified Public Accountants (C.P.A.s), lawyers, and financial advisers and planners.

Certified Public Accountants may be consulted for

all tax-related questions, financial and investment decisions, possible state and inheritance tax consequences,
anything related to such other plans as qualified employer plans, rollover possibilities, mechanics, and options. C.P.A.s also have the most experience in tax
return preparation and can relate best to the tax return
treatment of investment transactions, including IRA
transactions.

Many non-certified accountants are also well-quali-
fied. When selecting an accountant, inquire whether he
or she belongs to national accounting groups, is licensed
to practice in your state, and is an enrolled agent. The
latter means he or she may represent taxpayers in dealing
with the IRS—if your return is selected for an audit, for
example—and has demonstrated by examination qualification to practice in the tax area.

Some lawyers can do most of the things C.P.A.s do
and sometimes more, but try to select one who deals
regularly in tax matters. Many lawyers who have other
areas of specialization do not get involved in matters
closely related to IRAs and taxes. You need a lawyer
knowledgeable in preparing wills, trusts, prenuptial
agreements, and other documents in which IRAs might
figure. No other professionals are qualified to handle
those things. A lawyer should also be consulted if you
have questions about your IRA beneficiaries or beneficiary statement.

State or local C.P.A. or bar associations will furnish
you with several names from which to select if you do
not have a lawyer or C.P.A. Don't select any of these
people, however, if you don't feel comfortable with
them. As with any other kinds of services, a referral from
a satisfied client is frequently your best source for finding
a lawyer, C.P.A., or financial adviser. If you don't know
any, your friends, relatives, neighbors, or someone with
whom you work may be able to help.

Many financial planners are thoroughly trained and are registered, but anyone can call him or herself anything. Financial planners are known by any of a number of names; these include investment analysts, estate planners, investment or financial consultants, securities analysts, tax shelter consultants, investment representatives, and various combinations of these. The best are qualified to perform many of the duties lawyers and C.P.A.s do, but most will recommend that you consult a lawyer or C.P.A. for matters not specifically covered by their areas of expertise.

Don't hesitate, before consulting any independent professional adviser, to check credentials and get references. Ask the advisers about their membership in professional organizations, their practice, and their areas of expertise. Any honest, competent professional will be glad to explain exactly what he or she does or does not do.

Be wary of any professional who claims he or she can do anything and everything. Also, the more money involved, the less you should rely on one person for all your advice.

Getting the Most for Your Money

When you seek professional advice about an IRA you'll save money if you phone and make an appointment rather than dropping in unannounced. When you call, tell the adviser how you got his or her name, what you'll want to discuss, and what type of questions you'll have. In most cases the adviser should be able to tell you how long you'll need to meet and should be able to estimate the fee fairly closely.

When you go to the meeting, have your questions written out in advance so you'll be sure to touch on everything that concerns you. Be on time. Don't make small talk about irrelevant matters because the clock will be running. It will cost you as much to discuss the weather as it will to ask the most complicated technical questions.

In general, the fees charged by attorneys are highest. They range from a low of $50 to $60 an hour up to $100 or more, with the biggest fees charged in large metropolitan areas. Fees charged by C.P.A.s are slightly less than for lawyers, while fees charged by non-certified accountants are generally less than those charged by C.P.A.s by from 10 to 50 percent.

Financial planners may charge in a variety of ways, including hourly, a fixed fee, or a percentage of the value of the portfolio they manage. (Some who call themselves planners are paid for selling a product to you, and you should be wary of advice from these people.)

Many independent financial planners cannot deal economically with you unless a fairly large sum is involved. The fee they would have to charge to give advice on how to handle a small sum would simply not be worth it to you. Usually you should approach one with the idea of not just discussing your IRA, but of relating your IRA to all of your other assets.

Advice that Always Needs a Second Opinion

Wherever you go for information, you may hear some advice that should automatically cause you to seek at least a second informed opinion—particularly if the advice has been given to you by someone you don't know very well. Some examples are:

• I'll be your executor or trustee under your will or trusts.

• Long-term, the (stock market) (bond market) (any other market) will be your best deal.

• With an (annuity) (insured savings certificate) (anything else) you'll never have to worry.

• Go to any (bank) (savings and loan association) (credit union) because they're all the same.

• Put your money here and forget it until you're ready to retire.

• Sign here and we'll take care of everything.

• You *must* act now to take advantage of this opportunity.

• The results you'll attain with this plan are sure to beat the rate of inflation.

• Tell us where your IRA money is now, and we'll show you how you can get a much higher return.

• This is a little-known investment for IRAs and pays a lot higher than savings accounts, money market funds, annuities, and other things most people put their IRA money into.

• Forget everything you've heard until now about where to put your IRA money.

Does some of this advice sound familiar? Of course it does. Many of these same words and phrases were inducing people to make questionable investment decisions long before IRAs were invented.

15

The Battle for Your IRA Dollars

If you're a little confused by the barrage of advertising and promotional materials describing IRA savings and investment plans, it's understandable. Congress authorized the universal IRA at a time of great change and ferment in savings and investment markets. Most important:

• Savings rates at banks and thrift institutions are in the process of being deregulated.

If Congress follows through with its savings-rate deregulation schedule, total savings deregulation is still a few years off. But in line with the thrust toward deregulation, at almost the same time the universal IRA went into effect, federal regulators authorized a special new "wild card" retirement savings instrument for banks and thrift institutions. This new IRA and Keogh plan account has no interest-rate ceilings. It gives banks and thrift institutions an almost free hand in creating IRA savings plans, resulting in types of IRAs that would not have been possible before.

• The universal IRA was authorized when distinctions among the various types of traditional financial institutions were being blurred by consolidations, the creation of new financial conglomerates, and the breakdown of many historical barriers among financial institutions. To cite the most conspicuous example, mutual funds and brokerage houses now compete directly with banks and thrift institutions for household savings through money market mutual funds, which did not even exist before the 1970s.

Since the early 1930s, financial institutions in the United States had been structured along fairly rigid lines. Banks met a community's commercial lending needs, thrifts supplied money for housing, insurance companies stuck to selling insurance, and brokerage houses and mutual funds dealt in more risky investments. But in the 1970s, computerization and the new electronics technology brought about an increased blending of these functions—a process speeded by mergers of different types of firms. Even Sears Roebuck, the nation's largest retailer, has moved into the investment field and opened its own money market mutual fund.

The trend is toward new and ever-larger "baskets" of financial services at the same office. The companies and financial conglomerates offering these baskets of services see IRAs as a way to attract many new customers —and hope that in time these IRA customers will begin buying many of the other services they offer too.

These developments have further speeded changes in retail savings rates and services. Of course, the other side of that coin is that the more savers get paid for their savings, the more borrowers will have to pay for loans to buy homes, cars, farm equipment, or whatever. It's conceivable that eventually this could result in political pressure to lower the rates paid to savers, just as the low ceilings on many savings accounts resulted in pressure to increase rates to savers in the late 1970s.

But IRA sponsors—primarily banks, thrift institutions, mutual funds, brokerage firms, and life insurance companies—are competing vigorously for your IRA dollars with good reason. Increasingly, inflation has caused people to shift their savings out of long-term plans into short-term plans or into investments where it is available on demand.

Sponsors see IRAs as more stable sources of capital. Presumably IRA money is long-term money—or at least, it has been in the past. To the extent that financial institutions can attract more IRA dollars, the sponsors hope the trend to volatility in the flow of savings in and out of their investments will be reduced.

The Good News—and the Bad News

The good news about these developments is that you will have a far wider choice of investments than ever before, and that the intensified competition for savings capital will tend to keep returns to IRA investors high.

The bad news is that even if you wish to make the simplest kind of IRA investment today—namely, a federally insured account or certificate at a bank or thrift institution—you will be faced with some difficult investment choices.

In the past, these choices were made mostly by wealthier investors—or by the managers of financial institutions where people invest or deposit their money. These institutions are called financial "intermediaries," meaning that they are the middle-men between people with relatively small sums to invest and the larger markets where this money would be invested.

But now you must make your own decisions about such things as whether interest rates will go up or down —which in turn will depend on such things as the state of the economy, the government's fiscal and monetary policies, and the state of mind (always nervous and unpredictable) of professional money managers and investors. In effect, even at banks, thrift institutions, and credit unions, you no longer have a financial intermediary taking some of the money market risk off of your shoulders.

The money market risk is now yours to bear. Unless you are sure you know what interest rates and the financial markets are going to do—and top professionals in these fields are often wrong in making their predictions—you could run into trouble trying to second-guess these markets. One of the basic IRA retirement fortune-building rules is to diversify. This could include making different types of investments with the same IRA sponsor.

Relate Your IRAs to Other Retirement Income

To the extent possible, relate your IRA investments to your other anticipated retirement income. This includes Social Security, any other pension benefits, and income from personal savings and investments.

Obviously, if you are still many years from retirement, this will not be possible. But the closer you come to retirement, the more accurately you'll be able to make these projections.

Don't forget to allow for inflation. The purchasing power of any fixed-income payments you expect to receive after you retire will be progressively eroded accordingly.

On the other hand, in estimating your future income from investments, it might be prudent to be conservative. The odds are that sooner or later this current bout of inflation and extremely high interest rates will diminish, and investment returns will fall to what historically are more normal levels.

Periodically, the Social Security Administration updates tables showing what your retirement income will be for your age and income. These tables are available at your local Social Security office.

Factors to Weigh in Selecting Your IRAs

In general, most people preparing to invest in an IRA should play it safe. IRA money is retirement money. Unless you're assured of substantial retirement income from other sources, don't take chances with it.

That's not to say that when your IRA gets big enough you shouldn't consider diversifying by putting some money into investments that promise more gain although carry more risk. But it would be better to err on the side of being too safe than to make investments that could result in your losing some retirement capital.

If your IRA will be one of your most important sources of retirement income, you'll want to be the most conservative in selecting IRA investments.

On the other hand, if you are assured of a comfortable retirement income from other sources you can afford to take more chances. In fact, if you have a generous company plan and substantial personal investments, it would be perfectly appropriate to use your IRAs for highly speculative ventures (assuming you have the temperament for that sort of thing).

On a scale of safety, the safest IRA investments are U.S. government securities, followed by federally insured accounts and certificates at banks, savings and loan associations, and credit unions. Money market mutual funds and the types of securities in which they invest have relatively little market risk but are not insured. Mutual funds that invest partially or entirely in common stocks promise higher gains than investments that assure the return of your principal but also carry the risk of the loss of principal. At the top of the risk scale are self-directed plans where you make all of your own decisions in buying and selling stock but lack the downside protection afforded by the diversified portfolios you can get through stock mutual funds.

General Investment Strategies

Unfortunately, there is no magic formula for assuring the maximum investment success with an IRA any more than there is for assuring success in any other type of investment. With IRAs, as with any other type of investment, the time comes when the investor is on his or her own and must match investments to individual preferences and capabilities.

The basic IRA investment choices are to invest for income or to invest for growth.

There is no general consensus among financial advisers as to which is the best IRA investment strategy. Even if there were, there is no guarantee that it would be the *right* strategy.

The argument in favor of investing for income—in savings certificates, money market funds, bonds, annuities, utility stocks, and other big-dividend-paying stocks —is that you are making the most efficient use of IRAs because all interest and dividends are compounded tax-free until withdrawn.

Some analysts don't like using IRAs to buy stocks for long-term appreciation because when stocks are in an IRA they do not enjoy the favorable long-term capital gains treatment. Instead, no matter how long the period over which the gains are established, you would pay tax at the ordinary income rate when you begin withdrawing from your IRA. These experts recommend that when you make stock market investments it should be with other money, so you can take full advantage of capital gains provisions.

The basic argument in favor of investment for growth is that income investments won't give you nearly enough protection against inflation in the future—and that the only way to enjoy this protection is by going into mutual funds that invest in stocks or buying stocks yourself through a self-directed plan. In addition, because you are not concerned with capital gains and losses in an IRA, you may have much more latitude in making buying and selling decisions in a self-directed common stock plan than buying and selling stocks otherwise.

Whatever strategy you select—and there is no reason why you can't diversify by using both strategies to some degree—building a retirement fortune with an IRA will probably depend more on following the elementary fortune-building suggestions in this book than on tying all of your fortunes to one specific investment strategy or another. In particular, so long as you invest regularly and continue bettering the Consumer Price Index, you will be on the way toward carrying out a successful IRA investment program.

Guidelines for IRA Investors

IRA investors range from people with little or no experience or understanding of financial markets to top-level executives served by highly paid professional advisers familiar with the most sophisticated investment techniques. But whatever your investment know-how, here are some IRA investment guidelines that will keep you out of trouble:

• *Don't invest in anything you don't fully understand. This applies to the simplest IRA investments as well as the most complicated.*

Do you really understand what a floating-rate savings certificate is? Or how the index it is tied to works? Do you know what a mutual fund is or how it works? Do you understand the terms of an insurance annuity being suggested to you as an IRA investment, and the basis on which its return to you will be established?

If you don't know the answers to these or other questions about your IRAs, it's not difficult to get most of them. Usually you'll find the answers in literature prepared by IRA sponsors or in their disclosure statements. Read the literature and ask questions. Don't put yourself in the position of being vulnerable to an unpleasant surprise simply because you failed to understand how a particular investment works—or what the fees or penalties would be if you decided to get out of that investment before the end of an agreed-upon period.

Understanding how an investment works also means understanding what the IRA sponsor will do with your money—that is, how the sponsor plans to invest the money so as to be able to pay you and also make a profit. And, of course, it also involves understanding the risks in that particular investment.

Every investment carries risk of one kind or another. The risk of investing directly in stocks or in mutual funds that invest in stocks is that stock prices can go down—possibly way down—as well as up. The risk of an IRA investment with a fixed rate of return—particularly, one that requires you to tie up your money for a long period of time—is that serious inflation could erode its real buying power. The risk in money market funds and other short-term instruments is that if inflation ebbs and "normal" interest rate trends reassert themselves, yields could drop sharply.

In particular, don't sign up for any payroll deduction IRAs unless you fully understand what your money will be used for and what the risks are.

• *Don't invest in anything you don't feel comfortable with.*

Understanding an investment and feeling comfortable with it are two different things. You may fully understand the risk involved in a stock mutual fund or self-directed stock fund, and you may also have so much retirement income assured from other sources that in your financial circumstances you could easily afford those risks. But if you are the sort of person who can't sleep at night because you worry about the price of your stocks (or the stocks in your mutual fund) going down a few points, avoid such investments.

For one thing, it simply isn't worth the aggravation. IRAs are supposed to help ease your money worries, not add to them. If you build a large IRA (or roll a large sum into an IRA from an employer pension plan) and the money is in stocks or a stock mutual fund, relatively small fluctuations in market prices could vary the value of your IRA by thousands of dollars a day. This is in the nature of the investment and is no cause for alarm. But if paper losses would cause undue concern or depress you—and a steep and prolonged market break could result in substantial paper losses—seek IRA investments that assure the value of your principal.

Another reason for avoiding these investments if you do not have the temperament for them is that when you begin making decisions on the basis of fear, more often than not these will be bad investment decisions.

• *As a rule (but not always!) the higher the return on an investment, the greater the risk.*

There are some big exceptions to this. Most notable, low-yielding passbook savings accounts are no safer than any other savings instruments in a bank or thrift institution. But on the whole, any time you are held out the promise of a greater-than-usual profit or earnings it will be at the cost of some additional degree of risk. If higher returns are available in IRAs that invest in second mortgages, for instance, you can rest assured that this is because there is more risk in buying second mortgages than in many other IRA investments.

• *The younger you are, the more you can afford to take chances.*

If you make an investment mistake or two, there's time to rectify it. Also, you have long-term trends in investments like the stock market working for you. If you're investing in the stock market (or a mutual fund that invests in common stocks) for only a few years you may have to liquidate your investment during a down cycle in the market. Over the long-term, however, the odds are weighted more and more in your favor.

• *The closer you get to retirement, the more cautious you should be.*

As you near retirement, investment mistakes could have more serious consequences. In general, money in riskier investments should be moved to safer ones.

But even when you retire, don't overdo the emphasis on safety. With longer life expectancy and many people opting for early retirement, you may have another 20 or 25 years during which your IRA investments would be working for you. If you understand and feel comfortable with investments in stocks or stock mutual funds, it would be a mistake to pull out of these investments entirely just because of your age. Keep some of your IRA money in them as a hedge against inflation.

• *In general, be wary of investment concepts so new that they haven't had time to establish a track record.* The universal IRA is sure to spawn new investment ideas that may sound great at first but have hidden traps or disadvantages that become more obvious as time goes on. Don't allow anyone to make investment experiments with your IRA dollars.

IRA Investments to Avoid

Any investment that already shelters income from taxation is a bad IRA investment. These include all municipal bonds and tax-free money funds as well as All Savers Certificates at banks and thrift institutions.

These investments are already tax-sheltered. You gain nothing by putting them in an IRA to begin with. Because of their tax-sheltered status, they will pay a below-market rate. You can always earn a higher rate by putting non-sheltered investments into an IRA.

On top of that, even the lower earnings from municipal bonds, tax-free money funds, and the like would be taxable to you as ordinary income when you begin withdrawing them from your IRA.

Similarly, because they shelter earnings from taxation, IRAs are not appropriate for tax-deferred annuities. If you wish to invest in these annuities, they should be purchased on their own merits in addition to, not as a substitute for, an IRA.

BANKS AND THRIFTS

Savings accounts are still the most popular form of savings with Americans. And not too long ago, selecting a savings vehicle at a federally insured bank, savings and loan association, mutual savings bank, or credit union was a relatively simple matter.

All accounts and certificates had ceilings. You could deposit money in a passbook account, which paid the lowest rate but allowed you to withdraw as much or as little as you wished at any time with no penalty. Or, you could buy a savings certificate that paid a higher rate but required that you leave the money in the certificate for a specified period of time. If you withdrew money (other than interest the deposit earned) before the certificate matured, you had to pay a penalty.

The "Savings Revolution" of the 1970s

All this began to change in the 1970s. As inflation persisted and kept interest rates high, free-market yields on such money market instruments as U.S. Treasury bills, commercial paper, and bank or thrift institution certificates of deposit for $100,000 or more were often substantially higher than savers could obtain under the ceilings at banks and thrift institutions. But buying these money market instruments usually required much larger investments than most people could make.

This inspired the creation of money market mutual funds. By pooling investments from many small investors, the money market funds were able to invest directly in money market instruments and pay their investors market rates of return. It didn't take long for the funds to begin attracting some savings from banks and thrift institutions, and the number of money funds grew rapidly.

In an attempt to make accounts at banks and thrift institutions more competitive, federal regulators responded by creating savings instruments that also paid market rates: 6-month money market certificates (MMCs) that sold for a minimum of $10,000 and then 2½-year certificates, both with yields linked to changes in market prices for U.S. government securities.

Meanwhile Congress was under mounting pressure to deregulate all savings rates at banks and thrift institutions. This complex issue involved revising the whole structure of financial institutions in this country, which had been under intense study since the late 1960s.

Congress responded with the Depository Institutions Deregulation and Monetary Control Act of 1980. This measure called for the gradual removal of all savings rates at banks and thrift institutions over a 6-year period. The deregulation was to be carried out by a new government agency called the Depository Institutions Deregulation Committee (DIDC), whose members are the heads of the various federal financial regulatory agencies.

The DIDC's efforts to phase out savings ceilings at banks and thrift institutions have been controversial. Many banks don't think the DIDC has been moving fast enough, and many thrifts believe the DIDC has been moving too rapidly. This debate will probably continue until the DIDC completes its mission—assuming it ever does.

But after Congress approved the universal IRA, the DIDC responded by allowing banks and thrift institutions to offer an 18-month "wild card" certificate, which has no interest-rate ceiling, to buyers of IRA and Keogh plans. These new "wild card" IRA/Keogh retirement savings certificates are the major weapon in the savings war among depository institutions for IRA dollars and their principal weapon in competing with other IRA sponsors.

Savings Account Pros and Cons

Safety is a major reason savings accounts and certificates of deposit at banks, savings and loan associations, and credit unions are still the most familiar form of savings for most people.

This safety is in the form of federal savings insurance provided by agencies of the U.S. government and, in a few states, by state insuring agencies. In early 1982 the insurance ceiling was $100,000 for accounts in the same institution. There will, however, be attempts in Congress to increase this ceiling for retirement savings accounts, and it's likely they'll succeed.

For IRAs and Keogh plans, the statutory federal savings insurance ceiling is *in addition to* that for other accounts you may have in the same institution. You may have up to $100,000 in an IRA, another $100,000 in Keogh accounts as well as non-retirement accounts in the same institution and be insured for all of it.

There has been some pressure on the financial resources of the insuring agencies. Mostly, it has stemmed from the problems of thrift institutions forced to pay more for new savings than they were earning on portfolios of old, low-rate home mortgages. As a result, there have been some suggestions that savers with insured accounts in depository institutions would suffer losses if the resources of these agencies were exhausted and some institutions had to be closed.

However, it is unlikely that any Congress or president would allow this to happen. And in March 1982 both houses of Congress voted to reaffirm that the "full faith and credit" of the U.S. government stands behind all federally insured deposits, resolving that question.

On the other hand, savings above the insured ceiling are a different story. If an institution with accounts covered by federal deposit insurance must be liquidated—and the regulators will do all they can to avoid the last-resort step of liquidation—you will be paid off up to the insurance ceiling along with all other savers. However, everything in your IRA above the insurance ceiling will be at risk. You may get some or all of that money back eventually, but it may take time—perhaps several years—before the affairs of the liquidated institution can be settled. And during the time the affairs of the institution are being settled, the money remaining in your IRA may not earn interest.

Consequently when your IRA or IRAs at any institution get so large that their total value nears the insurance ceiling, it would be prudent to stop making additions to that IRA and open one elsewhere. You can have IRAs in as many different institutions with federal savings insurance as you wish. Accounts in each institution are protected to the limit.

Deposit insurance at commercial banks and mutual savings banks is provided by the Federal Deposit Insurance Corporation; at savings and loan associations, by the Federal Savings and Loan Insurance Corporation; and at credit unions, by the National Credit Union Administration.

Other Pros and Cons

Another big advantage of setting up an IRA in a savings and loan association, bank, or credit union is convenience. Most people live or work near one or more depository institution offices or can get to them easily. Other advantages are that there are usually no fees, or at most minimal fees, for opening, maintaining, or closing IRAs and that most people understand what these institutions are and what they do with your money.

If you buy a fixed-rate certificate, you'll also know exactly what it will be worth when it matures, a big help in making long-term plans.

But there are also disadvantages. At times you may have to settle for a lower return than you might obtain elsewhere—although the new "wild card" IRA/Keogh accounts should almost always be competitive. (And in 1982 all savings-rate ceilings were removed from all federally chartered credit unions, which will lead to their removal from many state-chartered credit unions too.)

A more serious disadvantage is the loss of liquidity, which means being able to get your money out quickly if you wish. With most existing savings instruments at banks and thrift institutions, you may be subject to a penalty if you withdraw money before the instrument matures.

On the whole, these penalties should be of less concern for owners of IRA accounts than for other savers. Presumably, people with IRAs are investing for the long-term. It's not likely you'd be forced to make early withdrawals from your IRA account simply to meet day-to-day living expenses.

Nevertheless, these penalties may discourage you from moving funds to another IRA. This could be to take advantage of a higher return elsewhere, because you're moving, or for any other reason.

In some cases, the penalties mandated by federal regulatory authorities could cut into your principal and lower your IRA's value. For most savings certificates opened or renewed after June 2, 1980, the penalty for withdrawing principal before maturity is the loss of 3 months' interest if the certificate's term is less than one year. If the term is one year or more—and this would include the new 18-month "wild card" IRA/Keogh retirement savings certificates—the penalty is the loss of 6 months' interest.

Example: You buy an 18-month savings certificate, but decide after 4 months that you want to move your funds to some other IRA investment. To do so, you would be penalized 6 months' interest. If the interest for 6 months totaled $120 but your IRA would have earned only $80 for the 4 months, you would lose $40 of your principal when you made the withdrawal.

For certificates opened or renewed before June 2, 1980, the penalty is the loss of 3 months' interest, with the interest rate for the remainder of the term reduced to the passbook rate. Obviously at this late date you could not lose any of your principal by taking this penalty.

If you are age 59½ or older, banks and thrift institutions may waive the penalty for pulling out of a retirement savings certificate before maturity—if they wish.

The option is all on their side. If you are near (or above) age 59½ and there is even the slightest possibility you may wish to withdraw principal from an IRA savings certificate before it matures, learn what the institution's policy is before buying the certificate. All things being equal, set up your IRA or IRAs in institutions that will give you the option of withdrawing without penalty after age 59½.

The deregulation process is still going on. For the next few years savings markets will remain in a state of constant change. Certainly the trend in new savings plans will be toward fewer restrictions on the rate of interest that can be paid and on how long money must be tied up to avoid a penalty for taking it out.

If you receive a large lump-sum distribution from an employer plan and decide to roll it over into an IRA or IRAs in a depository institution, it might be prudent to avoid committing all of it to a long-term savings certificate right away. Keep at least part in shorter-term, more liquid accounts so you'll be in a position to take advantage of any new IRA plans authorized in the next few years.

"Wild Card" IRA Savings Plans

Banks and thrift institutions were allowed to begin offering the new "wild card" IRA/Keogh retirement accounts on December 1, 1981, one month before the universal IRA became effective.

This account is a special time deposit category available only to people with IRAs and Keogh plans. Its minimum term is 1½ years. Its 2 most revolutionary characteristics are:

• *It does not have statutory interest-rate ceilings.*

Institutions can set the interest rate at any level they wish or allow the rate to go wherever an index will take it, if the rate is linked to an index. (However, institutions are free to set their own ceilings on how high they will allow the rate to go. They may also set floors, guaranteeing that they will pay you a specified minimum rate if the index goes below that.)

• *The interest rate can be either fixed or floating.*

Just as there are no statutory limits on how high the rate can go, there are no restrictions on how often the rate can be changed during the certificate's term—assuming it is going to be changed at all.

If an institution wishes, it may also offer these certificates in fixed-rate form with the same rate guaranteed for the life of the account. And in practice, many banks and thrift institutions offer both fixed-rate and variable-rate plans.

Rate changes for variable-rate certificates can be made in one of two ways. They may be linked to the movements of an index that is "readily verifiable and beyond the institution's control." Many institutions have selected market or auction rates of U.S. government securities as an index, and some have selected the Donoghue money market fund average.

As an alternative, rate changes can be made according to a predetermined schedule. An institution could promise to pay 11 percent for the first 6 months, 11.5 percent for the second 6 months, and 12 percent for the final 6 months.

Another important characteristic of the "wild card" is that *if the institution permits it, you may make additional contributions during the life of the certificate without extending the term.*

Not all institutions allow you to do this. If it is allowed, your right to make additions must be clearly stated on the certificate. Some institutions that permit additions do so only up to a certain point—perhaps for the first 6 months or year of the certificate's term.

While the IRA/Keogh "wild cards" have a minimum term of 18 months, institutions can offer them for longer terms if they wish, and some have offered them for up to 10 years.

The penalty for early withdrawal from a "wild card" is the same as for any insured account with a term of more than one year: the loss of at least 6 months' interest. If you made the withdrawal before 6 months had elapsed, you'd lose some of your principal.

When these accounts mature they'll be automatically renewed within 7 days unless the institution notifies you that it has decided not to renew. In that case it will convert to a passbook account until you do something else with it.

Read the renewal notices for these accounts carefully. Institutions have the right to calculate the interest rate in a different way or pay a different rate when the account is renewed. However, if the institution changes the basis on which interest is to be paid it must give you a written explanation at least 15 days before the term ends.

Which Way Will Interest Rates Go?

Basically, the "wild cards" require that you try to decide which way interest rates will go for the next 18 months —or longer, if your account has a longer maturity.

If you think interest rates will fall, invest in a fixed-rate certificate. This will "lock in" today's presumably high rate for the full term. With this option, you'll also know exactly what the certificate will be worth when it matures.

But if you think rates will rise, buy a variable-rate certificate. Presumably this will be paying an even higher rate as it nears the end of the term than it was in the beginning.

For most people, the problem is that trying to decide what interest rates will do for the next 18 months is like trying to decide whether a flipped coin will come up heads or tails. There's simply no way to be sure.

The future course of interest rates will be determined by a host of complex and unpredictable factors. To name just a few, they include the state of the economy, demand for money and credit, federal spending policies, the Federal Reserve's policies, economic and financial developments in other parts of the world, and such un-predictable contingencies as wars, great natural dis-asters, and financial panics here or elsewhere.

Many economists themselves have miserable records when forecasting interest rates, and the current mood in money markets can be misleading. It can change from euphoria to gloom overnight on the basis of a new set of statistics or on the presumed stance of the Federal Re-serve's Board of Governors.

This being the case, be wary of concentrating too great a proportion of your IRAs in investments that will do best if interest rates move in one direction. Unless you are convinced you know what rates will do, consider hedging your bets.

You could play it both ways from the start. If you've decided to open an IRA at a bank or thrift institution, put half of your money in a fixed-rate certificate that would be the best choice if interest rates fall during its term. Put the other half in a floating-rate account that would be the best choice if rates rise.

Then sit back and see how they compare. You won't come out as well as if you had put all of your money on the right choice. But you'll come out better than if you'd put it all on the wrong one.

Short-Term Rates Can Change Quickly

Many depository institutions that offer variable-rate IRAs tied to an index appear to be selecting indexes based on prices of securities with substantially shorter maturities than the 18-month "wild cards" themselves. If interest rates fall, this would put you at a disadvantage compared to big investors who buy money market securities directly.

Historically, interest rates for such short-term instruments as treasury bills, commercial paper, and negotiable bank CDs are more volatile than rates on money market instruments with longer terms. Big investors are willing to put up with this volatility because they know they won't be locked into that market for long. If rates plunge, they'll be able to get all of their money out in a few weeks or months as their investments mature, and they can then invest it elsewhere.

But if you have a variable-rate 18-month "wild card" paying a rate based on price fluctuations for 3-month treasury bills, you won't be able to get your money out after 3 months. If rates drop sharply after you buy it and the rate to you is greatly reduced 3 months later, you'll still be locked into that investment for another 15 months —unless you're willing to pay a penalty that will cut into your capital.

You should also be aware that most of the time, short-term rates are the lowest in the interest-rate spectrum. It is only in recent years that they have been higher than other rates, creating what economists call an "inverted yield curve." If history is any guide, if both the inflation rate and the interest rates drop, short-term rates will fall the furthest and fastest.

Of course if interest rates go up, short-term rates will rise the furthest and fastest. The point is, however, that the most reasonable variable-rate index would be one based on securities that mature at about the same time the IRA certificate does.

Other Insured Savings IRAs

If they wish, banks and thrift institutions may also offer any other account or certificate as an IRA. In those cases the rules for the other savings instruments apply. If you are allowed to make additions to the account, for instance, each addition may extend the certificate's term.

The principal savings instruments at banks and thrifts are

"Jumbo" Certificates—Rates and terms for these certificates are completely negotiable between the institution and the buyer. In early 1982 the "jumbo" minimum was $100,000, although the DIDC was considering a proposal to lower it. Under most circumstances, "jumbos" would be inappropriate as IRAs. But if you had a very large IRA or received a large rollover from a corporate pension plan and could find an institution that would sell you one structured as an IRA, this could be a high-paying parking place for your funds. If federal savings insurance is a concern, don't put more than the insurance limit in any single institution.

Other "Wild Cards"—Savings rates at banks, savings and loan associations, and mutual savings banks are being deregulated according to a timetable. In 1982 all rate limits were removed from new time deposits of 3½ years or more. As with the 18-month IRA "wild cards," banks and thrifts can pay what they wish on these accounts and structure rates and terms largely as they wish. Other than finding institutions that offer the highest rates, your basic choice is the same as with an IRA "wild card." It comes down to whether you want one with a fixed rate, which will be to your advantage if rates fall during the life of the investment, or whether you want one with a variable rate, which will be to your advantage if interest rates rise.

Presumably a few years from now all savings accounts and certificates will be "wild cards," and you can negotiate with your local thrift institutions and commercial banks for the best deal available at the time.

Market-Rate Certificates—Any new savings plans authorized by the DIDC in the future are likely to be of the market-rate type. Whether fixed-rate or variable-rate, rates are determined by changes in the market price of money market securities.

The first market-rate instruments authorized were the money market certificate (MMC) and the small savers certificate (SSC).

The MMCs have $10,000 minimums and 180-day terms. Rates are linked to weekly auction prices of 6-month U.S. Treasury bills, and rates to new buyers change each week. The $10,000 minimum limits MMCs to IRAs that have been maintained for some time or to employer-plan rollovers. Attempts are being made, however, to lower this minimum. And in 1982 the DIDC authorized a 91-day MMC with a $7,500 minimum, with rates tied to changes in the market price of 3-month treasury bills.

The SSCs have 2½-year terms and no statutory minimum deposit. Institutions may establish their own minimums, however, and many do. Interest rates are linked to market prices for 2½-year U.S. Treasury securities and change to new buyers twice a month.

The SSCs would be very appropriate IRA investments if you believe interest rates are likely to decline in the next 2½ years.

Passbooks—As long as passbook rates are substantially lower than other rates, passbooks should be used only as a temporary parking place for IRA funds. If you're given a lump-sum distribution from an employer plan or have rolled money out of an IRA and aren't sure what to do with it, you could park it in a passbook until you decide how to complete the rollover. But don't use a passbook as a permanent IRA unless passbook rates go much higher than they are now or market rates fall to passbook rates.

The exception may be in the case of some credit unions. All federally chartered and many state-chartered credit unions may now pay as much or as little on passbook accounts as they wish. Some may set their passbook rates high enough to make them acceptable as liquid IRA investments that could be held for a longer term.

Older Fixed-Rate CDs—Banks and thrifts are also authorized to offer a number of other CDs with fixed rates and terms. The rates these old CDs pay are unrealistically below the current market. They include a special IRA certificate that paid buyers 8 per cent and matured in 3 years.

Inflation has rendered these CDs obsolete. Most institutions won't bother telling you about them, and in no case should you seriously consider setting one up as an IRA. If you still have one of these old CDs, investigate now to see if it would pay to take the penalty and move the money into a higher-yielding IRA investment. If the switch wouldn't pay, mark the CD's maturity date on your calendar and make the move as soon as it matures.

MUTUAL FUNDS

The mutual fund industry's strength in the battle for IRA dollars is its broad spectrum of investments. These range from the most conservative—in the form of funds that invest only in U.S. government securities—to the most aggressive, which take risks in hopes of achieving superior capital gains.

They also include money market mutual funds, which invest directly in money market instruments formerly available only to institutional investors and the wealthy.

Mutual funds are companies that pool money from thousands of people and invest it in a broad range of investments selected by professional money managers.

Minimum contributions to set up an IRA at most mutual funds range from $25 to $500, although some requirements are higher or lower. As a rule subsequent contributions can be for smaller amounts, perhaps $50 or $100.

Some funds will also arrange to have withdrawals made automatically from your checking account and placed directly into the fund's IRA.

A major advantage of mutual funds is that they can provide a broad degree of diversification for a small investment. If you invest in a common stock fund, for $2,000 or less you can buy a stake in 50 or 60 companies or, if it is a balanced fund, in a combination of stocks and bonds. Your mutual fund investments can be spread over a broad range of industries or, if you wish, concentrated in the field where you think the possibility of gain is greatest. Some funds invest only in energy stocks, for instance. Others may concentrate their investments in such fields as precious metals, technology, or health care.

Families of mutual funds believe they have the special advantage of giving investors the ability to shift from one type of investment to another without being concerned about breaking IRS rules on rollovers and transfers. This flexibility has always been there, but in the past investors have not made great use of it. The universal IRA, however, has triggered a barrage of promotional materials emphasizing the advantages of this feature.

Typically, investors in a family of funds can transfer assets with just a phone call or by filling out a few forms. Some fund families charge you $5 to switch from one fund to another while others allow you to move for free.

Consequently the mutual fund industry sees the universal IRA as an opportunity to market its services to millions of new customers. Some will be people buying mutual fund shares through brokerage houses, insurance companies, or the funds themselves. Others will be people offered an opportunity to buy shares through IRA payroll deduction plans where they work.

Load and No-Load Funds

If you've dealt with mutual funds before you know that in addition to differing in their investment goals, there are two basic types of funds insofar as costs are concerned: load funds and no-load funds.

Every mutual fund has a management group that makes the fund's buying and selling decisions. This group charges annual management fees that vary between one-half and one percent of the fund's total assets.

In addition, *load funds* have sales organizations. Buyers of shares in load funds are charged a sales commission, usually 8½ percent of the amount invested. This is compensation for the registered stockbroker's representative, financial planner, or insurance agent who helps you select that fund.

The *no-load* funds don't charge a sales commission. In the past, it was much easier to find load funds than no-load funds. For years, the no-load funds rarely advertised, except in a few financial journals.

Now, the more than 200 no-load funds, including 18 families of no-load funds, are much easier to find. Many advertise in local newspapers and on local radio and television stations. Their trade group, the No-Load Mutual Fund Association Inc., sells a directory for $1 that lists all members and the key facts about them (see Chapter 14).

Many people have found load funds that best meet their investment objectives. With a load fund, you also get the personal service of the man or woman who helps you select that IRA investment. Over the years there has been no great difference in the general performance records of load mutual funds as compared to no-load funds. So, all things being equal—which they rarely are—you'll probably be better off buying a no-load fund that invests all of your annual IRA contributions rather than paying a big commission to a load fund.

Read the Fund's Prospectus

Every mutual fund has a stated financial objective that is spelled out in its prospectus, and before you can invest in the fund you must be given a copy of it. Some or most of it may be difficult reading because it has been prepared by batteries of investment professionals not always known for their clarity of expression.

It will be worth your while to try to read the prospectus anyway. Especially study the fund's objectives to be sure its goals are compatible with yours. If you are near or in retirement, for instance, and this IRA will be your main source of retirement income, be sure the fund is not committed to making relatively speculative investments that pay little or no dividends and may not reap major capital gains for years.

Then look at the specific investments in the fund's investment portfolio to see what it is going to do with your money.

As long as you continue to hold shares in the fund,

keep the prospectus, as well as any new prospectus the fund sends you and the periodic quarterly reports on how the fund is doing. If the fund's managers change the fund's goals or objectives, they will have to state that in a new or amended prospectus. Also, by comparing portfolios from one quarterly report to another, you can see which investments the fund has been buying—or selling.

The prospectus also gives you the fund's investment record over the years. To compare that fund's performance with other funds, consult some of the references described in the final section of this chapter.

Mutual Fund Performance

On the whole, mutual funds that invest wholly or partly in the stock market have performed well over the years. There would have been periods, of course, when, if purchases and sales were timed poorly, you would not have done well.

This suggests that purchases of shares in mutual funds that invest in the stock market should be made for the long haul. They would not be appropriate for anyone in or near retirement who may wish to begin withdrawing from the fund soon. And even in periods when funds as a whole are thriving, there are always some that substantially lag behind the market.

Consequently, if you've never invested in a mutual fund before and are given an opportunity to do so, perhaps in a payroll deduction IRA plan at work, keep in mind that the value of your investment can go down as well as up. In even the best-managed funds, values will drop if the overall stock market drops. If you're going to invest in a mutual fund, you must be prepared to live with that knowledge—and be able to sleep at night even if your fund's value has fallen since you bought it.

How well your mutual fund IRA will do depends on a number of things. These include the timing of your investments, how long you invest the money, and how well that fund does.

The Investment Company Institute, the trade group for the mutual fund industry, reports that the most conservative common stock funds—those that invest for both growth and income—would have grown to $288,000 by 1981 if you invested $2,000 at the start of each year for the past 30 years. The funds in this study were load funds, and all contributions were subject to an 8½ percent commission. This is an annual rate of return over the 30-year time span of about 9 percent, compared with an average passbook savings rate return of 4.1 percent.

Lipper Analytical Services, which primarily deals with institutional clients, reported at the end of 1981 that the mutual fund industry "is continuing to produce substantially better results than the market averages."

It said that general equity funds rose 119.38 percent over a 10-year period, compared with 62.69 percent for the Dow Jones Industrial average (reinvested) and 87.57 percent for Standard & Poor's 500 (reinvested). Over a 20-year period they grew 343.40 percent, compared with 184.17 for the Dow Jones Industrials and 270.75 for Standard & Poor's 500.

Fund Families and Types of Funds

Some mutual fund families have more than 20 individual funds, including stock funds, bond funds, and mixed funds of one type or another. But basically the essential elements of a mutual fund family are a money market mutual fund, a common stock fund, and an income fund.

The money market fund is for liquidity, for taking advantage of high short-term yields, and for parking funds when you are between investments. Common stock funds are usually for the growth of capital through the stock market. An income fund consisting of bonds, preferred stocks, or other high-yielding stocks such as utilities, can be used to lock in current yields for income and to achieve capital gains when interest rates are falling.

In this regard mutual funds are especially appropriate for the purchase of corporate bonds by small investors. A small investor must pay a premium price to buy an odd lot—and may find the bonds difficult to sell even at a large discount if the bonds must be sold before they mature.

Other basic mutual fund types include growth income funds, which seek to combine income and long-term growth; balanced funds, which seek to balance growth-oriented stocks with income-producing bonds and preferred stocks; specialty funds that specialize in the securities of particular industries or types of securities; and municipal bond funds, which are inappropriate for IRA investments because their income is already tax-exempt.

IRA investors may also wish to consider looking at so-called tax qualified mutual funds. When the universal IRA was authorized, there were only a handful of mutual funds designed especially for tax-sheltered investors. Formerly these funds were used only by pension funds, universities, and other tax-sheltered investors. But some of these funds will now accept IRA contributions from individuals.

The advantage of these funds to IRA investors is that their managers do not hesitate to take short-term profits, whereas managers of regular stock funds may be reluctant to generate too many short-term gains that would have to be passed on to shareholders. The managers of these funds actively seek investments in companies that may offer short-term gains because they may be involved in mergers, bankruptcies, consolidations, or other forms of reorganization.

Money Market Mutual Funds

Because they are virtually a cash equivalent, money market mutual funds are in a class by themselves. During times of high interest rates they can be used as a basic IRA investment. And they can be used to park money between IRA rollovers.

The money market funds have enjoyed remarkable growth. The first was organized in 1972. At the end of 1981 the assets of the nation's 160 money funds rose to more than $180 billion, more than doubling the $70 billion at the start of 1981.

This growth has been fueled both by large institutional investors and by individuals. The institutional investors move in and out of the money funds depending on whether they can get a slightly higher return by investing directly in money market instruments. Individual investors have taken to the funds both because they offer a high return and because the funds are liquid. There is no penalty for taking money out, and most funds offer what are in effect check-writing privileges (which of course will not be needed with an IRA unless you are age 59½ or older).

Money market mutual funds invest in money market instruments. Primarily, these are U.S. Treasury obligations, certificates of deposit issued by commercial banks and other financial institutions, and commercial paper, or corporate IOUs, issued by private corporations.

Maturities of these instruments are short-term. Consequently the yield on a money market fund is directly related to the volatile changes in short-term money markets. Historically, rates on short-term instruments are usually the lowest in the investment spectrum. But in the inflationary environment of the 1970s and beyond they have often been higher than other rates, resulting in generous returns.

During the 1977–81 period, the Investment Company Institute found that the average yield for money market mutual funds was 10.08 percent. In this case the "average" yield could be somewhat misleading. Money market fund rates are extremely sensitive to changes in short-term money market instruments, the most volatile in the interest-rate spectrum. In 1977, money market rates were down and the money funds' average yield for that year was only 5.0 percent. As inflation and economic policies pushed rates up in subsequent years, the money market fund annual yield rose to 6.9 percent in 1978, 10.0 percent in 1979, 12.0 percent in 1980, and 16.5 percent in 1981.

Many money market funds are operated independently and most are no-load. In addition, all "families" of mutual funds include a money market fund.

During periods when interest rates are at very high levels, money market funds may be among the highest-yielding IRA investments. Even when rates are down, money market funds can be a convenient parking place for IRA money until you decide what you want to do with it.

Money market mutual funds are *not* covered by federal savings insurance or by the Securities Investor Protection Corp. program that covers investments in securities held by brokerage houses. If a money market mutual fund runs into trouble, all of your investment is at risk.

The industry's safety record, however, has been excellent. Investor safeguards include regulation by the Securities and Exchange Commission, annual audits by independent certified public accountants, and the fact that all assets are held by an independent custodian bank.

But concerns have been voiced that under some market conditions, problems could arise. One would be if interest rates dropped sharply and investors began pulling money out of the funds for higher yields elsewhere. In addition to individuals, the investors in these funds include corporate and institutional cash managers and bank trust departments. These institutional investors stand to gain or lose huge sums at a slight difference in return, and in a plummeting market they would move assets out of the funds quickly. Under this extreme scenario, funds would have to liquidate some investments at a loss before they mature in order to meet withdrawal requests, and all fund holders could suffer some capital loss.

The other concern is that the financial system is so interrelated that major failures on one sector could affect others. It has been theorized that if one or more major corporate issuers of commercial paper went down, the commercial paper market could collapse—and money market funds heavily invested in commercial paper would suffer losses.

The safety of a money market fund's portfolio could also depend on the length of its investments. The further out its portfolio is committed, the more trouble it could get into if it guessed wrong on interest rates (or the better its performance would be if it guessed correctly). In spring 1982 the average money fund investment matured in about 30 days. The average period could change in the future—but to minimize this risk, seek maturities that are near or shorter than the average at the time you invest.

So far these safety concerns are only theoretical, but they have resulted in some controversial efforts to rate money market mutual funds by safety. "Money Fund Safety Ratings," a Ft. Lauderdale, Florida, investment newsletter, has ranked about 100 funds based on its analysis of their investment portfolios. It views the safest funds as those that invest in the securities of the U.S. government and U.S. government agencies that mature in about 30 days. But critics of the service say that the safety differences among funds are so small as to be insignificant.

Concerns over investor safety in general have resulted in a great expansion of money market funds that invest only in government securities. Their number grew from 18 in 1980 to around 40 by mid-1982. During this period their assets grew from about 5 percent to about 15 percent of all taxable money fund assets. The Lehman Government Fund grew from zero in fall 1981 to $120 million 6 months later. Sears, Roebuck attracted $120 million to its new money market fund in little more than a month of operations in 1982.

There's no doubt that if you want the highest degree of safety for your money fund, you should select one that invests entirely in U.S. government securities. But of course these funds will pay a slightly lower yield. One study found that over the last 10 years, treasury bill yields averaged 2 percent less a year than the yields on bank certificates of deposit. *Forbes* magazine reported that in early 1982, the U.S. government funds were yielding about one-half percent less than other money funds.

"Donoghue's Money Fund Report" found that the top general-purpose money fund 12-month yield as of February 26, 1982, was 17.09 percent, compared with 16.12 percent for the top government-only money fund.

During normal economic times, however, the chances of any money market fund getting into trouble appear minimal.

Switching Strategies

Investing in a family of funds gives you a wide range of options. You may pursue a single investment objective, or hedge your bets by splitting your IRA contributions into two or more funds. Investing in a family of funds also gives you a great degree of diversification not possible if you are investing as little as $2,000 a year or less in a self-directed plan at a brokerage house.

Investments can be switched either according to changes in your own circumstances or changes in the marketplace. If you inherit a big chunk of money and no longer need rely on your IRA for a substantial part of your retirement income, you can switch to funds that seek maximum capital gains by investing in small, fast-growing companies. But if you are nearing retirement and are concerned about the safety of your principal, you would switch to a money fund that is heavy in government securities or, if you believe interest rates will remain reasonably stable or come down, to a bond or other income fund.

You may also wish to switch to adapt to market changes. If the stock market is sluggish or declining but interest rates are high, you could keep most or all of your investment in the family's money market fund. But if interest rates fall and the stock market takes off, assets could be shifted out of the money fund and into a growth-oriented common stock fund.

Of course, this sounds simpler than it really is. It presumes that you—or someone advising you—will know when markets are turning: when interest rates are indeed peaking or hitting bottom, and when major turns are taking place in the stock market. The fact is that if you make a mistake, you can wind up losing money by switching from one fund to another—or at any rate not making nearly as much as though you hadn't switched.

If you've been successful in the past at calling turns in interest rates and tops and bottoms in the stock market, you'll probably be successful in switching from one mutual fund to another. But if you haven't been able to call turns in interest rates or stock market tops and bottoms, you're not likely to do any better by moving assets around in a mutual fund family. The versatility of a family of mutual funds gives you great flexibility, but you must have luck or the financial sophistication to exploit it. Otherwise you will be better off sticking to the one or two funds in the family that offer investments you understand and feel comfortable with, even if you are forgoing the chance for bigger gains.

The difficulty in calling market turns and interest rate peaks and troughs has given rise to a type of financial adviser called a market timing service. These services work primarily for institutional and other large investors and charge clients a flat fee for picking mutual funds in which to invest—usually one to 2 percent of the account.

Fact, the money management magazine, concluded that "there is no proof that the timers are any more adept at spotting the peaks and valleys of the stock market than are individual investors—or the portfolio managers of mutual funds."

In one sense, frequent switching from one fund to

another in the same family contradicts some of the rationale for investing in a mutual fund in the first place. It is that many people don't have the time, inclination, or training to study all of the information needed to make investments—and that mutual fund decisions are made by professionals who make it their full-time job.

So while the ability to switch from one fund to another in the same family gives you versatility, it won't ensure investment success. For most people, the ability to switch will probably be more valuable in adjusting to changes in their own circumstances—the need for safer and more conservative investments as you approach retirement, for instance—than in trying to "play" financial markets.

Learning More About Mutual Funds

The fact that most mutual funds may be gaining in value won't be much consolation to you if the one you selected falls.

If you have a stockbroker with reference materials, ask to see the latest reports from Wiesenberger Investment Companies Service, Johnson's Investment Company Charts, or Lipper Analytical Services. You may also be able to find one or more of these reference sources in a public library or a university library, if you have access to one. While past performance is no guarantee of future success, these references will enable you to make comparisons among results of specific funds. Any fund that consistently lags in performance should be avoided.

In addition, every August *Forbes* magazine publishes an annual report on mutual funds that grades them for performance in up and down markets.

Two industry trade associations can provide general information on mutual funds, including their addresses and investment goals. These are The Investment Company Institute, 1775 K Street N.W., Washington, D.C. 20006, and the No-Load Mutual Fund Association Inc., Valley Forge, PA 19481. For more on the information these trade groups can provide, see Chapter 14.

Several informational publications on money market funds are sold by the Cash Management Institute, 770 Washington Street, P.O. Box 641, Holliston, MA 07146. These are:

"Donoghue's Moneyletter," a bimonthly report on developments in money markets, the best performing money funds, interest rate trends, and new money market instruments. Twelve issues (6 months) for $49.

Donoghue's Money Fund Directory, a money fund listing with two-year performance records, phone numbers, addresses, and other information. Updated twice yearly, $15 per edition.

Donoghue's Mutual Fund Almanac, with 5- and 10-year performance records of more than 600 mutual funds. Published annually, $25 per edition.

Monthly performance comparisons of more than 400 mutual funds are available from United Mutual Fund Selector, a service of United Business Service Company, 212 Newbury Street, Boston, MA 02116. The service is bimonthly, and the comparisons are in the first issue of each month.

BROKERAGE HOUSES AND
SELF-DIRECTED PLANS

You'll find the biggest selection of IRA investment options at the large brokerage houses. And large or small, any brokerage house that wishes to can set up a self-directed plan through which you can buy and sell stocks, bonds, or other securities for your own IRA.

You can buy load mutual funds through a broker, and some will sell you an insurance annuity IRA plan or put your money in a savings account. Many of the large brokerage houses also have their own families of mutual funds in which you can switch from one to another just as with other mutual fund families.

The costs of taking the mutual fund approach at a big brokerage firm are less than with a self-directed plan. In early 1982 Merrill Lynch charged $15 to establish its mutual fund account, plus an annual custodial fee of $20. Dean Witter Reynolds charged $20 to set up its mutual fund IRA and $20 as the annual custodial fee. These charges were typical for the industry as a whole at the time. As with other fees at brokerage houses and most other IRA sponsors, these of course can be changed at any time.

Self-Directed IRAs

The type of IRA most associated with brokerage houses is the self-directed account, which works much like a regular brokerage account.

Legally your IRA is in the possession of a qualified custodian or trustee, usually a bank or savings and loan association, but you make all the decisions, giving you far more flexibility in controlling investments than with any other type of IRA. You decide how much risk you're willing to assume and direct the brokerage house to buy or sell investments, just as you would for your own account. In addition to the traditional stocks and bonds, these may include corporate bond unit trusts, limited partnerships in real estate and oil and gas ventures, zero coupon bonds, or any other investment not prohibited for IRAs by law.

Generally speaking, self-directed accounts should be used primarily by sophisticated investors. And while a self-directed account gives you the greatest latitude in making investments, it is also the most expensive way to go. In addition to the regular commissions for buying and selling securities, brokers were charging about $20 to $30 to open a self-directed account when IRAs became universal. They also charged annual fees ranging from about $20 to as much as $50 and may have termination fees as well.

At Merrill Lynch, the annual maintenance fee was the greater of $50 or two-tenths of one percent of the assets in the account as of December 1 each year. Bache Halsey Stuart Shields Inc.'s fees were $25 to open the account and a minimum annual fee of $35. Paine, Webber, Jackson & Curtis Inc. charged $25 to open an IRA, plus a $25 annual maintenance fee.

Most brokers will now put any cash that flows into the account—from dividends or interest, for instance—into a money market mutual fund until it's reinvested. These amounts will be small in the beginning, but over a period of time can substantially increase your overall return. Don't sign up for a self-directed IRA unless it has this feature.

Because you're dealing with the same trustee, with a self-directed IRA you're allowed to switch funds from one investment to another at any time without a tax penalty. But while you may trade pretty much as you wish in a self-directed account with a brokerage house, you're not allowed to sell stocks short. Because IRS rules prohibit using IRA assets as a pledge or collateral for a loan, most brokerage houses also interpret this to mean that margin trading in a self-directed IRA is prohibited. Even if you find one that interprets it otherwise, don't start trading on margin until you've checked it out with your own tax adviser.

Some brokerage houses also establish limitations to prevent customers from taking high-risk speculations with IRA money. And although brokers' accounts are the only way to make certain investments—options, for instance—most brokers limit IRA investors to writing covered calls, that is, buying stocks and simultaneously selling calls on them. This mechanism provides a way to increase the income on a stock, but you'd have to give up some profits if the stock's price rises sharply and the stock is called away from you. In any event, if you don't already know how options work, you don't want to start learning in an IRA.

Is a Self-Directed Account Right for You?

The great advantage of a self-directed IRA is its flexibility. You have many more investment options than with any other type of IRA. And while current law prohibits IRA investments in "hard" assets, a self-directed account can be used to buy stock in companies in the hard asset field—in gold and silver mines, for instance. But consistent success with a self-directed IRA requires one, and preferably both, of the following:

• *If you intend to rely primarily on your own judgment to make investment decisions, you should have already established a successful track record as an investor.*

If you've been consistently successful at making your own investment decisions in the past, it's likely you'll continue doing so with IRA investments. But if you have no experience in the types of self-directed IRA investments you're thinking of making, or your past record has been poor, the chances of your suddenly blossoming into an investment wizard with your IRA are not good—and the higher cost of a self-directed account makes the odds against you even greater.

Be honest with yourself. If you've been a successful investor, you probably have a pretty good idea of how profitable your investments have been. In fact the more successful you've been, the more likely it is you know just how far ahead of the game you are. When your stocks are going up, it's a lot of fun to sit down at the end of each week to figure out how rich you're getting. But when they're going down, it's amazing how many months you can put off sitting down with a calculator to see just how bad the news really is.

So if you have any doubts, before setting up a self-directed IRA in which you'd buy and sell common stocks, go over your investment records and tax returns for the last 5 or 10 years. Is your current portfolio of stocks worth more than you paid for it? And in past years have your capital gains been greater than your losses? If you can't answer "yes" to both questions, you have no business risking your retirement savings in the stock market unless your retirement income is already amply secured.

(On the other hand, if your retirement income *is* already amply secured—if you're so well off or have a guaranteed retirement income so large that you wouldn't worry if markets turned against you and you lost part or all of your IRA—go ahead and "play craps" with these tax-sheltered dollars. Who knows? You might score spectacular capital gains.)

• *If you do not have the knowledge and experience to*

make your own investment decisions, you should at least have a competent broker or investment counselor to make these decisions for you.

Ideally, this should be someone with a proven record in giving you sound investment advice in the past. It would not be prudent to set up a self-directed IRA if the investment decisions are to be made by someone who hasn't already demonstrated his or her competence to you—unless that person comes with high recommendations from a knowledgeable investor you know and trust.

There are thousands of highly competent customer's representatives at brokerage houses, but don't allow investment decisions involving your retirement money to be made by a total stranger. As in any other business, some customer's representatives are better than others. Not all have the experience or knowledge required to make investment decisions for you or would take enough interest in your account. Unfortunately, at some investment houses, accounts with small balances get little attention. Customers who don't trade often are known as "orphans." And just as with insurance agents and savings counselors at banks and thrift institutions, it would be unrealistic to assume that all customer's representatives at brokerage houses are familiar with the intricacies of IRA rules and regulations.

When Does a Self-Directed Account Pay?

If you're thinking of a self-directed account at a brokerage house in terms of buying and selling common stocks, you must decide at what point it will pay. If all you have to invest at the start is $2,000 or less, the fees—and particularly, the broker's commissions on each transaction—will probably eat up much or all of your profits, if any.

On the purchase or sale of 100 shares of a $20 stock, the commission at the typical full-service brokerage house would be about 3 percent, or $60.

You can substantially reduce those buying and selling commissions by dealing with a discount broker. But to take this route, you should be the sort of investor who doesn't need a broker's guidance on what to buy or sell and who does his or her own research on stocks and other investments. If you feel you must sit down and discuss your investment program and goals with your broker—and you'd want to rely on your broker's research facilities—you should continue dealing with a full-service brokerage firm.

The fees at discount brokerage firms vary widely. A 100-share purchase or sale of a $20 stock at a discount firm would cost anywhere from about $25 to about $45. Also, comparing discount broker fees is difficult because it's not easy when looking at their rate charts to see at a glance which broker really has the best deal for your circumstances.

Most brokers work on a sliding scale. The broker who charges the lowest commission on a relatively large block of stock may not charge the lowest for a small block. So if you're an independent-minded investor accustomed to going it alone, the discount broker can save you a lot of money over a period of years.

Realistically, whether you're dealing with a full-line brokerage house or with a discount broker, most advisers suggest having at least about $10,000 in your IRA before you start trading in common stocks.

With only $2,000 or less to invest, you'd be limited to buying stocks in odd lots, where buying costs are higher—or buying low-priced stocks, where investment risks are often greater. Some brokerage houses won't even buy a stock selling below a certain price out of concern that the risks for their clients would be too great.

If you're starting from scratch, you can build your IRA with insured savings certificates or a money market fund for several years. When it gets large enough, switch to a self-directed brokerage house IRA and begin building a stock portfolio.

Limited Partnership IRAs

Brokerage accounts are also being structured to offer limited partnership IRAs in oil and gas, real estate, and other business ventures. These IRA partnerships are designed to produce income rather than to produce tax write-offs, which traditionally have been the great attraction for these deals.

Primarily, limited partnership IRAs are for sophisticated investors or for investors who can afford sophisticated financial advice. Certainly they're not for everyone —and to participate in one you'll be required to meet certain income and net worth qualifications that can vary depending on the state in which you live.

A "limited partnership" is an agreement between a general partner, who presumably has the knowledge and expertise to operate the venture, and a group of "limited partners" who put up most of the money.

Until fairly recently, many deals of this type required investments of at least $10,000 or more in each unit. But now many partnership units are available through some brokerage houses at the $2,000 level and sometimes less, making them possible for IRAs.

The main advantage of limited partnership IRAs is that they give you the opportunity to invest in a venture you probably couldn't afford on your own. Through a limited partnership you can participate directly in specific oil and gas, real estate, or other ventures without any responsibility for their operations. At the same time, your liability is limited to your investment. If the venture runs into trouble, you cannot be assessed for more money.

An oil and gas income IRA involves producing properties with proven reserves. There is no high-risk drilling venture to worry about, and the cash flow usually begins quickly, often in the first year. But if you don't know much about these investment programs yourself, check the deal out with someone who does before committing any IRA funds.

The main thing to look for in checking any limited partnership proposal is that the company running the show has been in business for a reasonable period of time and has chalked up a successful investment record.

Through limited partnerships, IRA investments can also be made in income-producing real estate investments. These can involve income-producing office buildings, apartment complexes, and shopping malls as well as the financing of properties. In fact any income-oriented limited partnership, including those that lease computers, boxcars, or other business equipment, could be structured as an IRA.

Zero Coupon Bonds

With the universal IRA market still in its infancy, new IRA investment vehicles that can be marketed on a self-directed basis are sure to be devised—and new uses for older vehicles are being found too.

Already, a lot of interest and promotion has developed around so-called zero coupon bonds as IRA investments. They are also being marketed as unit trusts, which are portfolios of fixed-income securities, and some financial institutions have issued zero coupon certificates of deposit.

Zero coupon bonds, which have been around for some time, were designed chiefly for tax-exempt institutions and foreign investors with no U.S. tax obligations. But the universal IRA suddenly broadened the market for zero coupon bonds, as well as zero coupon notes and certificates of deposit.

These bonds pay no periodic interest. Instead, they are sold at a deep discount from face value. You may pay $2,500 for a bond that will mature in 5 years and be worth $5,000, doubling your investment.

If this bond were a taxable investment, the IRS would require you to pay tax on the "invisible" interest each year even though you didn't receive it. But if it is in an IRA, these "invisible" gains are sheltered from taxation. If purchased when interest rates are at relatively high levels, you have an investment where you know for sure that you could double or triple your money in 5 or 10 years.

Paine, Webber, Jackson & Curtis Inc. successfully offered the first fund composed entirely of zero bonds to the IRA market. Merrill Lynch, Pierce, Fenner & Smith Inc. introduced its own fund. Other competitors followed suit, and BankAmerica has marketed an offering that includes a $250 bond that would grow to $1,000 in 10 years. So long as interest rates remain relatively high, it is likely the zero bonds could grow to become a staple in the IRA investment market.

There is a sales charge, which varies from issuer to issuer. One major advantage of the zero coupon bond is that you know exactly what your investment will be worth 5, 8, or 10 years down the road, whenever the bond matures. In that sense it is just like a U.S. government E-bond that you buy at a discount for $75 and matures at $100. Another advantage is, because there are no interest payments during the life of the security, you don't have to worry about how to invest the interest.

But there are some negatives in this picture too. First, you have to look at the financial strength of the issuer of the bonds. Will the issuer be in a position to pay off the bonds 5 or 10 years hence? Most likely it will —but if it won't, your zero bond will have become a bad investment indeed. Buying zero bonds through a fund with a diversified portfolio will reduce the risk, but it is there nonetheless.

Second, a zero discount bond may be difficult to sell at a reasonable price before it matures. If you decide there's something else you want to do with the money, you may have a problem getting out of this investment. This being the case, a zero bond may not be the best IRA investment for older people who may need the money before the bond matures. It could also cause a problem for your heirs if you died before the bond matured.

Finally, despite all the excitement that zero coupon bonds have created—when brokerage firms began marketing them, they were publicized by a spate of articles in national magazines—basically they are just another play on interest rates. You buy them in hopes that interest rates will go down, allowing you to lock in a high yield for 5 years, 10 years, or whatever.

If you guessed right, you'd do well. If interest rates remain at roughly the same level over the period you hold the zero bond, you'd have come out ahead buying a coupon bond (which normally pays a slightly higher yield) and reinvesting the coupons at current rates. But you'd come out far behind if interest rates rise.

As a variation on the zero coupon theme, in 1982 Merrill Lynch was selling zero coupon certificates of deposit of the Crocker National Bank for IRA accounts. Unlike other zero coupon bonds and notes, these had federal deposit insurance protection on amounts up to $100,000.

Other Self-Directed IRAs

Through a self-directed IRA you can also play the interest-rate game with corporate and government bonds and, until you build an IRA of considerable size, with bond funds.

IRA sponsors are also adapting other financial instruments such as securities guaranteed by the Government National Mortgage Association. These are mortgage-backed securities with a monthly cash flow, representing monthly payments on home mortgages. While not direct obligations of the U.S. government, they are backed by the full faith and credit of the government.

The sponsors of the "Ginnie Mae" unit trusts see them as an investment alternative for people who have been settling for low interest in return for safety—and are now seeking a higher return. Units cost about $1,000 each, and monthly interest and principal payments are automatically reinvested if you wish. The fund's trustee will redeem units at any time, with the price determined by any principal repayments as well as the market price of the securities in the portfolio. If interest rates have gone up since you bought the units, the market price will be lower; if they have gone down, the price will be higher.

The price of the units includes a sales charge of a little more than 3 percent. In the past these securities have been totally repaid in about 12 years. However, because of the depression in housing markets and the trouble people are having buying and selling homes, people are remaining in the same home for longer periods of time. Consequently the payout period for investments made now may be longer than 12 years.

Self-directed IRAs have also been set up to invest in second mortgages and deeds of trust. These earn a high return—but carry a relatively high degree of risk. Unless you are a seasoned investor in this field and can afford higher risk, these and other riskier IRA investments should be avoided.

INSURANCE COMPANY IRAs

The life insurance industry's basic IRA product is the flexible annuity.

You decide how much and when you wish to contribute to the plan. You're guaranteed a minimum return every year or 6 months, but the company may pay you more than this if justified by the results of its investments. In recent years, they have paid more than the minimum.

When you're ready to start withdrawing from your IRA, the insurance company hopes you'll buy an annuity that will pay you a set income during your retirement. You're not, however, obligated to buy an annuity. If you wish, you can withdraw all of the money as a lump-sum distribution or transfer or roll it over into another IRA.

Typically the written guaranteed return over a long term is low, such as 3½ percent. The actual rate when you set up the IRA will be much higher than this. But the rate will change periodically depending on how the insurance company's investments are doing. (And if the investments don't do as well as the sponsor hopes, the high beginning return could diminish quickly.)

Costs May Vary Greatly

Some of the new insurance company IRAs give you a choice of several investments, including money market funds. Just as with a family of mutual funds, you're dealing with the same trustee and can switch from one fund to another without a rollover or transfer. The Metropolitan Life Insurance Company, for instance, offers a group IRA that includes 3 different stock funds, a money market fund, and a fixed-income fund with a guaranteed return that is adjusted periodically.

Insurance company plans that involve investments in specific funds are called variable annuities. While these variable annuities permit switching, they often provide fewer types of funds from which to choose than mutual fund families do and may charge higher management fees.

Charges can also vary greatly. Most life insurance is sold by agents who work on commission. Most IRA annuities are too, although some are marketed by brokerage houses.

The traditional way of charging a life insurance commission is to assess the fee at the beginning, a so-called front load plan. In marketing their IRA products, however, many insurance companies are adopting "back load" charges that will be assessed if you withdraw the money before a specified period of time has elapsed. Usually this will be up to 10 years.

Typically these "back load" fee schedules range from 6 to 10 percent of the IRA's value. The Prudential Insurance Company's "Pruflex IRA" charges a 7 percent withdrawal fee for the first to the fourth year and thereafter drops the charge by one percentage point for all future years to the tenth year, when it is one percent. There is no withdrawal charge after that, and withdrawal fee schedules are less stringent if you are age 60 or above.

Insurance IRA Pros and Cons

With IRA annuities you'll get safety and stability and, if you shop around, reasonable earnings rates. The trade-off is that during its accumulation period (the time during which you are making contributions and the IRA is building up in value) the average rate earned on these IRAs may be slightly lower than the rates paid by banks, thrift institutions, and money market mutual funds. Money market variations in the future, of course, could change that relationship.

Of all major types of IRAs, those sold by insurance companies are probably the most difficult to research and compare. There is a great variety in the way these plans work from one company to another, and there are no central sources you can consult to weigh the relative merits of one insurance company's IRA against others. And if it's not a mutual fund plan, you cannot keep track of how well or poorly your investment is doing by reading the *Wall Street Journal, Barron's,* or the business pages of a large daily newspaper, as you can with mutual funds and stocks and bonds.

The great variety of insurance plans also stems from the fact that insurance companies are not regulated by federal agencies, as are banks and thrift institutions. Insurance firms are regulated by state agencies in the states where they decide to do business. This is to your advantage in states with strong insurance departments and to your disadvantage in states with weak supervisory agencies.

Spokesmen for the insurance industry believe one of the advantages of their IRA is the personal service of the insurance agent who markets it, and who in many cases will come to your home to discuss and explain the product. Another advantage is that sponsors may provide a waiver of premium rider under which the company continues your IRA contributions if you become disabled.

If you decide to buy an annuity for your retirement, an insurance company IRA is also the only way where, if you wish, you can select a payout option that will assure that you'll never outlive your income from that IRA.

On the other hand, the person who provides personal services and sells you the IRA must be paid for his or her efforts, and this will come out of your capital. And the trouble with fixed annuity-type retirement payments is that their buying power can be eaten away by inflation.

Even at a 7 percent inflation rate, a low one by recent standards, a dollar's buying power will be cut in half in a decade. The $1,200-a-month pension you retire with today would be worth only $600 a month in today's buying power 10 years from now. If it's a lifetime annuity and you live long enough, selecting an annuity would prove a wise choice. But if you don't live long after retiring, it will not have been the best choice and, as is discussed later in this chapter, with some annuities your heirs could wind up with nothing.

If you've been successful in handling and investing money during your working lifetime, there wouldn't seem much reason for turning your assets over to an insurance company to manage when you're ready to retire. Because the insurance company must take some of your capital as its fee, you should be able to exceed an annuity's return with investments of comparable safety. You'll also be assured that if you die soon after you retire, the assets remaining in the IRA will go to your beneficiaries.

It's easy enough to compare what an insurance annuity would pay you with what your IRA would earn on its own. Check a few insurance companies and agents and get their quotations on how much annuity income the money in your IRA could buy. Then see how much your IRA would earn each month and each year in such other investments as treasury or corporate bonds, high-yielding mutual funds, "wild card" savings instruments at banks and thrift institutions, and money market mutual funds.

Unless the income from the insurance company is substantially higher, you'll probably come out ahead with one of these alternative investments. Until you reach age 70½, you don't even have to touch the principal of these other investments if you elect not to—and if something happens to you, your heirs will inherit all of it.

On the other hand, retirement income from an insurance annuity does have the advantage of being guaranteed, and you don't have to worry about any loss of retirement income due to the ups and downs of the economy. An insurance annuity would be also appropriate if you don't trust your own ability to handle and invest the money in your IRA in the future—or if you have a number of other sources of retirement income and wish to add an annuity's income in order to diversify.

Solid life insurance companies have an impressive history of safety over a long period of years. If you wish to go to the extent of doing your own research into the comparative merits of life insurance companies in general, A. M. Best & Co., a publishing house that specializes in the insurance industry, has manuals that provide a great deal of information ranging from the size of individual companies to the specific securities held by each firm. Many of the Best manuals are available at public libraries or through major insurance agencies. A Best rating of "A" or better would be an acceptable safety level.

Rules Similar to Those for Other IRAs

The IRS rules covering IRA annuities are similar to those for other IRAs. The annuity must be issued in your name as the owner, and either you or your beneficiaries if you die can be the only ones to receive the benefits or payments.

The amount in your account must be fully vested at all times, and the contract must provide that you cannot transfer it to anyone else. If you're given any refunded premiums, you must use them to pay for future premiums or to buy more benefits. This must be done before the end of the calendar year in which you receive the refund.

You may have a spousal IRA if you have a non-working spouse, and distributions from your IRA annuity must begin when you reach age 70½. Distribution rules after age 70½ are the same as for other IRAs.

Until November 6, 1978, the IRS allowed IRAs to be set up by buying an endowment contract from a life insurance company. An endowment contract is an annuity that also gives you life insurance coverage.

If you have one of these older IRA endowments, you are not allowed to deduct any portion of the premium that goes for life insurance, which means your immediate tax savings will be less than with other IRAs. If the total yearly premiums on all of your endowment contracts are more than $2,000, the endowment contracts will not be treated as an IRA. Each year the insurance company must give you a statement showing how much of your premiums went for life insurance and cannot be deducted.

To qualify as an IRA, the premiums on any insurance contract written since November 6, 1978, must be flexible. The company may establish minimum contributions, but you must have the right to make contributions whenever you wish—or, if you choose, not to make any contributions. Congress mandated this to assure that if people did not have income that qualified for an IRA because of a change in their circumstances, they would not be required to continue making payments on the investment. If you have an IRA insurance contract issued before November 6, 1978, that does not have flexible payments, you may exchange it for one that does.

As with all other IRAs, when you buy an IRA annuity you must be given a disclosure statement. The disclosure statements prepared by insurance companies are often difficult to understand. If you don't get clear answers to your questions, take the disclosure statement to someone who can explain it to you. Be sure you know what the fees to get in or out of the IRA will be, how much the company is actually guaranteeing to pay you, how the company will be investing your money, and how the payout provisions work.

Also, how will the return on your investment be calculated? Annual compounding will result in a lower total return than quarterly or daily compounding. And will it be calculated before or after fees or charges are subtracted? If it is after charges are subtracted, the actual yield on your total investment would be less than the stated rate of return. These little differences can make a big difference in how much your IRA will be worth over a long period of time.

Buying Retirement Income with an Annuity

If you decide that you'd prefer buying retirement income with an IRA annuity rather than investing the money yourself, whether you've built the IRA with an insurance company or in some other investment, take enough time to do some looking around.

Even though you may have accumulated your IRA with an insurance company, you're not obliged to buy your annuity from that company. When you're ready to retire, you can take the money and buy the annuity from some other insurance company.

Some annuities guarantee a certain payment for life and others guarantee payments for specified periods of time, but terms can vary greatly. The "NROCA News Letter" (P.O. Box 12066, Dallas, TX 75225), which analyzes insurance and retirement investments, observes that when buying annuity income you must shop with many firms to be sure you're getting the most for your money.

The newsletter points out that all companies do not pay the same amount of income even though you make identical payments to them. Companies base their payments on "their own ability to earn, their desire for a profit, and their tables on how long a life they expect buyers to have. And the more assurance you or your heirs have to receive back at least your original payment, the lower the income paid by the company."

Some companies set the amount they'll pay regularly and won't change that amount under any circumstances.

This leaves you vulnerable to the impact of inflation on a fixed-income retirement income.

Ironically, this is the very reason IRAs were created by Congress in the first place. Fixed-income retirement plans were losing purchasing power so fast that Congress acted to give people a way to protect their retirement purchasing power by investing money themselves. Unless you're convinced that the inflation rate is going to fall to zero and that actual price deflation is likely for some time to come, a fixed-payment IRA retirement annuity would seem a questionable investment. Other insurance companies have more flexible programs and will adjust your payments upward if their profits rise.

In addition to rate differences, there are also big differences in payout programs. Under some programs, if you die after you start receiving income from the annuities, your heirs won't get a dime. What the insurance people call a "life only" policy pays you only to the date of your death. No matter when you die, no more payments are made.

A "life and period certain" contract is a little more complicated. It will pay you to the date of your death, whether it is one or 30 or 40 years, assuming you could live so long. But it also contains a provision guaranteeing your heirs these payments for a specified period of time.

The longer this guarantee, the smaller the periodic income payment. Most commonly the agreement is for 10 years certain, but it could be for 3 years, 5 years, 20 years, or any other period of time.

If you outlive the specified period, you could very well come out ahead. But if you die before the specified period is over, the results could be very different. The insurance company would be obligated only to continue payments to your heirs to the end of the specified period, and then payments would stop.

To use a worst-case scenario, if you bought a "life and period certain" IRA annuity and the "period certain" was 10 years, if you died after 10 years your heirs would receive nothing no matter what the investment results of the money contributed to the IRA over the years.

Many other types of annuities are also on the market. If you're married, you'll probably want some type of a joint and survivor annuity, which will pay income as long as either you or your spouse lives. If you don't like the choices offered by one insurance company, see what the others have. Be sure the annuity you buy is right for you —and for anyone who may be depending on you for support during your retirement years.

INDIVIDUAL RETIREMENT BONDS

Sales of Individual Retirement Bonds were stopped by the Treasury Department in May 1982. The department decided that sales were so low that it was no longer worth the effort.

These bonds were authorized in 1974 by the same law that created IRAs. While they were risk-free, they were also one of the least desirable IRA investments. Although the rate they paid was increased periodically over the years, it was only 9 percent when sales were discontinued, less than for almost any other kind of IRA investment at the time.

If you bought any of these bonds while the government was still selling them, you should consider turning them in and rolling the money into another IRA. In addition to the low rate, they have other disadvantages.

IRA bonds stop paying interest on the first day of the month in which you reach age 70½. And if you don't redeem the bonds and roll the proceeds into another IRA by the end of that year, you'll be liable for tax on the whole sum in that year. Consequently, unless you're willing to pay tax on the entire sum, you must be prepared to redeem these bonds and make a rollover when you reach age 70½.

If you die before you reach age 70½, IRA bonds stop paying interest on the first day of the month you would have reached age 70½ or the fifth anniversary of your death, whichever is first.

You're not paid any interest on these bonds until you cash them in. The issue date is the first day of the month of purchase. Interest is compounded semi-annually. The bonds mature on the semi-annual interest accrual date that falls just before the date on which you reach age 70½ (or on that date, if both are the same).

One difference between these bonds and any other IRA investment is that within one year of the time you bought them, you may redeem them and get your money back without paying the premature distribution penalty. On the other hand, when you redeem bonds you've held for less than one year, you're not paid any interest. And if you don't roll this money over into another IRA you'll also lose the tax deduction.

If you redeem the bonds before age 59½ and you're not disabled, you'll have to roll the proceeds over into another IRA or IRAs or pay the 10 percent premature distribution penalty.

To redeem bonds, either personally bring them to a Federal Reserve Bank or branch or mail them to the Bureau of Public Debt, Division of Securities Operations, Payment and Reissue Section, Room 531-D, 13th and C Street S.W., Washington, D.C. 20226. When redeeming bonds by mail, write a covering letter requesting the payment. Then sign the back of the bond and have your signature certified by an officer of a bank or savings and loan association.

To give yourself a record of the mailing, it would be best to send your bond and letter by registered or certified mail. It should take no more than 6 weeks for the treasury to mail a check to you.

While you cannot buy or redeem these bonds at commercial banks, savings and loan associations, trust companies, and other financial institutions, these institutions may be able to help handle redemption requests, especially if you plan to roll the redemption proceeds into an IRA or IRAs sponsored by the institution.

COLLECTIBLES

Although the law that made IRAs universal also provided that tangibles and collectibles could no longer be purchased as IRA investments beginning in 1982, there's always a possibility this provision will be repealed.

Certainly the sellers of tangibles and collectibles—dealers in coins, stamps, antiques, art, gemstones, and the like—will try to persuade Congress to make tangibles permissible as IRA investments again. (If you put tangibles into an IRA before 1982, they are not affected by the ban. But you may not deduct contributions for any purchased after 1981.)

The rationale used by Congress for eliminating collectibles and tangibles as permissible IRA investments is that these investments don't encourage savings or capital formation. Presumably, Congress allows people to defer taxation on income in order to stimulate economic activity of one kind or another. And when people put IRA money in financial institutions it is loaned out to businesses and consumers, stimulating the economy and creating more jobs. But when you buy a collectible the money goes not to a financial institution that will reinvest it, but to a dealer who can do anything he or she wants with it, including putting it in a box and burying it in the backyard.

Collectors and dealers in collectibles retort that you are entitled to exercise your free choice in determining how you'll invest your money for retirement. They also argue that the ban on collectible investments stemmed more from pressure exerted on Congress by financial institutions who wanted more IRA money for themselves than from Congressional concern about the degree to which IRA money will stimulate economic growth.

There's something to be said for both sides of those arguments. But with it at least possible that collectibles will one day be made permissible as IRA investments, how do they rate?

Collectible dealers, of course, say they are ideal as IRA investments. So do many collectors. Spectacular long-term gains have been registered for coins, stamps, gemstones, art, and other collectible and tangible categories, although as the inflation rate began dropping in 1981 and early 1982, prices of many collectibles dropped sharply. Many investors viewed collectibles as an inflation hedge—but with the inflation rate falling and higher returns available elsewhere, they deserted the collectible market.

Aside from market risk, there are other disadvantages in buying tangibles and collectibles as IRA investments.

One is that to be successful you should be very knowledgeable in whatever field you are buying. Nobody knows more about any category of collectible than a serious collector. Collectors have spent years gaining this knowledge, including knowledge of values. If you're not an expert yourself, you'll always be at a disadvantage in making buying and selling price decisions. If someone else makes these decisions for you, you'll have to pay for the service.

Another disadvantage is that if your collectibles soar in value while in your IRA, you'll have to pay tax on the gain as ordinary income when you take them out of your IRA—which you must start doing when you reach age 70½, just as with any other IRA. On the other hand, if they were not in your IRA, you wouldn't have to start liquidating them at age 70½. If you did liquidate them, you'd pay the lower capital gains tax. If you didn't liquidate them, you may be able to turn them over to your spouse without any estate or gift tax liability.

Another consideration is that collectibles and antiques don't pay dividends or interest. By putting collectibles in an IRA you give up the tax shelter you could have received on such interest or dividend-paying investments as savings accounts, stocks, or bonds.

The novice collector also risks being defrauded by counterfeits or other deceptive practices. The value of a coin can vary greatly depending on marks of wear that may be virtually invisible to the naked eye. And in any collecting field, unless you're an expert you risk being duped by counterfeits or "reproductions," which are new items made to look as though they are old.

Finally, investments in collectibles should be made for the long haul. There is often a big spread between a dealer's selling price and the wholesale buying price. It may take years before the price at which you could resell a collectible would reach the point where you'd have a meaningful profit.

If Congress does allow IRA investments in collectibles again, it's likely the rules for making them will be at least as stringent as before they were banned.

Under the old rules, you had to do as you would with any other IRA. Rather than making the investments yourself, you had to direct them through a trustee in a self-directed IRA. Many trustees who handled the more traditional investments were unwilling to undertake the responsibility of handling IRAs made up of collectibles. Those that did charged extra fees for their services.

In late 1981 *The Collector-Investor* magazine prepared a list of more than 40 banks around the country that were willing to accept tangible investments in self-directed IRAs and Keogh accounts. Many would not accept certain tangibles, and there was a wide range of transaction and annual fees.

More important to many serious collectors, the old rules specified that you could not take personal possession of the collectibles in your IRA, even temporarily. The collectibles had to remain in the possession of the trustee or of a custodian appointed by the trustee. Obviously a bank trustee might not want to be responsible for storing rare works of art, vintage slot machines, antique automobiles, and other typical collectibles. These were turned over to a custodian, involving fees for custodial care.

Trustees made you agree in writing that they would not be held responsible for value estimates. The mechanics of getting the collectible to the trustee were also up to you. The dealer held the collectible for you, and you sent the money to the trustee along with an order to invest. You were not allowed to pay the money directly to the dealer. It had to go to the trustee, who sent it to the dealer to complete the transaction.

You could sell from the account at any time. But in addition to incurring sales charges, you were responsible for making all sales arrangements, just as you were responsible for buying arrangements. If the buyer wanted to see the asset, it would have to be at the facilities of the trustee or the custodian. To complete the sale, the transaction had to be between the buyer and the trustee because payment to you would be a premature distribution.

Complicated? Yes. But if collectibles are ever reauthorized as permissible IRA investments, it would be prudent to select a trustee convenient to where you live or work. If the trustee is located hundreds of miles away it will complicate (and make more expensive) all of your buying and selling transactions.

And as *The Collector-Investor* noted, "the mechanics of this sort of investment strategy can be tedious and expensive. You should only proceed into collectibles in a qualified plan if you're comfortable with the rules and plan to invest long-term."

16

Conclusion

Neither the authors of this book nor anyone else can spell out every step each individual must take along the road to building a retirement fortune or, if you're already near retirement, to building an IRA large enough to substantially increase your retirement income. We don't know enough about you, and we certainly don't know what will happen in financial markets in the future. But we do think this book will have pointed you in the right direction.

Some of you need little pointing. If you're a sophisticated investor you (or your advisers) already know how you'll handle your IRA investment program.

Most people aren't that fortunate. In contemplating an IRA investment program, they must make many difficult decisions.

The first is whether you should even set up an IRA. Yes, you can build a retirement fortune with one—but you may have more immediate needs. The sacrifices you'd have to make may not justify any kind of IRA investment program.

The next is what kind—or kinds—of IRAs to set up.

We hope that if nothing else, this book makes clear that there's no ideal IRA investment program for everyone—and that the program best for you depends on who and what you are.

You and your neighbor may have identical incomes, financial responsibilities, and financial resources—but your temperaments and personal preferences alone could dictate that each of you set up completely different IRA programs. One of you might understand and feel comfortable with IRAs whose value will rise or fall with ups and downs in the stock market, and the other may prefer fixed-rate insured savings deposits in local financial institutions.

And so while there's a wide range of IRA investment options, you'll have to find the answers to many questions in yourself, not in the pages of this or any other book. The best investment option or options for you may also change over the years, just as you will change. Your circumstances, your investment experiences, the contacts you make—all of these things, and more, will (or certainly should) contribute to an ever-changing investment outlook.

What it adds up to is that there is no one way to build a retirement fortune with an IRA. There are many ways. It can be done with insured savings deposits, with mutual funds, with self-directed accounts at brokerage houses, and with insurance annuity IRAs.

The route you take in seeking to build your retirement fortune with an IRA is not nearly so important as your decision to establish a disciplined IRA investment program and stick to it. If this book succeeds in demonstrating the value of an IRA and broadening your understanding of how IRAs work, what your responsibilities as the owner of an IRA are, and the importance of continually monitoring your IRAs and seeking professional advice when appropriate, it will have accomplished its purpose.

www.ingramcontent.com/pod-product-compliance
Lightning Source LLC
Chambersburg PA
CBHW022053210326
41519CB00054B/329